The Maginot Line

THE MAGINOT LINE

None Shall Pass

J. E. Kaufmann
and H. W. Kaufmann

PRAEGER

Westport, Connecticut
London

Library of Congress Cataloging-in-Publication Data

Kaufmann, J. E.
    The Maginot Line : none shall pass / J. E. Kaufmann and H. W.
Kaufmann.
      p. cm.
    Includes bibliographical references and index.
    ISBN 0–275–95719–5 (alk. paper)
    1. Maginot Line. 2. France—History—German occupation,
1940–1945. 3. Fortifications—France—History—20th century.
I. Kaufmann, H. W. II. Title.
D761.K36   1997
940.54′214825—dc21   96–39710

British Library Cataloguing in Publication Data is available.

Library of Congress Catalog Card Number: 96–39710
ISBN: 0–275–95719–5

First published in 1997

Praeger Publishers, 88 Post Road West, Westport, CT 06881
An imprint of Greenwood Publishing Group, Inc.

Printed in the United States of America

The paper used in this book complies with the
Permanent Paper Standard issued by the National
Information Standards Organization (Z39.48–1984).

10 9 8 7 6 5 4 3 2

COPYRIGHT ACKNOWLEDGMENTS

Permission to use drawings in Figure 5, 7, 8, and 19, which come
from *Hitler's Blitzkrieg Campaigns* by J. E. and H. W. Kaufmann
(1993) was granted by Combined Books.

Every reasonable effort has been made to trace the owners of copyright
materials in this book, but in some instances this has proven impossible. The authors and publisher will be glad to receive information
leading to more complete acknowledgments in subsequent printings of
the book and in the meantime extend their apologies for any omissions.

To our parents and Bessie

CONTENTS

Illustrations follow page 64.

ACKNOWLEDGMENTS

We would like to thank the following people for their help in preparing this book: William Allcorn, who helped us find key information as well as some important contacts; Raoul Heymes, who made us welcome at the ouvrage of Hackenberg and sent us documents; veterans Georges Dropsy and André Paquin, who guided us through Fermont; Georges Maistret, who made us welcome at Fermont and also provided documents; Raymond Mersch, who opened Immerhof to us; Jean-Bernard Wahl, who provided us with information on the ouvrage of Schoenenbourg, the RF of Lauter, and the Rhine Defenses. In addition, we give our thanks to the personnel of the archives of the Inspection du Génie in Paris, the Génie of Metz, Grenoble and Nice, who provided us with documentation and other information, especially Colonel Viennot of the Génie of Nice, who was particularly helpful.

Most of all, we must recognize the continuous help given us by Colonel Philippe Truttmann, who has helped us separate fact from fiction and as always he has been a rich source of information on this subject. If some errors have crept in this book, as they always seem to do in this type of work, they are not to be attributed to Colonel Truttmann who has done his best to educate us on this subject.

We would also like to thank Combined Books for allowing us to reprint Figures 5, 7 and 8 from *Hitler's Blitzkrieg Campaigns* (1993). Also, we would like to thank Wojciech Ostrowski for his drawings of cloches.

Special thanks to Dan Eades and Bruce Gudmundsson for making this book possible.

INTRODUCTION

World War II is not remembered for its fortifications and military architecture. It is usually associated with mobile warfare, tanks, aircraft and other paraphernalia that stole the show. It comes as a surprise, therefore, to realize that the few decades preceding the war marked the zenith of the development of military architecture.

The best known fortifications of the period, the Siegfried Line and the Atlantic Wall, are not the most outstanding product of the fortress-building period. Neither were they the only fortified lines in Europe. France, Belgium, the Netherlands, Czechoslovakia and other nations also spent the last years preceding the war erecting various lines of defenses wherever they felt a need for them. It was in France, however, that twentieth century military architecture reached its apex with the construction of the Maginot Line.

These lines of fortifications, usually represented as crenelated lines on the maps of military histories, intrigued us and sent us looking for them at first on dusty library shelves. We found that the descriptions of these fortifications were few and contradictory. Our quest eventually led us into the field, where we tramped through tall grasses, overgrown bushes, and underground tunnels in search of the truth. We visited the forts, interviewed old veterans and eyewitnesses, and searched through archives in six different countries. The *Service du Génie* of Metz and Strasbourg were gracious enough to give us copies of the original plans of the forts. We also had the luck to meet one of the foremost experts on the Maginot Line, retired Colonel Philippe Truttmann, formerly of the Génie, who wrote the most comprehensive and authoritative book on the Maginot Line and who gave us a wealth of information in his witty and humorous letters.

The image of the Word War II fortifications that emerged turned out to be quite different from the idea we had when we began the quest. We found that the forts did not have the mammoth proportions ascribed to them by propaganda and myth. They are, nevertheless, a treasure trove of human ingenuity. The architects who designed these forts had tried to solve, it seemed, all the problems that had cropped up during the preceding wars. We thought that other people in the United States would like to know more about these amazing forts and decided to publish what we found.

1

DEVELOPMENT OF LINES OF FORTIFICATIONS

One of the most obscure facts in the history of World War II and the period preceding it is the development of strings of interdependent fortifications along Europe's borders. The truth is that many European countries spent an astounding amount of their revenues and efforts in building and perfecting long lines of state-of-the-art forts. The concept of fortified lines is not new by any means. The Romans built stone walls across Britain and defensive "Limes" along their vulnerable borders in Europe and the Middle East. The Great Wall of China, contemporaneous with the Roman walls, is another famous example of fortifications designed to defend long stretches of territory. However, following the Roman period, continuous lines of fortifications ceased to be viable because no nation could field an army large enough to defend them. The small size of post-Roman armies only permitted fluid action or the defense of very limited amounts of territory. The situation did not change until after the Franco-Prussian War in the latter part of the nineteenth century.

There was one exception to this rule: the string of fortifications in Northeastern France dating from the Vauban period, which could be considered the precursor of the fortified lines of the twentieth century.[1] To be sure, Vauban's forts did not actually constitute a continuous line of defenses, being meant only to defend key towns rather than halt the enemy. Nonetheless, they guarded the same areas and followed the same course as the twentieth-century Maginot Line.

The end of the Franco-Prussian War brought about a radical change in the concept of fortification. The French, searching for a more effective method of protecting their borders from another invasion, came to the conclusion that a line of fortifications would meet their needs. Thus began a new cycle of fortification construction, starting in the late 1870s and culminating in the 1930s with the building of the Maginot Line.

The forts of Verdun stem from the first phase of this cycle. Part of the defensive system developed at the instigation of General Seré de Rivières in the 1870s, they were designed to meet the challenges presented by the ever-evolving military technology. The Crimean War and the American Civil War had demonstrated that masonry walls were obsolete in the face of advances in artillery, such as greater range and penetrating power. Military architects and engineers quickly realized that radical changes must be made in the design of new fortresses to resist the force and fury of the new weapons. From now on, forts would have to be sunk into the ground and their profiles reduced so that they would be better able to withstand the devastating effects of heavy artillery. The American Civil War also had shown that the new subterranean forts would need additional overhead protection in order to withstand the effects of heavy mortars, which, at that point, were able to deliver huge shells on top of their target.

The Verdun forts are classified as "ring forts" because they were placed in a circular pattern around the cities they protected. This system was extensively used by the French and Germans to protect key cities on or near their borders. These rings formed an almost continuous line in France, with isolated forts occupying key points in the gaps between them. The Belgians even went so far as to set up fortress rings in three of their major cities, leaving Brussels undefended. This was almost a return to the medieval castle system of defense when armies were small and the outcome of wars could be determined by the results of a few sieges. In some cases in the latter part of the nineteenth century, rings of forts were interconnected in order to create a continuous barrier. The range of the artillery determined the distance between the forts making up a ring and the area to be defended.

The French ring forts were built along the historical invasion routes, which were determined by topography. The Franco-German border was rather short. In addition, the steep, eastward-facing scarps of the Paris Basin did not allow easy access except through the river valleys cutting through them. Verdun, ringed by more than twenty forts and smaller fortifications, defended the exit out of the Meuse Valley and stood guard over the 1870 German invasion route. Its own fortress ring was linked to another one surrounding Toul, thus forming one of the strongest fortified zones in Europe during World War I. The other fortified zone consisted of the fortress rings of Épinal and Belfort, also linked to one another and barring another traditional invasion route. The border defenses along the Belgian frontier were not as modern nor as formidable as the other two zones because the French relied on the neutrality of Belgium to slow down any German advance from that quarter. Similar considerations would influence the layout of the future Maginot Line, which would, however, be built further to the east to guard territory recuperated after World War I.

While the French were busy erecting their fortifications to bar the 1870 invasion route, the Germans were similarly engaged in fortifying the sector between Metz and Thionville. Several of these German forts would eventually be assimilated into the Maginot defenses in a supporting role. They would also play an active role in the defense of Germany in 1944. More importantly, however, they would have a significant influence in the final design of the Maginot Line even though they did not see any major action in World War I.

Following the example of their French neighbors, the Belgians also constructed major defensive works during the pre-World War I era. The keys to the Belgian line of defense were the fortress rings of Liege and Namur, similar in design but not identical to the French systems. No doubt hampered by a shortage of funds and manpower, their designer, General Brialmont, neither linked the fortress ring of Liege to that of Namur, nor installed interval positions between the forts within the rings (Mallory and Ottar 1973, 25). This design would later prove to be disastrous, especially since it was coupled with inherent structural weaknesses in the forts. Brialmont designed his own mixture of concrete, not reinforced, which was intended to resist the heaviest weapons of the time: the German 210-mm mortar and the French 220-mm mortar (Balace 1981, 80). Unfortunately, shortly after the construction of Brialmont's forts, the Germans perfected the 420-mm Big Bertha howitzer. In addition, the new generation of high explosive steel artillery shells, called *torpedo shells* by the French, proved to have devastating effects on fortifications. Thus, unable to withstand neither Big Bertha nor the torpedo shells, Brialmont's forts became obsolete almost before their concrete had begun to set (Gaier 1981, 38).

One of the most serious flaws of Brialmont's design was the layout of his forts, which tended to be triangular in shape. A good example of these Belgian forts is Fort Loncin, one of the forts of Liege. Its weakness lay not only in its construction, but also in the emplacement of its weapons. The magazine was at the center of the fort and the majority of its gun turrets were overhead or nearby. Over seventy percent of the turrets stood within a radius of about 30 meters from the heavy gun turret located over the center of the fort, presenting the enemy with a cluster of targets and increasing the chances of a direct hit. Added to this, there were other serious faults in Fort Loncin's construction. A cheap grade of concrete was poured in two layers instead of a single thick layer, reducing its capacity to resist enemy shells. Once heavy artillery and shells were developed, these layers of concrete afforded practically no protection. Fort Loncin's turrets consisted of 20-cm of cast iron lined with two sheets of only 2-cm thickness each, which was too thin and could easily be pierced by shells (Mallory and Ottar 1973, 29; Balace 1981, 88). The consequences of these inherent flaws can be clearly observed today at Fort Loncin. Its turrets lie overturned and torn asunder after having literally popped out of their shafts following an explosion in the magazine, set off when a German shell penetrated the roof and detonated, triggering a tremendous conflagration and leaving a huge crater.

The French High Command, alarmed by the disaster that befell the Belgian fortifications in August 1914, concluded that France's own forts would suffer a similar fate at the hands of the enemy's heavy artillery. However, the French had underestimated the strength of their own fortifications. Unlike the Brialmont forts, the French forts received defensive support from specially constructed smaller interval infantry works. In addition, they had been modernized recently with thicker layers of concrete and sand for overhead protection against the heaviest explosive shells. As a result they could, and did, withstand the bombardment of the heavy 420-mm guns that had devastated Brialmont's forts at Liege (Mallory and Ottar 1973, 25). Furthermore, the French forts were irregular in shape, with four or more sides rather than being triangular, like Brialmont's. This design proved to be superior to the Belgian, allowing the forts to successfully conform to the terrain and making them less vulnerable to enemy artillery.

The layout and quality of the gun turrets in the French forts were also superior to the Belgian. The French gun turrets were few in number, but all of them were well spaced at a distance of about 50 to 100 meters from each other. There were a few exceptions such as the 155-mm gun turret at Fort Douaumont, which lay only about 25 meters from the machine gun turret and appears to have been a later addition (Fort Moulainville had a similar plan). What's more, the French turrets, unlike the Belgian, were made of steel and most were retractable (Mallory and Ottar 1973, 29).

Thus, the forts of Verdun were clearly superior in many ways to those of Liege. Unfortunately, the French High Command, unaware of this, began to disarm them in 1914, no doubt influenced by the disaster at Fort Loncin. The reduction of their own forts at Maubeuge, and the fall of their heavily armed fort, Manonviller an isolated position in Lorraine, to 420-mm cannons in August 1914 also must have weighed heavily on the minds of the French leaders and contributed to their decision.

The new German forts known as "*Feste*," found near the Metz and Strasbourg regions, were probably the best designed forts of the period, but they never saw action until World War II, so they have been largely ignored by history until recently. The Feste consisted of one or more batteries of 100-mm to 150-mm guns and thus had better range and more firepower than the Belgian or French. Unlike their rivals, the Germans separated their combat and garrison positions, scattering them over a larger area. This stratagem made it more difficult to put the fort out of operation by concentrating on a single position in the hope that near misses would hit other vital organs. Like the French, the Germans designed their forts to take full advantage of the terrain. However, despite the scattering of positions, the Achilles heel of the German forts was the large size of their blocks. A gun battery of three and four guns occupied a single block. It would take fewer well-placed hits to inflict greater damage on a German battery position than the more scattered French gun positions.

The Germans created strong fortress rings around the cities to be defended and effectively barred the traditional invasion routes. The great offensive and

defensive capabilities of the Feste made them the most powerful forts in exist-
ence until the creation of the Maginot Line. Germany's western frontier
included four major rings, further paired together in the following way: Metz-
Thionville and Strasbourg-Molsheim. Thionville and Molsheim consisted of
forts of the Feste type, Metz included this type, while Strasbourg had only
older forts.

The French, Belgian and German forts differed not only in their design and
construction, but also in their armament, size and garrisons. It appears that the
Verdun forts had less firepower than the Belgian and German forts even
though they were as large as the Liege forts. However, they were well
designed for their primary mission, close defense. The Brialmont forts
included infantry positions for the defense of the surrounding surface area of
the fort and coffres with weapons covering the encircling moat or fossé. The
moat was also covered with wire entanglements, but the side facing the rear
was relatively unprotected because attack was not expected from that quarter.
The French forts also included a surrounding fossé, but were usually defended
on all sides by coffres. The French machine gun positions were located in
such a manner that their weapons could sweep the surface of their forts with
fire. The design and armament of the French forts makes it apparent that the
French intended their forts to take part in an active front-line defense. The
German Feste, also built to take part in close defense, was in some ways less
vulnerable than the French forts, since its various organs were more widely
scattered. On the other hand, its batteries were more vulnerable than the
French gun positions because of their size and location on prominent terrain.

The French High Command's decision to disarm the forts of Verdun in
August of 1914 was justified in one respect. Its rationale was not only based
on the incorrect assumption that the French forts were no stronger than those
of Liege, but also on the belief that they would never be in the front line of an
assault. It was assumed, therefore, that these forts would prove of little value
as fire-support positions because of their lack of heavy artillery. Fort Manonviller, located in a relatively unsupported position near the frontier, fell to the
huge 420-mm German weapons. The French later found that its two Mougin
155-mm turrets had not stood up as well as its two retracting 155-mm turrets,
which had not escaped the ravages of the bombardment. Most importantly,
however, the garrison, incapacitated by the carbon monoxide released by the
explosion of the 420-mm rounds, had been forced to take refuge in the subterranean sections of the fort. As a result of this incident, military architects
and engineers would later pay special attention to the problem of gas in
developing new designs for the forts of the post-World War I period.

The fall of Fort Manonviller in the face of heavy bombardment led the
French High Command concluded that none of the other Verdun forts would
withstand the new siege artillery (Rocolle 1974, 308; Horne 1962, 49). Most
French forts mounted a few   75-mm guns in casemates and included a single
twin 75-mm gun turret. Few French forts included any weapon larger than a

75-mm gun. When the forts were disarmed, the weapons in the gun turrets were left in position because they had been designed for fortress mountings and could not be adapted for field service. On the other hand, most of the other guns in the forts designed for local defense and the 75-mm guns in casemates were taken out. Thus, the Verdun forts were left virtually defenseless.

When the Germans launched their assault on Verdun in February 1916, Fort Douaumont was only partially garrisoned and, with the exception of its turret guns, was virtually weaponless. Consequently, it fell quickly to the enemy. It was captured by German soldiers entering through one of the unmanned coffres after descending into the undefended fossé. After entering the coffre, a couple of German soldiers, later followed by more men, surprised the small garrison, which had been busy firing the fort's single 155-mm turret gun at a distant target (Hogg 1977, 122). Fort Vaux, with six hundred men, held out until June, slowing considerably the German advance. Fort Vaux's heroic resistance is all the more remarkable since it was achieved despite the fact that its only twin 75-mm gun turret was knocked out before the battle had begun. The ouvrage of Froideterre, a newer type of work, repelled a German infantry attack in June despite being pounded by heavy artillery and smothered with poison gas shells.

All of these events weighed heavily in post-war planning in France. The forts had proven to be the heart of the defense at Verdun and the French efforts had centered around such positions as Fort Souville[2] and the ouvrage of Froideterre. The Germans failed to seize Fort Souville and Fort Tavannes in a poison gas attack, and a solid ring of forts remained intact preventing a German advance into the Meuse Valley and Verdun. Some forts such as Souville and Tavannes, which were weaker than Douaumont or Vaux and lacked turreted weapon positions, were pounded into rubble. Still, they continued to provide a buttress from which the army could resist the enemy advance and return fire from well-chosen locations. They served to harass and impede enemy movements. The lessons learned during the first battle for Fort Vaux, and during the French effort to recapture Fort Douaumont, would heavily influence French planning of the post-war defenses. Indeed, one allied offensive after another had ground to a halt almost as soon as it began in the struggle to recapture the lost forts. Thus, later plans would also deal with the need for an interior defense system, absent from pre-war forts, which had had to rely on expedient field measures to defend the subterranean galleries once the enemy had penetrated their interior.

When the dust settled after the campaign, Marshal Philippe Pétain, who had exclaimed "*Ils ne passeront pas!*" (They shall not pass!) in the heat of the battle, attributed his success in stopping the enemy advance mainly to the fortress ring of Verdun. Most of the forts were still operational, having survived constant artillery bombardment. As a result, the French High Command, remembering its successes and failures at Verdun, would later place its faith in the superiority of fixed defenses.

After the war, Marshal Pétain, as Inspector General, pushed for the creation of a continuous line of fortifications across France's eastern border. Others, such as Marshal Joseph Joffre, favored defensive sectors similar to those constructed before World War I. These, thought Joffre, could be used as a base of operations from which to strike at the flanks of a bypassing enemy force (Mallory and Ottar 1973, 91-93). But Pétain, having experienced the drawbacks of such a system at Verdun, opted for stopping the enemy advance on the border. He wanted to avoid at all cost the possibility of an assault on French flanks and the creation of another "meat grinder" like that of Verdun in 1916.

Having opted for a modified version of Pétain's ideas, by 1929 France was preparing for the construction of a new line of defenses, which would take the name of the new Minister of War and war hero, André Maginot. Despite the name of the new line, most of the planning for this new system of fortifications had actually been done under the administration of Paul Painlevé, who was replaced by Maginot in 1929.

A veteran of Verdun, Maginot was a firm believer in and supporter of the newly proposed line of fortifications. He pushed for its construction and completion before the required withdrawal of the French army from the Rhineland in 1935. On January 4, 1930, the French National Assembly gave its blessing to the new defenses by authorizing approximately the equivalent of U.S. $120 million.[3] By the time the line was completed, cost overrun would amount to over twice the amount estimated originally. This has led many historians to conclude that the army had been forced to severely economize on its budget (Horne 1969, 27-28). The evidence, however, suggests that this was not the case since the large sums appropriated for defense were never even spent. The army had had the opportunity to redirect these funds towards other endeavors, such as the development of offensive weapons, but showed little interest in doing so. The French army did not begin to modernize its arsenal until about 1936 and when it finally decided to do so, it was never denied any funds by the French government (Goutard 1959, 21).

Faced with a shorter period of active duty service for conscripts in the early 1930s, the French military was not concerned with the development of new tactics or with any change in its training programs. When it did begin its rearmament program in 1936, many of the weapons selected proved unsuited to the development of new tactics. The blame lies with the High Command which: "alone selected the make of machines and made out the programme. In fact [they] acquired the weapons to suit the type of warfare [they] envisaged. Unfortunately, the Germans did not choose to fight the same type of war" (Goutard 1959, 21).

By 1939, the Maginot Line stretched from Longuyon, near the Belgian border, to the Rhine with additional sections extending to the North Sea and south of Switzerland to the Mediterranean.

NOTES

1. Sébastien Leprestre de Vauban (1633-1707), appointed General Commissioner by Louis XIV, fortified numerous border towns in France and took part in several sieges, including those of Lille in 1667 and Namur in 1692. His theories had a profound influence on the military architecture of his times.

2. Fort Souville had a turreted 155-mm gun located outside its peripheral fossé.

3. The monetary value is meaningless without making a comparison. In 1924 the U.S. Navy destroyed fifteen old battleships (twelve of which were predreadnoughts) built at a total cost of $197,418,620, which gave a return of just over $2,000,000. In 1927 the U.S. Navy's total operating cost, which included a fleet of eighteen battleships as well as new construction of smaller vessels, was $320,553,754 (Almanac 1929, 841-842). By comparison, the initial expense for building the Maginot Line is rather economical. One must bear in mind that France was trying to maintain the status of a great power whereas the U.S. was entering a period of isolationism.

2

THE MAGINOT LINE: PLANNING AND DESIGNING

By 1939 the famous Maginot Line included fortified sectors between Longuyon and the Rhine, the Maginot Extension from Longuyon to a point south of Sedan, the fortified sector of Maubeuge in the north, and the Alpine defenses adjacent to Italy. Other defensive fortifications, consisting mostly of lighter works, dotted the area between Maubeuge and the North Sea. In addition, coastal defenses sprouted on the southern side of the island of Corsica and a defensive line was built even in southern Tunisia. These additional fortified lines consisted mostly of fortifications of a later design (Service Techniques du Génie or STG type used for covering areas that were not part of the originally planned fortifications), which were also used to fill in the gaps in the Maginot Line (Truttmann 1988, interview).

The best known part of the Maginot defenses is the Maginot Line Proper, originally planned in the late 1920s and considered to be part of the "Old Fronts." It ran from Longuyon to the vicinity of Haguenau near the Rhine and consisted of two *Fortified Regions* (*Régions Fortifiées* or RFs) separated by the sizable Sarre Gap. The Fortified Regions were further subdivided into *Fortified Sectors* (*Secteurs Fortifiés* or SFs), while the Sarre Gap was subdivided into *Defensive Sectors* (*Secteurs Défensifs* or SDs). The SDs were more lightly protected than the SFs.

The Maginot Line Proper consisted of a soft skin of bunker-type positions with barbed wire and anti-tank obstacles. Forty-nine major fortifications known as *ouvrages* made up the backbone of the defenses.[1] These forts were stronger and better constructed than those of Verdun but their fire power was comparable. The French classified the larger works as *ouvrages d'artillerie* (artillery ouvrages) and the smaller as *petits ouvrages* (small ouvrages). The former wielded the firepower of the Maginot Line while the latter, usually lacking artillery, had mostly infantry-type support weapons.

The Alpine defenses, which consisted of several SFs, are identified in several English sources as the Little Maginot Line.   They too were included in the "Old Fronts" by the French.

The Rhine defenses, often erroneously included in the Maginot Line Proper, were actually several individual SFs with lighter defenses.[2] Added in 1934, the "New Fronts" included new SFs between Longuyon and Sedan that became an extension of the Maginot Line Proper (Claudel 1974, 2).   The Maginot Extension relied upon the rough wooded terrain of the Ardennes for its defense. It consisted of a single SF with two large and two small ouvrages of a new design and the standard interval positions. Because of the modifications, the Maginot Extension had inherent weaknesses that precluded its integration in the Maginot Line Proper.

The design of the Maginot Line emerged from a battle among the most influential military leaders of France in the 1920s. The Great War and the resulting Treaty of Versailles left the French leadership harboring serious doubts about their country's ability to deter a resurgent Germany. Neither the politicians nor the soldiers were convinced that the treaty, intended to cripple Germany, would work. France had suffered heavy losses in manpower during the Great War, so that it could not hope to muster enough men to oppose another invasion. It was therefore imperative to think of an alternative.

In March 1920 the Minister of War, André Lefèvre, ordered a study for the defense of Alsace and Lorraine, two provinces France had reclaimed from Germany in the Treaty of Versailles (Truttmann 1979, 34).   The *Conseil Superieur de la Guerre* was assigned the task. At the time it appeared that Germany would not present a serious threat as long as it did not violate the conditions limiting its military expansion and French troops occupied the Rhineland. However, the future seemed bleak to the French High Command because the French army was dwindling in size and the 1935 required withdrawal from the Rhineland was looming ever closer on the horizon. The men charged with studying the question of frontier radically disagreed on how to proceed. Some of them believed that the military should prepare for offensive operations while others insisted that a defensive war was more realistic.

In 1922 Marshal Joffre took charge of the newly formed *Commission de Défense du Territoire* (Commission of Territorial Defense) to study the problem of border defenses. Based on the experiences at Verdun in 1916, Joffre believed in developing strong fortified regions. Marshal Pétain, on the other hand, argued for a continuous line of light defenses, with what he termed *"parc mobile de fortifications"* (mobile park of fortifications) based on a belief in a flexible, in depth defense, such as the Germans would opt for in the late 1930s.   After Marshal Joffre resigned, General Louis Guillaumat, who replaced him, continued to endorse his ideas.

In the opposing camp, General Edmound Buat, a supporter of Pétain, died in 1923. His replacement, General Marie Debeney, allied himself with General Guillaumat and Marshal Ferdinand Foch against Pétain's faction. Between them, they opted for heavily fortified regions, deciding to use the gaps between them for offensive operations (Hughes 1981, 199; Truttmann 1979, 34-35). Paul Painlevé, then Minister of War, favored the concept of heavy defenses even though he was probably not unduly concerned about offensive operations. His support led to the creation of what, according to some, should have been called the "Painlevé Line" by the end of the decade. Their plans also included a modified version of Pétain's continuous line with heavier fortifications. In an article that appeared in the *Contemporary Review*, British journalist Dudley Heathcote went as far as to attribute the whole idea for these new French defensive plans to Painlevé (Heathcote 1929, 156).

The new defenses received neither Joffre's nor Painlevé's name. By the time the Joffre plans came to fruition, the old war hero, André Maginot, had been appointed Minister of War and the media would name the new defenses after him. In a way, Maginot deserved the honors. After all, he had endorsed the plans submitted by Joffre and Painlevé when he was a member of Parliament and had done much to turn them into reality even before he assumed the office of Minister of Defense.

The debate over frontier defenses continued as the military and international situations evolved during the 1920s. Although forced to bend on his ideas on defense, Marshal Pétain succeeded in replacing the army's square division (four regiments) of the Great War with a triangular division (three regiments) based on the fact that it was more mobile and would adapt to the changes in warfare, which included the need for armies to be more flexible.[3]

The need to protect to northeast frontier was heightened in 1925 when the Riff War in Morocco drew away troops from Europe, new legislation reduced active service first to eighteen months and later to only twelve, and the government announced its intention to withdraw from the Rhineland in 1930, five years ahead of schedule. The French army continued to shrink and could barely maintain twelve full-strength divisions, half of which were stationed in the Rhineland with the remaining half in reserve. Mobilization would result in a thirty-two division force. French war plans changed accordingly: before 1924 the army was to take the offensive from the Rhineland but by 1929 it was expected to retreat to the French border (Hughes 1981, 134-136, 192). The French leadership was probably inspired to opt for the fortification of the borders by the comments of the German military theoreticians Helmut von Moltke (writing before World War I) and Erich von Ludendorff (writing after the war), who stated that an attack on heavily fortified positions like Verdun would be excessively costly and drawn out (Heathcote 1929, 157).

The decision to fortify the borders did not go forward without strong opposition. Although public opinion supported the idea of a system of defenses, critics immediately pointed out that it would be impractical to erect large, mutually supporting concrete forts. Surprisingly, the loudest dissenting voice did not come not from the civilian sector, but from within the military establishment itself. The military opposition claimed that experiences during the last war and the new developments in military technology did not warrant such a commitment to fixed defenses (Heathcote 1929, 156). Some of them wanted to turn more attention to developing and maintaining the tank force and air force, while others simply wanted better equipment for the army. Unfortunately, their proposals were not practical for a nation whose armed forces were debilitated by shrinking numbers and one year of training for its recruits.

The *Commission de Défense des Frontières* (Border Defense Commission), with General Guillaumat at its head, went into operation at the beginning of 1926, drawing up plans for the set-up of the new defensive system. Undaunted by the previous rejection of his plans, Marshal Pétain continued to contribute to the development of the new fortifications throughout the 1920s and the 1930s (Truttmann 1979, 35). The resulting Maginot Line became somewhat of a hybrid between the original Joffre plans and Pétain's vision. Thus, instead of being a series of heavily fortified regions similar to the ring-fortress zones of the previous war, the Maginot Line took on a distinctly linear character after a number of alterations had been slipped in some time between the planning stage and the implementation stage.

Late in 1926 the *Commission de Défense des Frontières* prepared a report outlining the organization of the fortifications. On the Northeast Front, the report designated three fortified regions in order of priority for work needed: the RF of Metz, the RF of Lauter and the RF of Belfort. Each was to be separated by zones of either natural obstacles or barriers created by demolitions. The Northern Front, which consisted of the Belgian border at the time, was also to be covered by similar obstacles. It was in these non-fortified zones that the commission wanted to install Pétain's lighter works and "*parc mobile de fortification.*" The latter consisted of stockpiles of materials located at selected points to be used for erecting field defenses (Hughes 1981, 214; Truttmann 1979, 35-38). On the Southeast Front, mainly from the Swiss border to the Mediterranean, the plan called for several SFs to block invasion routes through the Alps (Truttmann 1979, 35-39).

A final report by the *Commission de Défense des Frontières* reemphasized the same priorities for the three RFs in the northeast. It also recommended the creation of a "frontier" position and a second line, a support line termed "barrage" or barrier position in each RF. The latter would consist of refurbished older defenses in the RF of Metz and Belfort and of new positions in the RF of Lauter. Following Pétain's recommendations in 1927, it was decided to build a barrier line of equal strength to the frontier line. Eventually, however, only the frontier line would be built (Truttmann 1979, 58-9). According to Lt. Colonel Philippe Truttmann, who did considerable research on the development of the Maginot Line during the 1970s, the fortifications envisioned in these initial reports were vastly different from those that eventually materialized on the terrain.

During the late 1920s concrete steps were taken to put the plans of the *Commission de Défense des Frontières* into action. In 1927 the Commission created the *Commission d'Organisation des Régions Fortifiées* (Commission for the Organization of the Fortified Regions, or CORF). The commission appointed the Inspector General of Engineers, General Fillonneau, as the president of CORF and assigned other high-ranking officers from each of branch of the army to the newly created organization. In 1929 General Belhauge replaced Fillonneau, heading the organization until it was dissolved in 1935 after the completion of its mission. CORF was responsible for drawing up the specifications of the fortifications, both large and small, as well as many other frontier defenses.

By the end of the decade the early withdrawal of French forces from the Rhineland became imminent, giving new urgency to the military planning in France. It was estimated that only two of the army's six full-strength divisions would be necessary to defend the RFs. The other four divisions would occupy the intervals and defend the frontier until the reserves could be mobilized (Hughes 1981, 206-207).

By 1929, the plans for the new fortifications had been drawn, the labor approved, and André Maginot, now Minister of War, was anxious for the work to begin. Finding a rare surplus of funds, the government authorized about eighty percent of the funds originally requested by the army. Thus, the Parliament apportioned 2.9 billion francs to the army for the period from 1930 to 1934. Unfortunately, this generous amount soon suffered devaluation with the onset of the Great Depression. The resulting lack of funds forced the military to change substantially the original plans of the *Commission de Défense des Frontières*, such as the elimination of the RF of Belfort (Hughes 1981, 195; Claudel 1974, 7).

In the 1930s it became necessary to raise additional funds, exceeding by far the original appropriations. By 1934 work on the fortifications had already consumed almost 7 billion francs, over twice the original government allotments.[4] Despite the additional funds, it became necessary to modify designs and plans in an effort to cut costs. After 1934 more money was required to finish work on the Old Fronts and begin work on the New Fronts. 1934 was a critical year for completion of the border defenses since Germany came under Hitler's control. Unfortunately, Marshal Pétain, now the new Minister of War, did little to further the cause of the border defenses. He requested only a small appropriation of funds for the New Fronts and did not even spend the money he received. He informed the Senate War Committee that the Ardennes were "impenetrable if some special dispositions are taken." He went on to state that if the enemy should advance through the Ardennes "we would close the pincers as he emerged. . . . This sector, therefore, is not dangerous." He went on to reiterate his past theory that fortifications along the Belgian border would be ineffective and that it was "essential for us to go into Belgium" (Rowe 1961, 86-88; Mallory & Ottar 1973, 107).

At the beginning of 1935, his successors had to get the work back on track. The Parliament was willing to appropriate more funds for the Southeast Front when relations between France and Italy deteriorated after the Italian invasion of Ethiopia. Despite the reduction in the scale of planned construction, the Maginot Line Proper and the partially completed Little Maginot Line of the Alps successfully carried out their mission at the onset of World War II.

Originally, the Maginot Line's mission had been both defensive and offensive. Indeed, Joffre and Guilaumat had visualized the RFs as firm bases with lightly defended intervals between them through which the army would be able to take offensive action into the Rhineland. In the 1930s the Maginot Line still retained its offensive mission. In fact, in 1939 the French launched an attack from the gap between the two RFs of the Maginot Line Proper. However, the effort was only a half-hearted, token gesture to show support for Poland.

The reason for the lack of a strong French offensive effort during war was not simply because of reliance on the fixed defenses, but because of French doctrine. The 1921 *Instruction provisoire sur l'employ tactique des grandes unités* drawn up under the guidance of Pétain and Debeney remained in force until the mid-1930s. Basically, it called for a well-prepared offensive force superior in numbers and firepower with a massive supporting tank force. This 1921 work simply adopted the techniques used by the French late in the war. Interestingly, aviation's role received more attention than that of armor. The creation of new mechanized and armored units in the 1930s slowly brought a change in policy.

In 1936 a new doctrine was prepared that replaced that of 1921 with General Alphonese Georges, who later commanded the Northeast Front in 1940, and air force general Bertrand Pujo in charge. Taking into account the new weapons of war, they made some important changes but retained some of the basic principles of the 1921 doctrine. So by the time the war began, the French had not deviated much from their plan to return to their slow methodical World War I tactics and needed many months to mobilize sufficient forces for such an operation (Corum 1992, 48-49; Gunsburg 1979, 9-10, 39-41).

The eventual debacle of 1940 was due, in part, to a crucial error made by the planners of the Maginot Line, particularly Pétain. Indeed, they left the Ardennes unfortified resulting in a wide gap between their defenses and those of the Belgian fortified areas. The latter stretched from Namur to Liege along the Meuse river. Many Belgians concluded that by fortifying the German frontier and leaving the Belgian border undefended, the French had deliberately and cynically channeled the Nazi forces away from France and into Belgium.

The reality was less sinister, however. Back in the 1920s some French politicians, like Painlevé, had been concerned that the Belgians might misunderstand any French effort to fortify the Franco-Belgian border. Building fortifications here might be interpreted as a lack of faith in the Franco-Belgian alliance, or, worse still, a desire to throw Belgium to the wolves. In addition, Pétain's assertion that the terrain in the Ardennes was virtually impassable to tanks lulled the French into believing that they were safe from attacks from that quarter. The terrain between Maubeuge and the sea, on the other hand, presented other problems. First of all, the important industrial city of Lille was too close to the border to defend. Second, the high water table in the area precluded the building of large subterranean forts.

As work began on the Maginot Line, the Ministry of War started to leak a careful blend of information and misinformation to the public.[5] At times Painlevé himself granted interviews to a select group of journalists. Thus in May 1928, the British *Daily News* erroneously reported that the French were planning a heavily fortified line from the Mediterranean to the North Sea. In September of the same year, Painlevé publicly stated that the Belgian frontier would not be fortified "in the face of our friends the Belgians." He then informed a British correspondent that France was constructing what was "a sort of continuous front line, an organized trench system of concrete and steel" (Rowe 1961, 45). From this point on, most news reports would describe the Maginot Line as a continuous line of defenses consisting of a trench system of concrete and steel. Even though contradictory information was later also released, the myth of a solid continuous line of fortification stubbornly persisted even after the war.

The Maginot planners had to place the new fortifications as close to the border as possible to protect the new frontier and to give a feeling of security to those living in the major cities of Alsace and Lorraine. However, the forts could not be placed so close to the border that they would not be able to take maximum advantage of the surrounding terrain. Thus, the main line of defenses had to be five to ten kilometers behind the border so that obstacles and clear fields of fire could be prepared on French territory since the Germans would not allow it to be done on their lands.

The RF of Metz had to protect the industrial zones of Lorraine, including the cities of Metz and Thionville. Although the town of Longwy was located too close to the Belgian border to be covered, the fortifications were placed close enough to Longwy and Longuyon to deny the enemy the opportunity to exploit the resources of the area. The section of the Maginot Line stretching from Longuyon to the vicinity of the Moselle faced the borders of Luxembourg and Belgium and was meant to prevent a swift German flanking movement through these neutral countries. These sectors were some of the most heavily fortified parts of the Maginot Line.

The SFs of the RF of Metz ran from Longuyon eastward across Lorraine to the vicinity of the Sarre. In the Sarre River Valley, which separated the RFs of Metz and the Lauter, the defenses thinned out in the area known as the Sarre Gap, a weak spot whose significance is often overlooked. It was here that the Prussian invasion of France took place in 1870, and it seems incredible that it was so lightly defended. It must be recalled that the plans drawn up in the 1920s suggested using this gap as the jumping off point for a French offensive into the Rhineland. As in the case of the area between Maubeuge and the sea, the water table was low, making it impossible to build large subterranean fortifications. However, the line could have had more depth as Pétain might have suggested. The defense of the area was to depend on large-scale flooding caused by diverting the waters of the Sarre River, and local canals and ponds. Unfortunately, the water barrier proved to be rather ineffective in 1940, largely because that year had been unusually dry and the water in the reservoirs had dropped to unexpectedly low levels.

On the east bank of the Sarre River the fortifications began again in the RF of Lauter and continued on to the Rhine, to a point just east of the town of Haguenau. Since the area between the Vosges and Rhine was not adequately fortified, plans had been drawn for additional ouvrages but work was never completed (Truttmann 1979, 241). The main reason why the construction of some of the petits ouvrages was canceled is that the water table was too close to the surface, which would have required more protection against humidity in the forts. This would have meant greater expenses at a time when the planners were cutting back on designs because of increased costs (Truttmann 1979, 241).

The RF of Lauter defended the approaches to Alsace and contained fewer major fortifications than the RF of Metz. Here the terrain was amenable to a more elastic defense, which depended on the thick woods and the Vosges Mountains for protection. Furthermore, this RF was low priority because it lacked major industrial centers. The sectors along the Upper Rhine, which were not part of the RF of Lauter, were protected by the great river and the mountains, which constituted a natural barrier against a German advance. Thus, the commission felt that there was no need for major positions in this area.

The most numerous fortifications in the Maginot scheme were bunker-like positions usually classified as casemates or blockhouses. The casemate usually contained a cloche (a small non-rotating steel cupola) and in many cases had two levels. The blockhouse was usually smaller, more simple and less sturdily built than a casemate. The larger works, classified as ouvrages, were actually forts with the mission to provide direct artillery fire support. They were the strong points of the Maginot Line.

The experiences derived from hand-to-hand battles fought in 1916 in the forts of Verdun heavily influenced the design of the ouvrages. Another, perhaps less important, source of inspiration for the French military architects was the newly acquired German Feste in Lorraine. Some of improvements that resulted included:

1. *Minimum exposure of the fort above ground level.* Even the German Feste of the previous generation had exposed court yards and casernes similar to those at Douaumont and other forts that were heavily damaged by artillery. In order to avoid the devastation, all facilities in the Maginot forts, with the exception of the actual combat positions, were sunk deep underground. All

the components of the forts were linked by underground tunnels so that no member of the garrison would have to brave enemy fire. The Maginot forts were made to withstand hits from the German 420-mm gun, some of the heaviest artillery with which the forts of Verdun had had to contend.

2. *Scattering exposed surface positions so as not to provide a visible outline or pattern of the fort.* At Verdun, the ouvrage of Froideterre, with scattered positions similar to those of a German Feste, had turned out to be less vulnerable than forts built in a more traditional manner. In the Maginot ouvrages, the entrances were placed far enough away to avoid being subjected to bombardment directed at the combat sections of the fort. However, the fossé or ditch was not eliminated from the plans because it was considered a valuable obstacle. Apparently the designers forgot that a fossé could help pinpoint a fort's position from the air. Fortunately, budgetary limitations prevented the completion of most fossés. The few that were built only covered part of a single side of a fort. Without the fossé the perimeter an ouvrage was more difficult to pinpoint.

3. *Blending of the fort into the salient features of the terrain.* In the past forts had dominated the terrain they were built on. Fort Douaumont, for instance, stood out in the distance. The German Feste were better concealed, but their larger blocks provided sizable targets. The positions of new Maginot ouvrages, however, were built into the terrain and each position was of medium or small size.

4. *All around defensive fires.* Most of the World War I era forts, even some with gun turrets, did not have the capability to cover their rear. For example, the Verdun forts had to rely on fires from the other forts in the ring for their defense. The Maginot forts, on the other hand, found themselves in a linear arrangements, so each ouvrage had to ensure its security by covering all its approaches.

5. *Location of forts in the main combat zone.* At Verdun, forts like Vaux had ended up in the midst of the front line and had managed to dominate the battle. It was decided, therefore that the new forts of the Maginot Line would be veritable fighting machines rather than support positions. This is one reason why they did not mount heavier artillery.

6. *A system of interior defenses.* The Verdun forts had been subjected to gas and infantry assault and had become helpless once the enemy was inside the fort. Chicanes inside Fort Douaumont and Fort Vaux had to be hastily raised to hold the enemy back inside the fort. To avoid such a situation, the new forts were equipped with such devices from the very beginning, like the German Feste, which had been prepared for such an eventuality.

7. *Total self-sufficiency.* Fort Vaux had had to surrender because of lack of water and deteriorating conditions outside (Horne 1962, 261-262). The new forts would be totally self-sufficient and include their own wells, efficient drainage and support facilities.

This combination of elements resulted in the strongest gun-firing fortifications in history. The plans drawn up by CORF did not create impregnable positions, but rather strong points that would buy time for the main army, time to mobilize and organize a defense or an offensive. However, the myth persisted that the Maginot Line was an invincible line meant to stand as a buffer between France and Germany. Later this erroneous perception would have adverse effects on war planning. The French High Command, however, never lost sight of the fact that the Maginot Line and its forts could not stand alone since they relied mainly on 75-mm guns and had no heavy artillery. Field units had to provide artillery support. Special heavy artillery pieces mounted on rail cars, such as the 340-mm railway gun, could also be rolled in on railroad spurs laid out behind the Maginot Line (Claudel 1974, 18). In addition, each ouvrage was covered by its neighbors, which were able to bring their firepower to bear upon its superstructure if the enemy broke through. The 75-mm guns could inflict little damage to the fort but they could pulverize anyone who ventured upon the fort's surface.

The casemates of the ouvrages faced away from the enemy and were not strong enough to withstand heavy artillery. This was done intentionally to avoid running into the difficulties encountered in recapturing Fort Douaumont in 1916. However, in 1944, when the allied forces advanced upon the Maginot forts then occupied by the Germans, they still found it difficult to penetrate these casemates.

The weapons of the Maginot Line were pretargeted on the whole terrain within their range in order to raise the probability of a first round hit. Unfortunately, the guns were not test-fired during peace time to verify their accuracy because such activity would have endangered civilians.

CORF established two basic types of ouvrages: the gros (large) ouvrage and the petit (small) ouvrage. The gros ouvrages were equipped with the artillery and for this reason were also termed as *ouvrages d'artillerie* or artillery ouvrages. The Petits ouvrages contained mainly an assortment of infantry-type weapons. Each was designed to support its neighbors as well as the small casemate and observation positions in the intervals.

The two segments of the Maginot Line Proper were divided into two regions: The RF of Metz and the RF of the Lauter further subdivided into four and three *secteurs fortifiés*, respectively, arranged as follows:

Région Fortifiée de Metz—14 gros and 24 petits ouvrages.
1. SF de la Crusnes—3 gros and 4 petits ouvrages. Purpose: To deny the enemy the industrial region of Longuyon and the nearby Briery iron mines.
2. SF de Thionville—7 gros and 4 petits ouvrages. Purpose: To protect the approaches to the industrial city of Thionville.
3. SF de Boulay—4 gros and 11 petits ouvrages. Purpose: To block the most direct route to Metz.
4. SF de Faulquemont—5 petits ouvrages. Purpose: To block the approaches to Metz. Here began the Sarre Gap, which fell under the jurisdiction of the adjacent *Secteur Défensif de la Sarre* and relied mainly on water obstacles and flooding for its defense. This sector was not part of either RF.

Région Fortifiée de la Lauter—6 gros and 5 petits ouvrages.

1. SF de Rohrbach—2 gros and 4 petits ouvrages. Purpose: To protect the northern approaches to Strasbourg. The petits ouvrages of Haut Poirier and Rohrbach were planned as gros ouvrages to strengthen the sector's flank adjacent to the weak SD de la Sarre (Claudel 1974, 10; Truttmann 1979, Plan 74).

2. SF de Vosges—2 gros and 1 petit ouvrage. Purpose: Same as Rohrbach. Both sectors had the defensive advantages offered by the Vosges.

3. SF de Haguenau—2 gros ouvrages. Purpose: Same as Rohrbach, but also to cover gap between Vosges and Rhine leading to Strasbourg. Plans called for the construction of several additional ouvrages in this sector. Two of these, Oberreodern and Kaaffenheim, were to be gros ouvrages located on either side of the forest of Haguenau. They would have covered the open terrain between the Vosges and the Rhine (Claudel 1974, 9; Truttmann 1979, Plan 74).

At the end of 1929 the government issued the contracts for construction. Early in 1930 work began on the first ouvrages: Rochonvillers and Hackenberg in the RF of Metz, and Simserhof and Hochwald in the RF of Lauter. These would be four of the largest forts. As time went by and resources dwindled, designs were modified and down-sized.

The RF of Metz contained most of the gros ouvrages to guard a key industrial region, only half of which faced the German frontier. The remainder were located along the border of southern Belgium and Luxembourg. The Maginot Line did not have considerable depth. In front of the main line of resistance, which included the ouvrages, a covering line was designed to warn of the enemy approach and attempt to channel and delay him. Behind the main line there were supporting positions, but they were not intended to act as a second line of defense as proposed in 1928. Almost as an afterthought, during the 1930s the army decided to create a stop line of lesser fortifications of a type known as Main d'Oeuvre Militaire (MOM), which were built by military personnel (Claudel 1974, 16). By the time the war started, these small MOM bunkers were not completed in sufficient numbers to create an effective barrier. As a result, the Maginot Line was essentially a shallow, linear position, which required a reasonable number of field divisions to help it protect the frontier effectively. Today, the true nature and purpose of the Maginot Line are still frequently misunderstood as people continue to believe that it was an impregnable wall that failed to fulfill its mission.

NOTES

1. Before World War I, the term *ouvrage* was used to refer to smaller interval positions between forts, but after the war it was applied to any works or forts. In the present work, the term will be used to refer to the forts of the Maginot Line.

2. German documents during the war incorrectly identified virtually all the defenses from the North Sea to the Swiss border as part of the Maginot Line (see *Denkschrift: Über die französische* 1941).

3. It took the U.S. Army another twenty years to realize this (Hughes 1981, 124).

4. In 1936 American sources estimated the amount spent at $350 million (Johnson 1936, 14).

5. Vivian Rowe (1961), who first described the Maginot Line, noted that the British press was especially privileged with the "secret" information.

3

THE OUVRAGES D'ARTILLERIE

The media dubbed the Maginot Line a "super trench." In reality, it was a series of subterranean forts, whose most innovative feature was the location of their interior positions, deep below the surface. The largest Maginot works were the artillery forts, or *gros ouvrages*, underground positions usually about 30 meters below the ground and linked by subterranean galleries.

The ouvrages' armament consisted of three basic types of artillery: 75-mm guns, 135-mm howitzers and 81-mm mortars.[1] The 75s and the 135s constituted the real artillery of the new forts, which mounted a total of 137 of these weapons in casemates or turrets from Longuyon to the Rhine.[2] The turret-mounted weapons included over fifty percent of the 75s and eight-five percent of the 135s. The petits ouvrages did not include either of these two weapons and the 81-mm mortar was their largest piece.

Theoretically the average Maginot Line Proper fort, based on the total number of weapons and positions deployed, would consist of:

1. Six pieces of 75-mm or 135-mm artillery as follows:
   —Four or five 75-mm guns
   —One or two 135-mm howitzers
2. Two 81-mm mortars.
The above weapons would be mounted as follows:
   —one or two twin 75-mm gun turrets
   —no or one twin 135-mm howitzer turret
   —one twin 81-mm mortar turret
   —remainder of weapons casemate mounted.

Two of the twenty artillery ouvrages, Bréhain (A-6) and Anzeling (A-25), fit precisely this model.[3] Another ouvrage, Soetrich (A-11), was almost identical but had two 81-mm mortars in casemates instead of a turret. With the exception of Rochonvillers (A-8) and Grand-Hohékirkel, each ouvrage contained at least one twin 81-mm mortar turret. Hackenberg (A-19) and Schiessek each contained two twin 81-mm mortar turrets.[4] Every ouvrage had 75-

mm guns with the exception of Galgenberg (A-15), which only had 135-mm howitzers. All the positions, with the exception of Latiremont, mounted one or two twin 75-mm gun turrets. Thirteen of the twenty ouvrages had 135-mm howitzers and at least one twin 135-mm howitzer turret (Bruge 1975, 375-379). All of the turrets had a 360 degree field of fire, whereas the guns in the casemates were limited to only 45 degrees.

A further breakdown of the artillery of the Maginot Line shows:

One hundred and twenty-nine guns and howitzers plus several
75-mm guns in caponiers:
  —Ninety-one 75-mm guns
  —Thirty-eight 135-mm howitzers
RF of Metz—ninety tubes
  —Sixty-six 75-mm guns
  —Twenty-four 135-mm howitzers
  —Turret mounted weapons from the above:
  —Forty-two 75-mm guns in twenty-one twin gun turrets
  —Twenty-two 135-mm howitzers in eleven twin gun turrets
RF of the Lauter (including the SF of the Sarre):
  —Forty-three tubes
  —Twenty-nine 75-mm guns
  —Fourteen 135-mm howitzers
  —Turret mounted-weapons from the above:
  —Fourteen 75-mm guns in seven twin gun turrets
  —Ten 135-mm howitzers in five twin gun turrets (Bruge 1975, 375-379).

The RF Lauter packed half the firepower of RF Metz even though it had less than one third of the Maginot Line's artillery ouvrages (six of twenty). However, its positions lay closer to the German border than anywhere else—one of them was as near as five kilometers—so that the greater firepower may have been considered necessary for their survival.

In the RF of Metz eleven of the fourteen gros ouvrages defended Thionville and the approach routes to Metz. These ouvrages occupied a section about forty kilometers long, giving an average of one ouvrage in less than four kilometers, not including the petits ouvrages. This constituted the greatest concentration of firepower in the Maginot Line.

The artillery ouvrages were massive subterranean constructions, consisting of one or two entrance blocks and several combat blocks. The block was a position that had to be partially exposed to the surface in order to preform the functions assigned to it. A fort usually incorporated three basic types of combat blocks: observation, artillery and infantry. The observation blocks generally consisted of fixed observation cupolas known as cloches. Although they are not classified as combat blocks by all historians of the Maginot Line, their cloches could, and in most cases did, mount light weapons. In addition, they directed most of the ouvrage's combat activities, so they should be classified as combat blocks. The artillery block was either a casemate, a turret, or a combination of both. Finally, the infantry block consisted of a casemated position for anti-tank guns and machine guns and/or a machine gun turret. Every ouvrage had at least one infantry block with a machine gun turret.

Construction of most gros ouvrages began in 1930 after surveys and plans had been prepared and approved in 1929. The work on these great forts consisted mainly of initial excavations at the sites in 1930. In a few ouvrages, such as Hackenberg, building started in late 1929. Work on the subterranean galleries, underground facilities, and surface positions was well under way by 1931. By the end of 1933, most of the subterranean positions and the combat and entrance blocks were completed. During 1934 workers began outfitting the interiors of the ouvrages with equipment necessary for transmitting electricity and ventilation and installing lifts or elevators. Finally, in 1935 the forts were ready for service and the army began installing the anti-tank obstacles. The installation of the weapons was not as speedy as the construction. Thus, it was not until 1937 that the 37-mm and 47-mm anti-tank guns were finally installed (Hohnadel and Truttmann 1988, 4-5; Hohnadel and Varoqui 1986, 40-41; Collin and Wahl 1981, 37).

This construction schedule applied to the gros ouvrages of the Old Fronts, not to the two forts built in the New Fronts or in the Alpine sectors. In the Alps the building proceeded much more slowly. Work did not speed up until Mussolini's Ethiopian adventure and the creation of the Axis in 1936 convinced the French leadership that there was a real threat on France's southeastern border.

Although CORF prepared the plans for the fortifications, the chief engineer in charge of fortifications for each region took charge of the construction of the ouvrages and other works in his area. This type of effort required the use of civilian contractors, some of whom employed foreigners. These workers were entrusted with a variety of tasks ranging from excavating the subterranean galleries, to building the blocks, and installing the equipment. As late as 1940, civilians still had access to the forts, which still needed some refinishing. According to French public opinion, which is now supported by documental evidence, German intelligence employed some of these workers as spies although there is no evidence that they engaged in sabotage.

The internal operation of the fort relied on electric power, which could be either generated inside by diesel engines or imported from the outside. However, although blueprints for external power had been drawn up in 1930, the actual link to the civilian power grid was delayed until 1938-1939. The ouvrages were then linked to the outside grid through underground cables. The civilian districts were linked up, in turn, with other regions of the interior in case the enemy destroyed their power-generating plants. The central heating system and the searchlights in some of the combat blocks were installed between 1939 and 1940. The need for a heating system became apparent when the forts were manned in response to the German occupation of the Rhineland in 1936. Showers for gas decontamination also had to be added in the entrance blocks (Hohnadel and Varoqui 1986, 40-41; Weisbecker 1985, 5-9; Hohnadel and Truttmann 1988, 6-7).

FERMONT (A-2)

The ouvrage of Fermont is fairly representative of the Maginot forts. This ouvrage of average size comprised seven combat and two entrance blocks. Its garrison consisted of approximately eight hundred men led by a captain. Some of the other ouvrages came under the command of a *Chef de Battallion* (equivalent to major), or, in a few cases, a lieutenant colonel. The combat blocks of Fermont, relatively well concealed on a hill, mounted a total of five 75-mm guns and two 81-mm mortars. Nearby, on Fermont's left flank, lay the petit ouvrage of Chappy, the western terminus of the Maginot Line Proper. Behind Chappy, two casemates and an observatory flanked Fermont. Five casemates and another observatory covered Fermont's right flank to the east. These positions fed information to Fermont, helping it direct its artillery fire. They also protected the fort and were, in turn, covered by its supporting fires. According to the Maginot Line concept, all the fighting was to be kept in front of these positions. Fermont and Chappy were designed, like other ouvrages, to bear the brunt of it. Fermont and the nearby ouvrage of Latiremont also covered each other with defensive fires. This type of supporting fire was a primary feature of the Maginot positions.

Fermont had two entrance blocks, a relatively standard feature for an artillery ouvrage. One entrance block was exclusively for the men, while the other served as an entry for supplies. The entrance blocks had the firepower of an infantry block and were not as weak as in the World War I era forts. The only access to the ouvrage other than the entrance blocks was from a small number of well-concealed emergency exits. In addition to the exterior obstacles, many surprises awaited intruders within the fort. The capture of Fort Douaumont by German soldiers climbing through firing positions in the coffre was not to be repeated again in any of the modern fortifications.

The Men's Entrance (*entrée des hommes*—EH) was located in the side of a hill. Its massive rectangular facade faced the rear of the fort. Above the block two lookout cloches, each armed with light machine guns (*fusil mitrailleur*—FM) and a 50-mm mortar, facilitated 360 degrees of observation and small-arms fire coverage. A large iron grate barred the entrance, which was also covered by a machine gun position. In front of the grate a moat, or *fossé*, formed an additional obstacle. In peace time it was spanned by a portable metal bridge. In time of war it would also serve as a receptacle for pieces of concrete splintering off the facade, thus keeping the firing positions from being masked.[5] Not far behind the grate, the entrance tunnel made a 90 degree turn to the left in front of the FM crenel. The end of the entrance passage was sealed by an armored door. Three large crenels pierced the block's exposed face. Two of these positions mounted light FMs, while the largest crenel housed a special fortress model of the same type of machine guns on a twin mount (*Jumelage de Mitrailleuses*—JM). The gunners could swing the JM mount back against the wall and replace it with a 47-mm anti-tank gun slung from an overhead rail. One of the light machine gun crenels was angled so it could cover the fossé and the face of the block. Inside the block, a two-ton elevator and a stairway led down to the bowels of the ouvrage.

About 250 meters from the EH, but not in direct line of sight, was located the much larger Munitions Entrance (*Entrée des Munitions*—EM). Two lookout cloches on top of this structure also served as observation and defensive positions. In addition, a special type of cloche, almost flush with ground level and containing a single vertical opening to accommodate a 60-mm mortar, supplied close defensive fires. However, the army did not succeed in perfecting and mounting the mortar in time for the war. Thus its cloche, which could serve no other purpose, remained unused. Like the EH, the EM was protected by a fossé the facade. A small concrete bridge spanned the moat in front of the block, leading to a double gate of iron bars. Four crenels in face of the block were angled in such a way as to permit cross fires. The larger crenel had the same type of special fortress machine guns, JM, and anti-tank weapons as the EM.

Behind the heavy entrance grates of the EM a corridor about 3.5 meters long and covered by a light machine gun led to a large armored door. Between the grate and the armored door lay a three-meter deep trap covered by a rolling bridge, which could be withdrawn into the wall in war time. Entrances designed for truck traffic usually had a wider entrance tunnel and no bridge-covered trap. A short distance behind the first armored door, two bunker-like positions defended a second armored door. From there the tunnel continued towards two elevators—one of five-tons and the other of two-tons—and a stairway connecting the entrance floor to the main underground gallery. The only access from the EM to the garrison area and the engine rooms (the *caserne* and the *usine*), located at about 30 meters below the surface, opened behind the second armored door.

Although most EMs contained features similar to those of Fermont, level entrances, which facilitated logistical work, were preferred to elevator shafts. On the other hand, elevators were favored in the EHs because they had additional defensive value.

The firing chambers of the entrance block presented standard features throughout the Maginot Line. Each was equipped with a special tube for ejecting grenades into the fossé. In the cloches above, observers maintained contact with a soldier in the firing chamber below via a voice tube. The floor of the cloche could be lowered so that a wounded observer might be easily removed, obviating the need to lower the victim through the narrow access hatch and ladder. This mobile floor also facilitated the movement of ammunition for the FM and breech-loaded 50-mm mortar from the bottom floor to cloche level (Dropsy 1979, interview).

A small-gauge railroad track linked Fermont to the military railway. Rail cars crossed the concrete and the rolling bridges into the EM where they were off-loaded. In the forts where the EMs were not linked to a rail line, the munitions were delivered by truck. At Fermont, the cargo was placed on the fort's small rail wagons, which were rolled into the elevator and lowered into the main gallery. They exited the elevator through a gate on the opposite side from which they had entered, were hooked up to one of the three electric train engines, and were towed to their final destination. In emergencies, these vehicles could rely on man power for short distances.

At Fermont the elevators opened at the end of the main gallery, a short distance from the main ammunition magazine of the fort, M-1. There were three types of magazines in the fort: M-1 (only one per fort), M-2, and M-3. Near the magazine was a workshop for the train engines. The gallery, extending for about one kilometer, linked the M-1 to the heart of the fort located under a hill.

The gallery was served along its length by the narrow-gauge railroad or subway known as the *Metro*. It branched off into several smaller galleries leading to the various combat blocks. These secondary galleries were too low to hold an overhead power cable, which powered the little metro engines. Armored air locks, also with a low clearance, further restricted the use of overhead cables in these access galleries. So the cars had to be moved by man power through these sections. When necessary, however, a special attachment allowed a power cable to hook up to the main power line with the aid of a winch. Thus powered, the engine could proceed into these galleries (Dropsy 1979, interview).

Concrete shelves lining both sides of the central gallery carried duplicate sets of telephone and power cables. Along the ceiling of the tunnel stretched the electrical power cable for the subway engines. The Metro rails ran along one side of the gallery while the troops marched along the other side. The crew of Fermont had to walk because the underground train was reserved for the transportation of munitions. Unlike King Minos' Labyrinth, Fermont's underground maze of galleries was user-friendly because all the lights on the walls pointed towards the entrance. It seems, however, that this ingenious system was not commonly used outside of Fermont. The main gallery branched in two directions near the M-1 magazine, one corridor leading to the M-1 and the elevator shaft of the EM and the other towards the garrison area.

Fermont consisted of seven combat blocks, divided among three basic types: the casemate, the turret or special observation cloche, and a combination of both. Each block functioned primarily as an observation, infantry or artillery position. The blocks were about one hundred or more meters apart in order to reduce the fort's vulnerability. Thus, if one position was damaged, the others would still remain fully operational. In closely spaced position, on the other hand, a well-aimed hit could destroy the whole fort, as in the case of Fort Loncin.

The most effective combat position in Fermont, and indeed most of the Maginot forts, was the twin-gun turret for the 75-mm guns. However, these turrets were so expensive to build and put so much stress on the fort's energy supply, that they were used sparingly by the designers (Dropsy 1979, interview). The more turrets an ouvrage had, the greater were the power demands on its generator system and the greater the consumption of reserve fuel supplies. Thus, to operate a large number of turrets a fort would require more machinery and space, which was at a premium. For these reasons few ouvrages were equipped with many turrets, especially those mounting the largest, the 75-mm guns. The turrets could also be controlled manually, in an emergency. Their design was very similar to that of the World War I era. In fact, turrets from the Great War had been installed in some of the other Maginot forts. Only one of these actually housed a pair of 75-mm guns and the others received 25-mm guns.[6]

Block 1 at Fermont consisted of a gun turret with two 75-mm Model 33 guns. These canons, with a rapid-fire rate of up to thirty rounds per minute and an effective range of 12,000 meters, had considerable firepower (Truttmann 1979, 121; Truttmann August 1982, correspondence). Its ability to retract or eclipse reduced the turret's exposed surface area so that only a direct hit by a heavy-caliber weapon had any chance of knocking it out.

The turret with all its components weighed 265 tons (including a 30-ton roof). The steel roof was 0.35 meters thick and the turret wall was 0.30 meters thick. All of this was sunk into 3.50 meters of concrete (Maistret 1978, 11). At Fort Vaux only a direct hit had managed to remove a similar, albeit weaker, position and it had taken a round from a 420-mm weapon!

The turret crew consisted of seven men. Three loaded and fired the guns inside the turret. Loading as well as ejection of the shell casing was automatic on the 75-mm Model 33, which accounted for its rapid rate of fire. Below, in the control room, were four other artillery men. Two men served an apparatus called a *monte-charge* (charge mounter), operated either electrically or manually, which carried the 75-mm rounds from the M-3 magazine to the turret. The ammunition was carried into the control room in a case slung from an overhead rail. All of the ammunition was moved in these cases throughout the ouvrage. The other two crew members operated the controls to raise and lower the turret. Below the block other soldiers operated the M-2 magazine, the munitions elevator, and other equipment. The control room was equipped with a phone and a special type of naval-like order transmitter, which received and relayed firing instructions. Below the control room was a chamber housing the 18-ton counterweight for eclipsing the turret. Although it was electrically powered, it could also be operated manually by one man in an emergency. At the control-room level another man could manually rotate the turret (Paquin 1978, interview).

On the surface, near the gun turret, protected by a heavy screen, was the air vent for the block, which drew air into the filtering system designed to take out poison gas. High air pressure inside the fort also prevented the infiltration of gas. Also exposed on the surface was a cloche for light weapons and observation known as a *Guêt Fusil-Mitrailleur* (GFM). It was equipped with a light machine gun (FM) and a breech-loaded 50-mm mortar. The GFM cloche, being the most common type of cloche, was found in the majority of the Maginot combat blocks. Its armament was standard. The thickness of its steel varied from 0.25 to 0.30 meters and half of its armor structure was implanted in the concrete roof of the block (Maistret 1978, 9). The cloche's interior was large enough for one or two men who maintained communications with the block below by telephone or voice tube.

An additional position on the surface was known as a *cloche lance-grenade*. It had a single tube-like opening made for a special, automatically loaded and fired 60-mm mortar, which was to shower the surrounding area with bombs and keep the enemy off the superstructure. It was the same type of position as the one already noted on the EM (Truttmann August 1982, correspondence).

There was no exit to the surface of Block 1. Nothing less than a direct hit by a large-caliber gun or a demolition team with powerful explosives could breach it. Its roof cover was so thick that it was capable of withstanding direct hits from 420-mm rounds.

Block 4, the other artillery position, consisted of three 75-mm Model 32 guns. This position had less firepower than the turret because its weapons were only semi-automatic and had to be manually loaded. The practical effective range of these guns was about 10,000 meters. This type of position gave its guns only a 45 degree angle of fire. Its exposed concrete facade, 1.75 meters thick, could only withstand hits from 160-mm caliber rounds. These casemates were more lightly protected than the roof because they faced to the rear of the fort and were out of the direct line of fire from the enemy's heavy artillery. In the Maginot forts, rearward positions like this casemate were thinner in order to facilitate the recapture of the fort without having to go through an ordeal such as the bloody 1916 battle for Fort Douaumont, which resulted in a veritable carnage (Claudel 1974, 2). In addition, expecting plunging artillery fire rather than direct fire on these rear walls, the Maginot designers felt that heavy protection would not be crucial on this side of the fort. The roof of Block 4, like that of Block 1, could withstand heavy-caliber artillery fire. The casemate itself could supply supporting fires to flanking positions, which included the nearby ouvrage of Latiremont. It could also cover the approaches to the entrance blocks from the fort's right flank.

Block 4 included three firing chambers for the 75-mm guns on its upper level and an M-3 magazine. Each gun was served by a crew of nine men (Dropsy 1979, interview). A crenel for a light machine gun covered the fossé in front of the block's facade and another interior crenel protected a small armored door that opened onto the moat. On the lower level of the block, which included the filter room, the garrison had a rest area. A GFM cloche rose above the block. Another cloche, built into the surface of the roof and mounting special fortress twin 7.5-mm machine guns (JM), fired over a single section of the fort's surface. It had only one weapons crenel and two small observation openings.

The emergency exit of Block 4, about half the size of a normal door, opened right over a fossé. In order to reach the surface of the fort, the soldiers would have to cross this moat via a small, portable metal bridge. It was through this door that the crew of the fort could come out and patrol or repair the surface area. However, according to Georges Dropsy, a veteran who served in the fort, the Fermont crew normally used a wooden plank instead of the metal bridge.

Two munitions elevators and a stairway served the block and connected it to the fort's interior deep below where the artillery block was linked to the main gallery by a subterranean access gallery. A set of armored doors, similar to those found on ships, acted as air locks in this access gallery. They also served as defensive positions, thanks to small openings for light weapons. Curving access galleries made direct fire down their length impossible, further strengthening the internal defense system. These measures were taken to avoid the recurrence of the situation that developed during World War I at Fort Vaux, which had lacked interior defenses.

Block 5, with a mortar turret, was also considered an artillery position and was served by artillery men. The turret was only half the size of the 75-mm gun turret. Its armament included two specially designed 81-mm mortars with an effective range of only 2,800 meters. Their breech-loading mechanism was designed for firing from an interior position and their rifling increased their accuracy. However, their rate of fire was only about fifteen rounds a minute. These mortars had to be water cooled like most of the other weapons in the fort. The surface and most of the interior features of Block 5 were similar to those of Block 1. However, the elevator of Block 5 weighed 1 ton instead of 2.5 tons, since ammunition loads for the mortars were not as heavy as those of other artillery. Block 5 also had a GFM cloche and covered the approaches to the ouvrage and its surface.

Block 6 mounted a machine gun turret and included two GFM cloches. This was an infantry position and required no elevators for heavy loads, but it did include a monte-charge for carrying the light ammunition loads. This position covered the right front of the fort as well as its surface.

The same type of block was found in every artillery ouvrage and in many petits ouvrages. At Fort Vaux, where there had been no similar positions, the garrison had been forced to operate from exposed positions on the surface, eventually losing control of the superstructure. However, Fort Vaux was not necessarily typical. Other forts of that earlier period had been equipped with machine gun turrets. Thus, the Maginot machine gun turrets were not an innovation, but they had more armor protection and were less exposed.

The machine gun turret block was similar to the other turreted positions.

At Fermont it is represented by Block 6, which had two cloches, and Block 2, which had one cloche. They both served a similar function, but different sides of the fort.

The machine gun turret was only slightly smaller than the 81-mm mortar's and it was run by a four-men crew. Two operated the machine guns in the turret and the remaining two maneuvered the turret and sent up the ammunition from the control room (Truttmann August 1982, correspondence). These turrets also had a mounting position for a 25-mm cannon, which was not delivered in time for the war. On the upper level was also the air filter room connected to an armored air vent like that of Block 1. In casemated blocks, such as Block 4, the air vent was usually located on the facade instead of the roof. Block 2 was connected to the subterranean access gallery, which was reached by a stairway. There was no need for an elevator or an M-2 magazine because the machine gun ammunition was small and easy to transport.

Block 7 of Fermont, an infantry casemate, had the normal two-level arrangement. On the roof, there was an observation cloche and the empty emplacement for a special 60-mm mortar similar to that of Block 1 and the EM. A firing chamber with two crenels on the upper level housed twin machine guns or JM. One of the JM could be pulled out and replaced with a 47-mm anti-tank gun as in the entrance blocks. A third crenel, which flanked the fossé, was designed for a light machine gun (FM). An armored searchlight stand was at the corner of the block. These searchlights were a feature found on some infantry blocks for night time surveillance of the area, especially to the flanks and rear. The air filters and a rest area for the block's garrison were located in the lower level. In many ouvrages the lower level of the infantry casemates was equipped with an emergency exit opening into the fossé. It was closed by a small armored door covered by an interior crenel situated behind it. At Fermont, Block 7, located just down hill from Block 4, provided protection for that position against direct enemy assault by infantry or armor. In addition, it covered the rearward approaches to Block 5.

One of the most important positions in Fermont was Block 3. Designated as an observation block, it occupied a key position on the highest part of the hill. Like all the other blocks, it too had two levels. Its importance lay in the fact that it housed the command post of the ouvrage in several rooms located at its lower level. It comprised four cloches.[7] Two mounted twin machine guns whose limited field of fire swept the vulnerable areas of the fort's surface. They were similar to the JM cloche of Block 4 and were purely defensive positions with no accommodation for observation. The third cloche was a standard observation cloche (GFM) with its normal armament. The fourth cloche included special optical instruments, including a periscope, for observation with no room for weapons with its narrow observation slits. This observation block and the headquarters below it constituted the brain center of the fort. Coordinating information from other observation cloches of Fermont, outside observatories and the interval troops, the command post sent firing instructions to all the artillery positions. Large maps and aerial photos and tables for pin-pointing targets lined the walls. Between 1935 and 1939, as part of the training program, the army's topographic service helped create the maps and firing charts for each ouvrage, collating data from the artillery and infantry services on each type of weapon and projectile employed in the ouvrage. In addition, geographical panoramas were painted on the walls of the firing chamber in all the ouvrages and casemates in order to give the gunners precise information on the distance and angle of the various points lying in front of each weapon (Truttmann 1979, 450-451). The orders from the command post were sent by telephone or through a special order transmitter similar to those used on a ship. The observation block of Fermont was located in a forward position because the terrain where the fort was built demanded it. However, this was not a typical arrangement; normally the observation block was placed further back.

The combat blocks were like semi-independent fortifications linked to each other and the rest of the fort by subterranean galleries. Fermont's underground features were, so to speak, its vital organs. Its main magazine (M-1), garrison area (*caserne*), power house (*usine*), and water and fuel stores were located by the entrances. Its central gallery sloped back toward this area, allowing seeping water to drain down towards the EM and out through an underground passageway. This drain could also be used as an emergency exit and was closed off at the main gallery by an armored door covered by a firing crenel. As long as the fort remained in operation, this drainage system was highly effective. However, after Fermont was decommissioned, mineral deposits blocked the drainage gutter, flooding the elevator shafts (Paquin 1978, interview).

In the caserne area, a cistern collected drinking water. In an emergency the garrison could also draw water from a well. An infirmary complete with operating room took care of the soldiers' basic medical needs. Unlike the officers and the NCOs, the soldiers in most ouvrages had no individual bunks because the barracks could only accommodate about a third of the crew at a time. In peace time the troops were quartered near the ouvrage in a standard above-ground army camp. The garrison operated in three shifts, which kept most facilities in constant operation as each shift rotated (Claudel 1974, 2-4).

Despite some shortcomings, the amenities for the troops were a vast improvement over those of the pre-World War I era forts. Eating facilities were rather cramped, since there was no dining hall. The men ate on folding tables, actually shelves or drop-leaf tables, attached to the walls of the corridors. Latrine facilities were available in all the blocks and the caserne. The showers, on the other hand, were only available in the living quarters. At Fort Vaux, for instance, the garrison had found it almost impossible to continue the struggle in 1916 after the latrines had been captured by the enemy (Horne 1962, 258-260). Brialmont, in Belgium, had even forgotten that men had to relieve themselves occasionally, and neglected to install the proper facilities near the fighting positions in his late nineteenth century forts.

Beyond the caserne, another armored door separated the usine with its four diesel engines from the living quarters. The caserne's air filters occupied a large chamber nearby and an access gallery led off to the Men's Entrance. Two engines sufficed to meet the ouvrage's daily electrical requirements. The current was sent at double the necessary voltage so as not to lose power in the transmission, then reconverted at a substation near Block 4 from whence it was redistributed to each block area. The usine also had its own storage area for large stocks of diesel fuel, engine oil and water (Maistret 1979, interview).

The diesel engines operated only when normal sources of power were cut and/or the fort was isolated. A fortified substation linked to the main civilian power grid redistributed electricity to Fermont and other nearby ouvrages to which it was connected with special military power line. One or two kilometers before each ouvrage, the aerial cable went underground to prevent detection in the battle zone. This measure also prevented the enemy from locating the ouvrage from the air by following the lines. Some ouvrages could supply power to one or more neighboring positions, including other ouvrages, through underground emergency cables (Truttmann August 1982, correspondence). Time and lack of funds impeded the completion of all planned links between ouvrages.

The emplacement of the usine was carefully selected so that the exhaust fumes from the engines would have a minimal distance to travel to reach the exterior of the fort. The best place was usually the vicinity of the EH or EM. At Fermont, the fumes vented through an outlet located by the fossé of the EH. However, the noise generated by the engines could become a problem for the crew, so at Fermont the usine was placed far enough from the living quarters to avoid irritating the troops. Unfortunately, the usine could not always be so conveniently located. In some ouvrages, such as Anzeling, a special chimney block surrounded with barbed wire and rail obstacles was added and was protected by an adjacent combat block.

Fermont's barracks area, windowless and painted regulation gray and white, was rather small, dank and depressing. Bunk beds stacked three high lined the cold concrete walls. A small metal partition separated the men's heads from each other. Each room was heated since, at 30 meters below the surface, the temperature was constant but rather cool.

Some old photographs show soldiers sun bathing under solar lamps to maintain their health. However, the veterans of Fermont, who do not remember ever using such lamps, point out that they had sufficient time above ground to enjoy the sunshine (Paquin 1978, interview). No doubt, these lamps were used more extensively in ouvrages where the garrison had little opportunity to spend time at the surface at reasonable intervals.

Fermont, like all other ouvrages, had a small recreation area equipped with a radio and phonograph and little else. Living conditions were spartan at best. The only advantage Fermont and similar positions offered their occupants was a relative sense of security.

HACKENBERG (A-19)

The ouvrage of Hackenberg is interesting because it was one of the two largest of the Maginot forts. Its thirteen 75-mm guns and 135-mm howitzers (not including one 75-mm gun covering the anti-tank ditch) made it the most heavily armed ouvrage of the Maginot Line. Hackenberg consisted of a total of nineteen blocks, while the next largest ouvrage, Hochwald, had only fourteen; the average artillery ouvrage consisted of nine or ten. Hochwald would have been much larger had it been completed as planned (Bruge 1975, 375-379).

Both Hackenberg and Hochwald included two distinct combat sections. Since these ouvrages were the best known of the Maginot Line, many erroneously assumed that all artillery ouvrages consisted of two distinct combat areas. In reality, most gros ouvrages did not follow this pattern, which had been dictated by the terrain rather than the size of the ouvrage.

The ouvrage of Hackenberg was literally cut into a large hill. Its magazine and garrison lay beneath one of the highest parts of the hill. The fort included almost ten kilometers of tunnels, about one third of which were served by a Metro (Heymès 1979, interview). The main gallery ran through the hill for over 350 meters, from the caserne to a point where it branched off in two different directions leading to the combat sections. One of these two galleries, which passed under the highest part of the hill, ended on a spur to the northwest where the combat positions sat.

The other gallery continued in an easterly direction to a second group of combat positions on a ridge of the hill. About 100 meters from the junction of the two main galleries, the western tunnel branched off once more, leading to two observation blocks located in the highest part of the hill, between the two groups of combat blocks. Each of these blocks was outfitted with the normal combat/observation cloche (GFM). In addition, it included a special periscope cloche consisting of a single opening and a movable metal lid through which the periscope could be projected. The western section of the ouvrage lay about 700 meters from the caserne while the eastern section was almost 1,200 meters away.

As at Fermont, a ridge separated Hackenberg's Munitions Entrance (EM) block from the Men's Entrance (EH). However, at Hackenberg these two positions were about halfway up the side of a steep and much larger hill than at Fermont. About 18 meters of the EM's width were exposed to the surface. The block stood about 8 meters high. Two firing chambers similar to those of Fermont covered the sides of the entrance with two crenels each. The EM was surmounted by the usual two GFM cloches. Most features were similar to Fermont's: fossé, rolling bridge, etc. However, there were two machine gun crenels in front of the armored door instead of one. The armored door split in two and slid into recesses on either side of the entrance wall, like Fermont's. A smaller doorway, cut into one of the armored halves, allowed the men to enter the fort when the large main doors were closed to vehicles. Past the entrance, the curved passageway was covered by three bunker-like positions similar to those in all EMs. In Hackenberg the entrance gallery connected directly with the main gallery and had no elevators like Fermont. A third type of EM, found in some other ouvrages, had neither elevator nor level access to the main gallery. Instead, an incline led down to the gallery, requiring a cable to lower the cars into the main gallery. The level approach for EMs, like at Hackenberg, was the ideal.

The gallery from the EM led to the caserne after passing by the nine-cell M-1 magazine, which was the largest of the Maginot Line (Bruge 1975, 377). Special armored doors, similar to those of Fermont, protected the garrison area from a potential explosion in the magazine. The caserne was similar to that of Fermont, only larger. The troops either walked through the large expanse of galleries and corridors or rode on special folding bicycles (Heymès 1979, interview). Since the garrison was large, about 1,200 men, Hackenberg had larger facilities and provided a greater number of services than other forts.

Beyond the caserne lay the combat blocks previously mentioned. The headquarters or command center of the ouvrage was located on a separate level between the observation blocks and the access gallery. This arrangement was rare, existing only in the few forts with a great difference in elevation between the main gallery level and the observation blocks (Claudel 1974, 2-3).

The western part of Hackenberg consisted of three artillery blocks. One casemate of three 75-mm guns, Block 8, provided defensive fires to the west as far as the Moselle, covering all the fortifications in between. Block 9, with a turret of two 135-mm howitzers and one casemated 135-mm howitzer, provided general support for the nearby positions. Block 10 had the turret for 81-mm mortars. To Block 10's defensive fires were added those of an infantry casemate, Block 7, which also mounted a machine gun turret. With the exception of the 135-mm artillery block and the combination casemate-turret infantry block, the combat positions were similar to those of Fermont.

A wide and deep anti-tank ditch extended for 250 meters along the western side of Hackenberg, then turned and moved towards the east. It extended from Block 25, about halfway to Block 24 and was then replaced by a wall spanning the remaining distance to the eastern section of combat blocks. The anti-tank ditch was covered by infantry positions. Block 25, the infantry casemate, at the end of the ditch served as a caponier. Its 75-mm gun was positioned so that it could fire through the anti-tank ditch as well as above and beyond it. The gun had a limited field of fire, which reached just beyond the ouvrage of Michelsberg. The ouvrage of Hochwald also employed 75-mm guns in similar positions. However, other ouvrages such as Simserhof lacked this type of position because CORF eventually canceled the construction of anti-tank ditches, replacing them with anti-tank rails, an adequate but less expensive alternative.

Most of Hackenberg's infantry casemates were only armed with 37-mm rather than the newer 47-mm anti-tank guns, because the already completed embrasures were too small to accommodate the new models. The larger guns went only to positions in newer forts and those not already completed.

Block 9 of Hackenberg, an artillery position, was armed with 135-mm howitzers, only one of which was in casemate. A machine gun position at moat level covered the face of the block because the two cloches above the casemate could not effectively protect the facade at close range. Although this type of defense was common in most artillery casemates, it did not give adequate protection from the rear. As a result, it was necessary to build other positions to cover these blocks from the rear.

The howitzers of Block 9, with a rather limited range, were able to supply fire support only to positions about five kilometers away. The turret, smaller than a 75-mm gun turret, was set in a concrete depression and kept a low silhouette even in the firing position. This arrangement was possible because howitzers, like mortars, have to be fired at a high angle and are not hampered by the depression. In a nearby block, a twin 81-mm mortar turret sat in a similar position. Curiously, the two GFM cloches of the block, as in most blocks, presented a more visible target than the turrets in their firing position.

In the western section of Hackenberg, the cloches were given masonry camouflage, which still remains in places. It was designed to confuse the enemy and hide the location of the weapons and observation crenels. Hackenberg was also outfitted with lighter decoy cloches and cupolas to give the impression that there was a combat block where in actuality there was none. This ploy was also used in other ouvrages.

Hackenberg's eastern section of combat blocks was similar to that already described. The western section had four blocks plus the infantry block at the end of the anti-tank ditch. The eastern group included six blocks plus a block at the end of the anti-tank wall which mounted nothing more than machine guns and a 50-mm mortar. Block 5 was an artillery casemate similar to Block 8, but it covered the right flank. Block 2 was a 75-mm gun turret position which was missing from the other group. A 135-mm howitzer turret made up Block 6, which did not have a casemate position like Block 9. Block 3 was an 81-mm mortar turret similar to Block 10. The machine gun turret of Block 1 covered the approaches to the ouvrage like Block 7, but like Block 6, it had no casemate position. In addition to Block 21, three other blocks with cloche and casemates covered the anti-tank wall, but they had direct subterranean connections to the main gallery. Some writers have confused the few ouvrages like Hackenberg which had two groups of combat blocks, and labeled each group as a separate fort, but this was not the case.

At Hackenberg, as in most ouvrages, as much of the natural vegetation as possible was preserved to provide concealment. Most of the combat sections appeared to be clearings in the forest and were carefully camouflaged. However, in the nearby woods trees were judiciously removed to clear fields of fire. No two ouvrages were identical. Fermont and Hackenberg, which are open to the public today, remain two of the best examples of Maginot Line gros ouvrages.   The first represents the average-sized forts, while the other embodies the original concepts that had to be canceled later.

NOTES

1. The 135-mm weapon was called a *lance bombe* or *bomb thrower*.   Some sources classify it as a mortar, but it appears to have characteristics closer to those of a howitzer.   Philippe Truttmann states that it was a 1926 French copy of the German 170-mm minenwerfer designed to strike at troops in protected positions.   Only the Maginot fortifications employed this type of weapon (Truttmann November 1982, correspondence).

2. A few of these 75s were used only to protect an anti-tank ditch and had a limited ability to act as supporting artillery.

3. Each ouvrage was identified by the letter A and a number designation. Likewise, interval casemates were identified by the letter C and a number and oberservatories with the letter O and a number.

4. In the RF of Lauter, Schiessek and the other ouvrages did not have an "A" designation number.

5. This feature was clearly a reaction to the Verdun experience.   Pictures of Fort Souville at Verdun show the entrance blocked by their own debris after heavy bombardment.

6. See section on weapons for more information on this subject.

7. There was no standard number or type of cloches for an observation block.

4

COMPONENTS OF AN OUVRAGE

Each ouvrage of the Maginot Line is unique because it had to be modified to adapt to the surrounding terrain. Although guidelines and standards were set for all types of ouvrages, the engineers had to modify them to meet local needs. These modifications included adding extra protection above the ouvrage where the water table prevented it from being placed at the required depth, placing pumps inside to drain the water where it was not practical to create a water drain which might have to extend a kilometer or more beyond the ouvrage, or putting elevators where the terrain did not permit the construction of a level or inclined entrance tunnel (Truttmann 1979, 240-241). Despite these differences, most gros ouvrages have many characteristics in common, giving them a certain degree of uniformity. These standardized elements consist mainly of the basic design, equipment, and certain features in the layout of the fort. It is, therefore, possible to identify and catalogue the main components of a typical Maginot fort.

THE BLOCKS

With the obvious exception of a few petits ouvrages of the monolithic type, the designers organized the forts into separate sections known as "blocks," which usually, but not always, were connected to the others by subterranean galleries. These blocks are classified by function and/or form.

If divided by function, the blocks fall into two main categories: the combat blocks and the entrance blocks. The combat blocks can be further subdivided into infantry, artillery, and observation blocks, not found in all ouvrages. The observation blocks, whose main purpose was to act as artillery observation posts, served also as infantry positions with respect to firepower.

If classified in terms of their form, the blocks fall into three basic types: casemate, turret, and mixed. As its name implies, the third type is a combination of the first two. Most observation blocks can be classified as turret-type positions even though they do not normally hold turrets but only cloches. No block held more than one turret but most consisted of two levels. In terms of function, the blocks could be classified into four categories: infantry, artillery, observation, and entrance.

a. The Infantry Block
   This type of block usually includes one or more of the following types of positions:
   i. *Mitrailleuses* turret (heavy machine guns).
   ii. One or more cloches for machine guns (FM or JM), light anti-tank gun, 50-mm mortar and/or observation.
   iii. Casemate position for anti-tank gun, machine guns (FM or JM) and a grenade thrower (a tube for dropping grenades into the fossé).
b. The Artillery Block
   This block includes one or more of the following types of positions:
   i. Turret for a heavy mortar, howitzer or gun.
   ii. Cloches for machine guns (FM or JM), mortar and/or observation.
   iii. Casemate position for heavy mortar, howitzer or gun and light machine gun (FM) and grenade thrower.
c. The Observation Block
   This block served primarily for artillery observation and contains one or more of the following:
   i. Cloches for machine guns (FM and JM), mortars and/or observation.
   ii. Special cloches which contained nothing more than a periscope for observation.
   iii. In a few instances a casemate with a crenel for observation and signaling.
d. The Entrance Blocks
   These blocks come in three basic types:
   i. The Munitions Entrance (gros ouvrages only). Type A was designed for rail cars from a special military railway and Type B for trucks only. Type B is much wider. Some ouvrages, like Schoenenbourg, with a Type B entrance received a rail link just before the 1940 campaign (Wahl 1982, interview). EMs were not normally used for the passage of troops.
   ii. Men's Entrance (found in most gros ouvrages). It was used exclusively for the movement of troops. Small containers of munitions could be moved through when necessary. Most are equipped with elevators for handling small loads unlike infantry blocks, which normally have only a stairway down to the gallery. The EM was armed like an infantry block.
   iii. Mixed Entrance (gros and petits ouvrages). It was used for both troops and munitions and exists in gros ouvrages that have a single entrance. Some are as large as Type B EMs while others are as small as an interval casemate's entrance.

Right before the war started, many infantry and artillery blocks and some entrance blocks were being equipped with a bomb throwing cloche for a special, automatically fed, breech-loaded 60-mm mortar. As fate would have it, the weapon was never perfected in time for the war.[1]

The weapons positions usually included in these entrance blocks are:

a. Cloches with FM and 50-mm mortars.
b. Casemates for anti-tank guns, machine guns (FM and JM) and a grenade launcher for the fossé.
c. Almost any type of weapons positions typical of a petit ouvrage, when the fort has no special entrance block and one or more of its combat blocks also serve as an entrance block.

The Munitions Entrance comes in three basic designs:

a. Level Entrance
   The main gallery was at the same level as the block. The designers preferred this type of entrance because it was cheaper to build and facilitated the quick movement of munitions, especially where rail cars were involved.
b. Inclined Entrance
   The main gallery was below the entrance and was reached by an incline of 25 or 45 degrees (Mary 1980, interview). In this type of entrance, munitions movement was slower and more laborious. Usually a special type of engine moved the rail cars down the incline. This design is found in ouvrages where the main gallery is located not too far below the EM.
c. Elevator Entrance
   If the distance between the main gallery and the entrance was too great, this type EM was used. The supply wagons were lowered with elevators. This type of entrance was not popular with the designers because, besides being very costly, the elevator could seriously hamper operations if it broke down. In addition, munition movement from the entrance level to the gallery level via the elevator was considerably slower than in the other entrances because the wagons could be lowered only one at a time. However, this type of entrance has defensive advantages because the elevator shaft can be easily defended.

Ideally, elevators were reserved for the EHs where they presented some defensive advantages. The EHs were usually placed at a higher elevation than the EM, enabling them to give additional fire coverage to the rear. However, the terrain did not always permit this type of arrangement.

In all the ouvrages the EM opened on a trap several meters deep designed to create an obstacle between the outer armored doors and the gate at the entrance. In the Maginot Line Proper this trap was covered by a mobile floor or rolling bridge, which could slide into the adjacent wall, exposing the opening. In the Alps an armored drawbridge replaced the outer gate and was lowered across the fossé to allow safe passage for vehicles. The mixed entrances of most of the petits ouvrages and some Type A EMs did not have this trap by the front gates.

As a rule, the blocks, whether combat or entrance, had two levels. The lower level was usually outfitted with the equipment necessary for the smooth operation of the block. The upper level, on the other hand, was reserved for the crew and the firing positions. However, there are numerous exceptions to this rule. Combat blocks and entrance blocks alike were connected to the main gallery by stairways. The combat blocks often had elevators in addition to the stairs, depending on the type of weapons they were designed to house.

THE CLOCHES

The cloches are the most characteristic and visible feature of the Maginot defenses. They stood out like giant armored mushrooms on the surface of the ouvrages and could be visible for miles. They were also the most vulnerable part of the fortifications. These cloches housed everything from anti-tank guns and machine guns to observation equipment, believing that the crew, never having to expose themselves, were safe from just about everything except a direct hit by heavy artillery.

When the forts were in use, they not only provided most of the close-range defensive fires for the ouvrages, but also served as its eyes. The garrison of a block was completely isolated from the outside world since the ouvrages were soundproof. The only members of the crew who had any clue of outside events were those serving in the cloches. One could assume that the cloches might also have acted as the ears of the ouvrage. However, according to the men who served there, the compressed air of the ouvrages whistling out through the sides of the crenels created such a din that the observers were effectively deafened. Thus, the cloche was able to act only as the eyes of the ouvrages and not its ears.

CORF employed several types of cloches:

a. The Observatory
   There are two basic types: one with only a periscope, the other with a periscope and an episcope for direct vision. These cloches were placed in optimal positions for observation and sometimes in an observation block built especially for them.
b. The GFM (*Guêt/Fusil Mitrailleur*) or Lookout and Light Machine Gun Cloche
   There are two basic types: A and B. They came in large and small sizes. Model 1934 B had a special place for a periscope while the older model 1929 did not. A few cloches of this older type were modified to take the periscope at a later date. These cloches had between three and five crenels with a field of fire of 72 degrees each. Special mounts for FM and a breech loaded 50-mm mortar were fitted into the crenels (Truttmann 1979, 172-177).
c. The JM (*Jumelage de Mitrailleuses*) or Heavy Twin Machine Gun Cloche
   These cloches used to mount JMs firing through a single crenel with a limited field of fire. They were strategically located to protect the vulnerable sections of the fort's surface and periphery. Three different 1932 models of large and small cloches were used (Truttmann 1979, 182). These cloches were less exposed than the GFM type and were better concealed because of their mission.
d. *Armes-Mixtes* Cloche
   This type of cloche came in both a large and a small size. The most commonly used model was the 1934. This cloche had two crenels set close together, yielding a field of fire of about 90 degrees. In the past it housed a 25-mm gun sandwiched between a set of heavy machine guns. The single JM was swung out into the desired crenel. This type of cloche supplemented the firepower of smaller and weaker ouvrages built in the Maginot Extension and the Alps.

e. *Lance Grenades* Cloche

Cloches of this type were added to many ouvrages shortly before the war. However, even though some of their apparatus was installed, none became serviceable. This type of cloche was to have supplied local defensive fires on the surface of the blocks. They were almost flush with the surface and a metal cover slid over the orifice through which a 60-mm breech loaded mortar was to fire its bombs.

All these types of cloches and their various models not only came in different sizes, but also had, in many cases, different armor protection. In the Maginot Extension and the Alps, cloches and turrets from the World War I era supplemented the inventory. They were modified and brought back into service for reasons of expediency. They were usually placed in secondary positions and not in ouvrages (Mary 1980, interview). Shortly before the war, the Germans studied the Czech fortifications with similar cloches, uncovering their vulnerability to direct artillery and sniper fire.

THE TURRETS

Most of the turrets of the Maginot Line were, at one time, part of the forts's artillery and, thus, were manned by artillery men. The only exceptions were the machine gun turrets and the *armes-mixtes* turrets. They rotated 360 degrees and retracted, leaving only their heavily armored domed roof to deflect shell hits. In some ouvrages, the terrain precluded a firing angle of 360 degrees. There were five basic turret types:

a. 75-mm Gun Turret

It came in two sizes: a small turret that used to mount two 75-mm Mle R 32 and a larger turret that used to house two 75-mm Mle 33 guns. This turret, which sat slightly above the level of the surface of the blocks, had three embrasures: two for the guns and one for observation.

b. 135-mm Howitzer Turret

This turret was slightly smaller than the 75-mm gun turret and had only two embrasures (none for observation). It sat in a depression on the block's roof in order to reduce its surface profile. This arrangement was only possible because it was designed to hold weapons with a high angle of fire

c. 81-mm Mortar Turret

Like the 135-mm howitzer turret, it sat in a depression and had only two embrasures for the two breech-loaded mortars it was designed to house. However, it was smaller than the 135-mm howitzer turret.

d. *Mitrailleuse* Turret

The mitrailleuse turret was the smallest, sitting slightly above the level of the block, like the 75-mm gun turret, to increase its field of fire. Turrets of this type had four openings for JMs and observation. The extra embrasure was intended for a 25-mm gun, which was not ready until mid-1940.

e. The *Armes Mixtes* Turret

The army authorized the development of the *armes mixtes* turret primarily to increase the firepower of the petits ouvrages. However, a few of these turrets were also installed in gros ouvrages. There are two types of *armes mixtes* turrets:

i. A-1 Armes Mixtes with a 50-mm mortar.

It had five embrasures: two for machine guns, one for a 25-mm gun, one for observation, and one in the roof at the rear of the turret for a 50-mm mortar. This mortar could be fired even when the turret was retracted (Truttmann 1979, 206). This turret was larger than the 81-mm mortar turret.

ii. A-2 Armes Mixtes.

This was a refurbished World War I 75-mm gun turret. It was redesigned to mount a 25-mm gun sandwiched between two heavy machine guns and was similar to the 75-mm gun turret. Two of its embrasures were designed for the weapons. A smaller opening located between the gun embrasures held the observation paraphernalia (Mary 1980, interview).

THE CASEMATES

The majority of the blocks of the Maginot line were of the casemate type. The army built so many different styles that a description of all the variants would be too long and tedious. Suffice it to say that the engineers designed each casemate to meet the need of specific locations. The casemates included one or more embrasures for firing positions.

Despite the great variety of forms, casemates can be divided into two basic types according to their function: artillery and infantry. The artillery casemate, usually larger than the infantry casemate, was linked to the galleries below by an elevator and a stairway. The infantry casemate, on the other hand could usually only be reached by a stairway.

a. The Artillery Casemate

The artillery casemate usually mounted one to three pieces of the same type. In the Alps, however, artillery blocks had a different design from the Maginot Line Proper and often housed cannons of different types. In the Maginot Line Proper, casemates usually contained one of the following sets of weapons:

i. 75-mm guns. Usually three to a casemate.

ii. 135-mm howitzers. Usually a single gun to a casemate.

iii. 81-mm mortars. Normally mounted in pairs.

There are, however, a few exceptions to these rules. Even in the Maginot Line Proper a few mixed assortments of these three weapons were installed. In the Alps a casemate mounting a pair of 75-mm guns and a pair of 81-mm mortars was not uncommon. In some cases the firing chambers were located on both levels.

b. The Infantry Casemate

Normally it consisted of a firing position for JM, which could be replaced by an anti-tank gun, and a second firing position for another set of JM or an FM.

Artillery and infantry casemates alike usually had one or more GFM cloche and sometimes cloches of other types.

THE WEAPONS

The heaviest weapons consisted of medium-sized artillery: the 75-mm guns and 135-mm howitzers. The 75-mm gun was a modified version of the vintage "75" of World War I fame, which was still in service. This weapon was a gun-howitzer that had the qualities of both weapons, as most modern guns do. The various models of 75-mm guns employed in the forts differed mainly in barrel length and method of feeding ammunition into the breech. The French classify most of these weapons as *obusier* or howitzer because of the trajectory of fire. However, most English sources do not consider this to be a pure howitzer-type weapon.

The casemates employed:

75-mm Mle 1929—maximum range 12,000 meters—30 rounds per minute.
75-mm Mle 1932—maximum range 12,000 meters—12 to 30 rounds per minute.
75-mm R Mle 1932—maximum range 9,000+ meters—12 to 30 rounds per minute.
75-mm Mle 1933—maximum range 12,000 meters—(semi-automatic) 12 to 30 rounds per minute.

The turret employed:

75-mm R Mle 1932—maximum range 9,000+ meters—13 to 18 rounds per minute.
75-mm Mle 1933—maximum range 12,000 meters—30 rounds per minute.
75-mm R Mle 1905—maximum range 8,700 meters—data not available on rounds per minute (Truttmann 1979, 121, Hohnadel and Truttmann 1988, 100).

Only the ouvrage of Le Chesnois had Mle 1905 weapons, which were located in a single turret. These were considered to be howitzers but could only fire at only about a 30 degree angle, which accounts for their limited range.

The 135-mm howitzer, known as the *lance-bombe* de 135-mm or 135-mm bomb thrower, provided the necessary plunging fire to defend the approaches to the ouvrages and cover areas that were out of reach of the 75-mm gun. This weapon was mounted in casemates as well as in turrets. The main model used in the Maginot Line was the 135-mm Mle 1932—range 5,600 meters—(semi-automatic) firing eight rounds per minute and placing plunging fire at points which the 75-mm guns could not cover (Claudel 1974, 25; Truttmann 1979, 121).

In addition, the mortar, a smaller piece of artillery, not only protected the surface with its plunging fire, but also covered certain avenues of approach with a more rapid rate of fire than the 135-mm howitzer. The following two mortars were in use in the Maginot Line:

81-mm Mle 1932—range 3,600+ meters—12 to 16 rounds per minute.
75-mm Mle 1931—range 5,900 meters—12 rounds per minute.

Both of these mortars were breech loaded and were much larger than the normal infantry mortar (Claudel 1974, 25; Maistret 1978, 8; Truttmann 1979, 121).

The only other type of artillery weapons used in the ouvrages consisted of four naval guns of 95-mm at the ouvrage of Janus in the Alps (Mary 1980, 288).

The infantry weapons were of a mixed variety. Except for the 25-mm gun, the ouvrages normally included all types, including FMs, JMs, 37-mm or 47-mm anti-tank guns and 50-mm mortars (Claudel 1974, 30). The main infantry weapon for the forts' defense was the twin machine gun or JM mounted in turrets, cloches and casemates. The light machine gun or FM was mainly used in cloches and casemates.

Three types of machine guns were used most frequently in the Maginot forts: the JM Reibel, the 7.5-mm FM Mle 24/29, and the Hotchkiss Mle 1930. The *Jumelages de Mitrailleuses* Reibel (JM), designed by General Reibel, consisted of two 7.5-mm FM MAC 31s mounted together. They were a modification of the Mle 25/29 machine gun, had an effective range of up to 1,500 meters, and fired alternately at a rate of 750 rounds per minute.

The 7.5-mm *Fusils Mitrailleurs* Mle 24/29, also employed in tanks, had an effective range of 600 meters and a rate of fire of 500 rounds per minute. This highly effective light machine gun remained in use for most of the century (Fitzsimons 1978, 582-583).

Finally, the 13.2-mm Hotchkiss Mle 1930 was a heavy machine gun with a range of over 800 meters. Considered a light anti-tank weapon, it was installed in casemates in the Vosges. It was also deployed as an anti-boat weapon in the Rhine casemates (Truttmann 1979, 149-150).

The infantry and entrance blocks usually included anti-tank guns for use against enemy armor. There were three types of these weapons: the AC 37-mm Mle 1934, the AC 47-mm Mle 1934, and the AC 25 Mle 1934. Originally the designers planned to make the casemate embrasures large enough to accommodate the *Anti-Char* (AC or anti-tank) 37-mm Mle 1934. Although the AC 47 Mle 1934 turned out to be more effective, many of the casemates had already been completed and could not be changed to take this newer weapon. Therefore, they were included mostly in newer casemates whose designs were altered during construction. The smaller AC 25 Mle 1934 guns, weighing half as much as the other two, also came into use. All these guns had an effective range of about 1,000 meters. Only casemates mounted the larger calibers; the smaller weapon was found in some cloches and turrets (Claudel 1974, 24; Maistret 1978, 8). In addition to these pieces, 47-mm naval guns were placed in interval casemates to make up for a shortage of anti-tank guns.

When the anti-tank gun was not in use in the casemate, it was swung back on an overhead rail, away from the embrasure, making room for a JM. In the turrets, the 25-mm gun was not mounted separately, but with a JM.

Finally, the infantry was to have two types of mortars at its disposal: the 60-mm mortar and the 50-mm mortar. The 60-mm mortar or bomb thrower, which was to be installed in its own specially built cloche, was never perfected. The breech-loaded 50-mm mortar Mle 1935, with a range of 800 meters, was housed in GFM cloches. A few of these weapons were also found in casemate mountings or an *Armes Mixtes* turret. The special casemate crenel was found in a few unusual positions like the infantry casemates covering the anti-tank ditch and wall at Hochwald and Hackenberg (Maistret 1978, 8; Mary 1980, 244, 274).

CONCRETE PROTECTION

The concrete protection given to all the positions varied according to their location. More concrete was added to those ouvrages that could not be dug to the regulation depth because of the geological structure of a particular site. The minimum roof protection for a gros ouvrage was 3.5 meters to which was added the cushioning effect of the earth and rubble covering the blocks.

Four types of standard protection were employed. They ranged from protection number 1 with 1.75 meters of reinforced concrete, which could withstand a hit from a 160-mm round, to protection number 4, 3.50 meters thick, which could resist a hit from a 420-mm weapon. Walls consisted either of protection number 1, 2 (2.25 meters thick) or 3 (2.70 meters thick). All the exposed positions of a gros ouvrage received protection 4, except the rear-facing casemates, which had only protection 1. The petits ouvrages, usually had no more than protection 3, which could withstand a 300-mm round (Mary 1980, 82).

The interior walls of the blocks were about one meter thick. In those ouvrages too near the surface the roof was lined with a metal sheet about 5-mm thick, which reinforced the ceilings and was meant to prevent flaking of concrete during intense bombardment (Maistret 1978, 9; *The Small Fortification of Immerhof 1979, 1*).

TURRET AND CLOCHE ARMOR PROTECTION AND STATISTICS

Most of the armor protection was found in the form of steel turrets and cloches. There were also armored shields that covered the crenels and an *avant-cuirasse*, or frontal armor, which surrounded the turrets to prevent near misses from damaging the blocks' concrete and jamming the turret mechanism.

The standards for armor thickness were as follows:

a. The Turrets:

i. | Armor Thickness | Roof (cm) | Walls (cm) |
|---|---|---|
| 75-mm/33 Mle gun | 35 | 30 |
| 75-mm/R 32 Mle howitzer | 30 | 30 |
| 135-mm howitzer | 30 | 30 |
| 81-mm mortar | 30 | 30 |
| *Mitraileuse* | 30 | 30 |
| A-1 *armes mixtes* | 30 | 30 |
| A-2 *armes mixtes* | 28.5 | 18.5 |

ii. | Other Statistics | Weight* (tons) | Number installed |
|---|---|---|
| 75-mm/33 Mle gun | 265 | 21 |
| 75-mm/R 32 Mle howitzer | 189 | 12 |
| 135-mm howitzer | 164 | 17 |
| 81-mm mortar | 125 | 21 |
| *Mitraileuse* | 96 | 61 |
| A-1 *armes mixtes* | 151 | 7 |
| A-2 *armes mixtes* | 135 | 12 |

*The weight includes the turret, the *avant-cuirasse* and all the other associated parts of this type of position such as counter-weights, mechanisms, etc. (Truttmann 1979, 206).

b. The Cloches
i. Armor Thickness. The thickness varies with each type of cloche, reaching a maximum of 25 to 30-cm. A standard feature of all cloches is the tapering off of the thickness of the armor towards the bottom. The casting of the cloche left weak points around the crenels, a problem that was corrected in Type B cloches with their distinctive circular plate (Maistret 1978, 9; Truttmann 1979, 173-175).
ii. Weights. This also varies with each model. The smaller cloches weigh about 10.5 tons and the larger, about twice as much. The cloches for JM were relatively small, weighing 11 tons. The larger could weigh up to 28 tons. The *Cloches d'Armes Mixtes*, the last to be designed, were the heaviest, at 35 tons (Truttmann 1979, 182).
iii. Size. The interior diameter varies, staying within a range of 1.0 to 2.0 meters. The interior of the Type A GFM cloches measured 1.2 meters in diameter, Type B, 1.3 meters, JM cloches, 1.39 meters, and the *Armes Mixtes*, from 1.5 to 1.9 meters. The length of the cloches went from 1.7 to 2.8 meters, half of which was normally embedded in concrete (Truttmann 1979, 182).

THE OPTICAL EQUIPMENT

The Maginot fortifications were outfitted with a splendid variety of optical equipment for observation, range finding, and so on. Certain cloche models of the GFM type had an opening in the roof for a small periscope. The crenels of a cloche were also designed to accommodate an episcope. Some weapons such as 75-mm cannons in casemates, JMs, FMs, anti-tank guns and mixed arms combinations were fitted with telescopic sights (Truttmann November 1982, correspondence). Turrets with direct-fire 75-mm weapons had a crenel for the scopes.

Over a dozen types of optical equipment were used in the Maginot Line. Cloche periscope ranged from 12x magnification power in observatories to as little as 1.1x in GFM positions. Telescopes, 8x power binoculars, and episcopes were also commonly used. The larger periscopes weighed up to 300 kilograms while smaller scopes for direct vision for the cloche weighed 30 kilograms (Mary 1980, 149-150; Bruge 1973, 25; museum display at Simserhof).

Thanks to this large variety of optical equipment, the forts' garrisons could remain within their positions, secure from enemy fire. The only problem was that the optical equipment was vulnerable to sniper fire. However, no ouvrage was ever neutralized or even lost its effectiveness because of damage to its optical equipment.

SUBTERRANEAN SECTIONS

The subterranean organs of an ouvrage include the main gallery, the caserne, the magazines, the usine, the ventilation and filter rooms, and the command and communication centers. The design of each of these locales was determined by the needs of a particular ouvrage but they all shared certain characteristics.

Every ouvrage had a single main gallery which linked the combat blocks to all the major facilities of the fort. In the larger ouvrages the distance between the facilities of the fort and the combat blocks was quite considerable. In many forts the distance between the caserne and the combat blocks was about one kilometer or more. The main gallery, leading from the combat area to the EM, was the only link between the two parts of the fort. It was usually connected to the EH by access galleries.

In most of the gros ouvrages, the main gallery was large enough to accommodate a small train known as the Metro. The forts equipped with this subway also had a garage area for the engine and cars. The rails for the train occupied one side of the main gallery so troops could circulate freely on the other side. The rail cars carried almost exclusively munitions and supplies and, on special occasions, VIPs. The wagons were not intended for moving troops across the fort. Overhead electrical cables supplied the engine with power, but they did not normally extend into access tunnels like the rails. In these access tunnels, the engines could move with an extension cable which was normally wound on a pulley attached to it. The soldiers usually pushed the cars into these access tunnels. For reasons of safety the engines did not operate in the M-1 magazines although tracks ran into the magazine.

In most ouvrages, strategically placed niches about midway down the main gallery contained enough explosives to seal off the combat section of the ouvrage from the support areas in the event the enemy penetrated from either direction (Mary 1980, interview). Electric and telephone cables ran along both sides of the main gallery's walls and over the entrance ways of adjoining access galleries. In some cases these cables were placed on specially built ledges. Usually, a duplicate set cables would back up the main system.

A drainage channel under the floor collected seeping water along most of the main gallery and discharged it outside, at a convenient distance from the ouvrage. Further, the gallery itself was sloped in such a manner that the water would flow naturally out.

The vaulted galleries had concrete walls and cemented stone or cobble roofs. The walls were often painted and even decorated with geometric motifs in the most frequented areas such as junctions of galleries, or in well-lighted sections.

The caserne included all the necessities for the soldiers' survival. The men slept in large chambers with three-level iron bunks. Their sleeping quarters were sparsely furnished with metal stools, and racks and hooks for their clothing and equipment. Small heaters struggled to heat the chilly rooms. The NCOs and the officers lived in smaller, equally spartan quarters.

According to some of the veterans, the barrack areas were rather depressing. Others have fonder memories of the forts. The company, which was plentiful, they claim, more than made up for the shortcomings of the living quarters. The officers, on the other hand, had to pay for their privacy with less conviviality to break the monotony of their days underground.

The caserne also included a kitchen with large electric ranges and ovens as well as running water. The pantry could store enough staples and wine for a period of up to three months. In addition to a well, which supplied most of the water needs for the fort, there were large water storage tanks.

The hygienic facilities of the ouvrage showed great improvement over those of Verdun. Each fort had not only proper latrine facilities and toilets, but also showers with cold and hot water. These facilities were not only located in the caserne but, with the exception of the showers, also in and below most of the combat blocks. If there was a problem with the plumbing, it was because the men had a tendency to dispose of their trash in the toilets, causing the septic tank system to fail (Bruge 1973, 26). The forts were even equipped with a special garbage collection area; however, the designers had underestimated the refuse-generating capacity of the ouvrages. As a result, the refuse had to be taken out at frequent intervals, even after the hostilities started. Thus, some cases, volunteers had to venture forth at night to take out the garbage (Bruge 1973, 26).

In addition to the living quarters, the caserne area also included a small detention area and an infirmary. The prison cell was of small dimensions, painted in regulation gray, windowless and sparsely furnished. Its only access was a door that shut the outside world away from the miscreant. The prospect of being locked up in this cubicle must have deterred many a man from infringing on the rules.

The infirmary varied in size according to the dimension of the ouvrage it served. The largest forts had operating rooms, doctor's offices, pharmacies, dentist's offices and a sick bay for the wounded. However, few of the ouvrages offered all of these medical facilities. The average fort included a doctor's office and an operating room for battle casualties.

Each ouvrage also had a number of magazines where the ammunition was stored. Special annexes housed sensitive items such as fuses. There were three types of magazines in the Maginot Line: M-1, M-2 and M-3.

The M-1 magazine, or main magazine, was found in most artillery ouvrages. It was used to store the majority of the fort's ammunition. It held enough ammunition to allow an ouvrage to continue fighting for a month or more, depending on expenditure rates in combat when isolated. The M-1 magazine consisted of a series of storage cells, each with a chicane-like entrance at two ends to prevent accidents. The magazine was accessed through one of two entrances off the main gallery.

Since the possibility of an accidental explosion was very real in this area of an ouvrage, several measures were taken to lessen potential damage. For instance, the short corridors leading to the entrances of magazines curved away from the caserne in order to deflect the shock waves away from the garrison area. In addition, niches placed on either side of each storage cell would attenuate the effects of the blast. Furthermore, a special seven-ton armored door in the main gallery was designed to slam shut automatically in the event of an explosion, thereby protecting the main gallery and caserne. Finally, a sprinkler system, located in the magazine itself and activated by rising temperatures, would avert disaster before it had a chance to happen (Mary 1980, 109).

The M-2 magazines acted as distribution points for artillery blocks armed with 75-mm and 135-mm weapons. They were located beneath the blocks, at the end of the access gallery. The ammunition was loaded from these magazines into nearby elevators and sent up to the M-3 magazine situated above them, in the combat block.

The M-3 magazine supplied the immediate needs of the block's main weapons. From the M-3, the ready ammunition was moved into lockers adjacent to the block's artillery. Other, smaller rooms served as storage space for small-arms ammunition, grenades, and so on.

Monorails were fixed to the ceiling of the M-1 and M-2 magazines for loading and unloading ammunition cases. Positions mounting 75-mm and 135-mm guns were also outfitted with a monorail, which carried the ammunition from the M-3 magazine to the combat area. M-3s were not found in the majority of petits ouvrages, since few had artillery weapons.

Behind the 75-mm and 135-mm weapons stood a device called *entonoir*, which served as a sort of funnel for spent shells. These slid down to the gallery below along a slide called a *toboggan*. Along the stairway, at different levels between the block and the gallery, inspection points allowed for unclogging any blockage that might occur. The shells could easily be collected and even recycled. This system of shell evacuation not only prevented accumulation of expended shells and their poisonous fumes in the combat block, but also eliminated the necessity of hauling the shells down to the gallery.

The usine, or power plant, normally situated near the EH, used the entrance block as an outlet for its exhaust vents. In those ouvrages where the usine was too far from an entrance block, a special chimney block became necessary to vent the deadly fumes.

The usine made it possible for the ouvrage to operate for an extended period of time in complete isolation from the outside world. If the power-generating equipment of an ouvrage failed for some reason, a limited amount of energy could be supplied by neighboring ouvrages through underground cables. However, not all ouvrages had links with their neighbors. In addition, power cables connected the ouvrages to outside fortified substations which, in turn, were tied into the civilian power grid. One substation usually served several ouvrages so that the forts would not find it necessary to use their own generating systems until actually under combat conditions. High-tension lines of a military style linked the ouvrage to the substation. In the vicinity of the fort, the cables went underground in order to lessen their vulnerability to bombardment and to keep the exact position of the fort secret.

Everything necessary for the transmission and production of electrical energy could be found in the usine. Each usine contained two to four diesel engines: two in petits ouvrages and four in gros ouvrages. Since the gros ouvrages occupied a larger area, they were also equipped with a set of transformers located near the engines. These transformers raised the voltage level in order to transmit electrical power along the main gallery to a substation near the combat blocks. The voltage received from the civilian grid through the fortified substation was lowered when it entered the fort. In addition to the transformers, the usine had converters, that changed the alternating current into direct current after the voltage had been reduced. Storage tanks containing diesel fuel, oil and water allowed the usine to produce its own power when access to the civilian grid was shut down. These tanks held up to three months supply of fuel (Claudel 1974, 28).

Under normal operating conditions, a usine ran two diesel engines at a time. The other two engines served as reserve and replacement. The electrical current produced went into the transformers where it was stepped up before it was directed towards a substation in the combat block area. Once there, the voltage was stepped down again by transformers and changed to direct current by convertors. The usine also supplied power to the garrison area where the electric current required fewer steps in transmission.

VENTILATORS AND FILTERS

A special chamber was reserved for air filters near the usine. These filters were designed to purify the air for the caserne and the galleries and, more importantly, to filter out poison gases. Each block was equipped with its own individual system and air-intake vents on the surface. In blocks with no casemate positions, armored air intakes with small, screen-covered openings protruded just above the surface. In casemate blocks, the air intakes were not as heavily protected, but they were situated in inaccessible places.

In addition to the filtering system the forts relied on air over pressure to keep noxious gases out. The interior air pressure was maintained at a higher level than the exterior pressure, reducing the possibility of gas infiltration from the outside. In addition, a set of armored air locks in the access galleries prevented the compressed air from escaping though the crenels of the combat blocks and also kept gases from seeping into the rest of the fort (Maistret 1978, 15). Finally, in the event of a successful poison-gas attack, the garrison could always fall back on its gas masks for protection.

THE COMMAND POST

The command post or headquarters of the ouvrage was normally located in the combat area and was its nerve center. It housed the offices of the commanding officer, the chiefs of the artillery and infantry units of the fort, and all the supporting staff. Data coming from observation positions on the fort's surface and from interval positions were collected and processed here. Here, too, orders were given to other units, requests received, and action coordinated with the combat blocks and outside positions.

In some ouvrages, such as at Hackenberg and Fermont, the command post lay directly beneath a special observation block with a commanding view of the surrounding terrain. In others, such as Simserhof, it was situated in a central position in the fort, but not in a specially built block. The command post was normally located at the subterranean gallery level. However, in rare instances, such as Hackenberg, it was placed at its own separate level above the main gallery but below the level of the blocks.

The headquarters were linked to other ouvrages and the French High Command by telephone as well as radio. Telephone cables linked adjacent ouvrages and interval positions to each other and to the rear area. They were usually buried underground to avoid detection or destruction from air or artillery bombardment. The interval troops could use special relay points to connect into the telephone system. These relay sites, which were numerous, consisted of a small underground chamber in the field. The greatest advantage of this system was that contact between upper and lower echelons could be made with a minimum of security risk. Inside, the telephone lines connected all the positions of the ouvrage to its the command post.

The radio served as an alternate form of communications, but the French army was lagging behind in this form of technology. Radio antennas were arrayed across the upper face of the entrance block and some combat blocks with casemate positions. Although appearing quite impressive, they were vulnerable and not very effective. Their range extended only to about twenty-five kilometers.

Inside the combat area of the Maginot forts, the communication technology was varied. The observers in the cloches communicated with their comrades on the lower level by means of a voice tube. They could also contact the command post directly by telephone. The command post, on the other hand, sent orders to the artillery blocks through various types of order transmitters, a method borrowed from the navy. Most models of these transmitters included a warning bell and a red light to alert the operator that new instructions were being sent. Commands indicating the type of ammunition and fire to use and other such information were conveyed by the movement of needles on the transmitter. It took only seconds for the orders to be sent, verified, and executed.

These were some of the most basic features of an ouvrage. The French engineers made numerous modifications to the original CORF plans in order to tailor each of the forts to the nature and exigencies of the surrounding terrain. Compared to the fortifications of the previous era, the Maginot forts showed more sophistication.

NOTE

1. LTC Philippe Truttmann in his extensive study of the Maginot Line has found only one incomplete example of this type of weapon. It was located in Block 6 of Simserhof (Truttmann November 1982, correspondence).

5

THE PETITS OUVRAGES AND LESSER FORTIFICATIONS

Smaller works covered the intervals between the gros ouvrages. These included petits ouvrages, casemates, blockhouses, observatories, and troop shelters. Some of these positions were actually in front of, or to the rear of the gros ouvrages and most were covered by its guns. In advance of these fortifications, which occupied the main line, was an outpost line of even smaller works to give advance warning of an enemy attack.

THE PETITS OUVRAGES

Although similar in many ways to the gros ouvrages, the petits ouvrages, as indicated by their name, were much smaller and did not have or require all the features necessary in an artillery fort. They were usually built in places where it was deemed unnecessary or impractical to establish a gros ouvrage, but where a strong fortification was required. In some cases, petits ouvrages were erected in locations where the original plans had called for a gros ouvrage. These small forts, with concrete protection number 3, were mostly surface structures without important subterranean sections, even though they included underground galleries that linked the combat blocks to an underground caserne and usine. Although there was no standard plan for the petits ouvrages, the French popular historian Robert Bruge (1975, 375-379) divided them into four basic sizes with a more or less standard array of weapons.

The first type consisted of a single massive monolithic combat block usually with a machine gun turret and the standard cloches. It included casemate positions for 47-mm anti-tank guns. Bois du Four, designated A-5, also had casemated 81-mm mortars. The RF of Metz had all six petits ouvrages of this type.

The second type of petits ouvrages had two blocks with cloches and casemates. These ouvrages had a machine gun turret and emplacements for 47-mm anti-tank guns. There were three ouvrages of this type in the RF of Metz and none in the RF of Lauter.

The third type consisted of three blocks and a machine gun turret as well as casemates positions for 47-mm anti-tank guns. Eight of these ouvrages were located in the RF of Metz and three in the RF of the Lauter. Two of the ouvrages in the RF of the Lauter had a mixed arms turret and 47-mm anti-tank guns, but the ouvrage of Lembach had only 47-mm anti-tank guns and no turrets.

The fourth type of petits ouvrages consisted of five or more blocks. There were five ouvrages with four blocks in the RF of Metz. Except for the Annexe Sud de Coume (A-32) and Immerhof (A-10), they had a machine gun turret and 47-mm anti-tank guns. The A-32 had no machine gun turret and A-10 included two machine gun turrets and an 81-mm mortar turret. In the RF of the Lauter, there were two of these ouvrages. Both had a machine gun turret and 47-mm anti-tank guns. Of these, Haut Poirier also had a mixed arms turret while the ouvrage of Otterbiel mounted an 81-mm mortar turret (Bruge 1975, 375-379).

There were two petits ouvrages of more than four blocks in the RF of Metz. Laudrefang (A-37) was the only five-block ouvrage. It was designed to have two machine gun turrets and to mount casemated 81-mm mortars and 47-mm anti-tank guns. One of the five blocks, Block 3, was not completed. It would have been identical to Block 1 with a machine gun turret, a 47-mm anti-tank gun and two 81-mm mortars in a casemate positions, as well as two GFM cloches. Bovenberg (A-27), the only six block-ouvrage, had a machine gun turret and a position for a 47-mm anti-tank gun. Block 3, an infantry casemate, was not completed and served as a double casemate without a subterranean gallery. Another block consisted of nothing more than an observation cloche, and two other blocks had nothing but cloches. Block 1, the entrance, was the only casemate type position. Having only a single block with a casemate was not unusual for petits ouvrages (Mary 1980, 261, 263).

The machine gun turret and the 47-mm anti-tank gun were standard features in most petits ouvrages. The cloches and firing chambers were similar to those of the gros ouvarges. They also carried the standard assortment of weapons: FM, JM, 50-mm mortar, 25-mm anti-tank gun (normally mounted in old 75-mm gun turrets in pairs, each with a set of JM).

Although the petits ouvrages tend to be less standardized than the gros ouvrages, a description of a few can serve as an illustration of this type of position. Chappy (A-1), being the first ouvrage on the Maginot Line Proper, holds a special significance. It is situated at a short distance from Fermont, right under its guns. With only two blocks, it was not exceptional. Block 1, nearest to Fermont, consisted of two firing chambers, each mounting a 47-mm anti-tank gun and two sets of JM. Two GFM cloches and a JM cloche provided observation and defensive fires. Block 1 also served as the main entrance to the limited subterranean facilities, which included a caserne for the 110-man garrison and a usine. The second position, Block 2, included a machine gun turret and the same number and type of cloches as Block 1. The emergency exit was located at the rear of the fort, in the drainage system (Maistret 1979, interview).

To the North of Thionville lies Immerhof, one of the largest petits ouvrages. It included an *Entrée Mixte*, or combination men and munitions entrance, of the size of an EH of a gros ouvrage. In other words, it was smaller than the *Entrée Mixte* of a gros ouvrage. The standard array of weapons protected the entrance: a 47-mm anti-tank gun, JMs and FMs. Above the block, two GFM cloches provided all around defense and observation. Immerhof also had the cloche for the special 60-mm mortar, which was never perfected.

Like most petits ouvrages, Immerhof had number 3 protection: 2.5 meters of concrete, which can resist 305-mm artillery rounds. Since the subterranean sections were not very deep below the surface, protective metal sheets lined the ceilings to prevent fragments of concrete from breaking off and littering the floor (*The Small Fortification of Immerhof* 1979, 1-5). In this respect, Immerhof was similar to Chappy because neither had a large natural hill to protect it nor deep subterranean galleries. Immerhof's main gallery, leading from the entrance to the combat blocks, was about 200 meters long and only wide enough to accommodate small supply carts and the men who pushed them. Like the galleries of the gros ouvrages, Immerhof's was equipped with armored doors and air locks. At the intersection of the main gallery and the two access tunnels to the machine gun turret blocks three bunker-like positions covered the three corridors.

Immerhof's communications center was located in the entrance block. The usine and caserne were adjacent to the artillery block, about midway between the entrance and the infantry blocks. The usine used to house two generators, which supplied enough power to operate the fort and its three turrets. The drainage system was like those of the artillery ouvrages.

Immerhof's two infantry blocks consisted of little more than a machine gun turret and a pair of GFM cloches. The artillery block included an 81-mm mortar turret, a GFM cloche, and an infantry casemate that faced the rear of the ouvrage. The fort used to be protected by a line of anti-tank rails and anti-personnel obstacles.

Bois du Four, located in about the middle of the SF of La Crusnes, was one of the few monolithic petits ouvrages. Unlike the combat blocks of most of the ouvrages, which follow a standard pattern, this single-block ouvrage had little in common with others of its own type. The only feature that Bois du Four shares with other monolithic ouvrages is the machine gun turret. In its heyday, Bois du Four sheltered a garrison of about 140 men whereas further east, in the RF of Metz, Sentzich held less than 70. Another other single-block ouvrage in the RF of Metz was also manned by 70 men, and two other such forts had garrisons of about 80 men. Coume-Annexe Nord, a very small ouvrage for only 36 men, resembled a casemate more than a petit ouvrage. However, it was endowed with a machine gun turret (Mary 1980, interview; Truttmann 1979, Plate 76).

Bois du Four is of interest because it was a very large, two-level block with a machine gun turret. Its field of fire did not reach 360 degrees because its location on the terrain did not permit it. Each of its flanks was covered by an 47-mm anti-tank guns and a JM. Two 81-mm mortars were mounted in the fossé at the lower level of the eastern firing chamber.

Unlike most single-block forts, Sentzich and Oberheid had an elongated plan. The tips of their two wings may be likened to casemate positions while the area between them, which held the usine and caserne areas, may be compared to the main gallery. At Sentzich, which lay along the gentle slope of a hill, the difference in elevation between the northern and southern casemate positions was 8 meters. Sentzich was originally designed to be two separate casemates. However, when a machine-gun turret block between the two positions was planned, it was decided to transform the position into what became a monolithic petit ouvrage (Mary 1980, 241).

Sentzich presents many of the features found in most gros and petits ouvrages. The garrison's quarters, midway between the two casemates, resemble those of the gros ouvrages. They used to hold enough bunks for twenty of the fort's sixty enlisted men. Adjacent to the men's billet, a room about half its size was reserved for six NCOs. Down one flight of stairs, near the southern casemate, were the kitchen and latrines. Next to the northern block are the usine, its fuel storage area, and a small infirmary. The filter system and a wine storage were located in chambers below the northern block. A rest area for six men and the M-3 magazine were under the nearby turret block. Other chambers below the southern block housed a rest area for eight men, more wine racks, the fort's well, and a store of charcoal.

Some of the petits ouvrages in the east end of the RF of Metz, located beyond the range of the guns of the gros ouvrages, fell to the Germans in 1940 after the withdrawing interval troops left them at the mercy of the enemy. Among these ouvrages are the multi-block ouvrages of Kerfent (four blocks), Bambesch (three blocks) on one side of the Sarre Gap and Haut Poirier (four blocks) and Welschoff (three blocks) on the other side. At least Haut Poirier and Welschoff had one *Armes Mixtes* turret for protection. The other three were much more vulnerable since they had only machine gun turrets to hold the enemy artillery at bay (Mary 1980, 252-267).

However, not all the petits ouvrages were doomed to failure. For example, the petit ouvrage of Laudrefang (five blocks), situated at the end of the RF of Metz, successfully supported two of its neighboring ouvrages with its 81-mm mortars. Of the ouvrages that surrendered, none had any weapons as large as this (Mary 1980, 262-64). This fact demonstrates that a properly armed ouvrage, properly buttressed by its neighbors could ward off attacks even without the support interval troops.

Like the gros ouvrages, the petits ouvrages were CORF creations. Construction on them began at about the same time as on the larger forts and reached completion between 1930 and 1935. Additional petits ouvrages were built in the New Fronts after 1935.

LESSER FORTIFICATIONS

The ouvrages of the Maginot Line were not designed to stop an enemy advance on their own. Instead, their mission was to provide the main points of resistance. Originally, it was planned that in the intervals between the ouvrages other, lighter, defenses would help delay the enemy by providing the interval troops with strong points from which to fight.

As a fortified line, the Maginot Line had little depth. The main line consisted of the ouvrages with an assortment of interval positions. In most places, it was little more than one kilometer deep, the average distance between the entrance and combat blocks of most gros ouvrages. Between the ouvrages, and in some cases in front or behind them stood lighter positions such as casemates, abris and observatories, which had been included in the original plans of the Maginot Line.

After the dissolution of CORF in 1935, the *Génie* (French Corps of Engineers) was directed to build supplemental positions. These new field fortifications, built and designed by the *Service Techniques du Génie* (STG), were expected to cover areas left unprotected by the CORF works. Their construction began after 1938, mainly in the Sarre Gap. In addition, the *Main d'Oeuvre Militaire*, or MOM (military construction workers), erected many small blockhouses (Hohnadel and Truttmann 1988, 5-6). However, the MOM fortifications were not built according to any specifications and turned out to be weak and useless.

As the war approached, General Belhague, who was recalled to duty in 1939, pushed forward a plan to build a Stop Line. This line would incorporate the old World War I era forts, which were conveniently situated and already armed. For the most part, however, it would consist of additional positions at the rear of the main line whose mission would be to provide a second line of defense in case the front line buckled under pressure. Built as an afterthought, the Stop Line would include mostly bunkers. Its construction was entrusted to MOM. However, a shortage of man power and equipment severely limited the number works actually completed and in use as supporting positions for the main line (Rocolle 1990a, 173).

In 1939 the army created the *Commision d'Étude des Zones Fortifiées* (CZEF) under the direction of General Belhague, who was replaced by General Philippe in 1940. The mission of the CZEF was to give more depth to the Maginot Line by adding two lines of defense and cover the gaps in the main line with STG-type blockhouses. These plans never came to fruition because time ran out. The CZEF accomplished little beyond the fortification of some positions in the Sarre Gap. In addition, a mixed labor force of military personnel and volunteers proved inadequate for the job (Bruge 1973, 82-83; Hohnadel and Truttmann 1988, 7; Truttmann 1979, 402).

The area in front of the main line, sometimes called *Avancées de la Ligne Maginot*, was a lightly defended zone acting as an outpost line. Located two to three kilometers in front of the main line, this line consisted of defensive positions that would sound the alarm, delay the enemy at key points, and possibly deflect his advance. Work on these positions took place between 1936 and 1937. The most common positions were fortified houses (*maisons fortifiées* or *maisons fortes*) and the *avant-postes*.

The *avant-postes* were found, often in clusters, along the German frontier and in the Alps. They usually included a single- floor barracks, a blockhouse for light machine guns, an anti-tank obstacle placed across a road, and a mined site. They were located in or near towns and crossroads between the frontier and the main line. In the Alps the *avant-postes* were much more elaborate. Built by the MOM under the supervision of the *Génie* of the XIV and XV Army Corps between 1935 and 1938, they included an underground gallery system and several concrete positions for observation and machine guns (Truttmann August 1982, correspondence).

The fortified houses were mostly used along the border of Luxembourg and the Ardennes. Their mission was to support the *avant-postes* or even replace them in some areas of restricted terrain, such as the border with southern Belgium. The fortified houses also served to protect key crossroads or entries into villages. They fell into two basic categories: single and double level. The first type consisted of a blockhouse structure added to one or both sides of a one-floor edifice. The second type consisted of a two-level building whose lower floor was actually a bunker with concrete walls. Today, they are hard to spot because the whole structure was made to look like a regular residence and the locals have taken up residence in them (*Grosses Orientierungsheft Frankreich* 1937, 87-89; Truttmann 1979, 394-395).

The fortified houses and *avant-postes* were often reinforced with a variety of obstacles. In the Northeast and Southeast Fronts, holes were drilled into important roads to accommodate steel rails to quickly create obstacles. Concrete positions with steel beams and as well as an assortment of other types of barriers could quickly be positioned to close roadways. In addition, cradles full of boulders were placed along some roadways to form barriers (*Denkschrift: über die französische* 1941, 346-355).

Covering troops operated forward of the main line's interval units. These troops included the *Garde Republicaine Mobile* (professional soldiers of the Gendarme). They occupied the *avant-postes* and the fortified houses from where they were to sound the alarm in the event of attack. They were also expected to delay the enemy, channel his forces, and if possible, withdraw into the main line before being overrun (Truttmann August 1982, correspondence).

The front-line defenses did not form a continuous line, but were built to hold key points (Truttmann August 1982, correspondence). Many of these positions that made up the *avant-postes* may not have been permanent structures since little remains of them today (Viennot March 1981, correspondence).

Giving depth to the Maginot Line had not been a priority consideration during the initial planning and construction phases. In the 1920s the advocates of the RFs had only wanted to delay the enemy long enough to buy the army time for a counter-offensive. On paper, the Maginot Line was relatively thin, especially compared to the German West Wall, but it was, in fact, stronger than it appeared.

The West Wall consisted of numerous small bunkers designed only for machine guns and small-caliber anti-tank guns. The German positions relied to a great extent upon the supporting weapons of defending field units. However, the main difference between the French and German lines was a new invention in modern warfare: vast fields of anti-personnel mines. These minefields, covered by defensive fires from bunkers and supporting artillery, were also protected by a continuous anti-tank barrier of concrete "dragon's teeth" and wire obstacles. This arrangement proved to be surprisingly effective in 1939, when it successfully repelled a French advance.

The Maginot Line, on the other hand, completely lacked anti-personnel mines, relying mainly on anti-tank barriers, other obstacles and supporting fires to stop the infantry. The French developed a heavy anti-tank mine for fortified areas in 1931 and a lighter mine later on. However, there is no evidence that they had anti-personnel mines even though some war time sources claim that they were already on the drawing table (Rocolle 1990a, 107). Anti-personnel mines would have rendered the Maginot Line extremely difficult to penetrate and would probably have allowed a reduction of interval troops.

During 1930, civilian construction firms erected many of the abris and casemates that served as the primary interval positions between ouvrages. The abris, or interval shelters, was probably one of the most important positions for the interval troops. Abris were usually found to the rear of the line of ouvrages or casemates. There were two basic types: a large monolithic structure and a cavern-like shelter with only small surface positions for access. The second type offered greater protection to the troops because all its facilities were located deep underground and its small entrance blocks were well separated from each other. The abris were used as shelters and headquarters for the interval troops and housed all the facilities needed for independent operations such as a usine, filters, stores, etc. They also provided fire support to the nearby blockhouses used by the interval troops. Most abris accommodated between 100 and 200 troops, a few smaller ones held a maximum of fifty to sixty.

The abris had their own defenses. Normally one or two GFM cloches controlled the surface and a fossé protected the facades of the monolithic structures. The embrasures allowed FMs to defend the entrance. A few shelters included not only a JM, but also a 37-mm anti-tank gun. Since the abris were not designed to hold key points, but to provide shelter for field troops, they were built into hillsides, facing away from the enemy.

The abri of Zeiterholz in the RF of Metz was a fairly typical monolithic shelter. Two armored doors open on each side of its exposed face and the remainder of its facilities were built into the hillside. Small, removable metal foot bridges span the fossé, which runs the length of the facade. Two GFM cloches overlooked the surface. The interior consisted of two levels. The lower one housed the usine and kitchen. Troop accommodations occupied both levels. Typically, most of the space was dedicated to the troops. As in most abris and smaller ouvrages, the cooking at Zeiterholz was done on a rather hazardous charcoal-burning stove rather than on electric stoves of the type found in gros ouvrages (Bernard 1979, interview).

Zeiterholz, one of thirty-three abris completed in 1935, was located between the petits ouvrages of Aumetz and Bovenberg, in one of the most heavily defended parts of the Maginot Line in the RF of Metz. In the RF of Lauter an additional twenty-five abris were located between the petit ouvrage of Welschoff and the Rhine River. Among these were several of the cavern type, such as Gasserloch, also finished by 1935.

Gasserloch consisted of two small entrance blocks with a crenel for an FM and a GFM cloche. Its fresh air intakes are located on the block on the southeast corner. Its exhaust vents used to emit the fumes from its usine over the other entrance, located below the southeast block. The main part of Gasserloch was situated about 20 meters below the blocks. It consisted of five large subterranean chambers and several smaller ones designed to house about 145 men. In addition, there were offices, storage facilities, kitchens, and all the other facilities usually found in the caserne area of an ouvrage. The drain pipe, which carried the water out of the ouvrage at a point between the entrance block, but at a lower level, also served as an emergency exit (Collin and Wahl 1981, 47-53).

The Rhine defenses also included abris: three were north of Strasbourg and seventeen were spaced out rather evenly between Strasbourg and Mulhouse. An additional abri was located near the Swiss border. The abris of CORF manufacture along the Rhine looked more like blockhouses than shelters in the interval positions of the Maginot Line Proper. Between 1935 and 1940 STG and MOM abris, some with emplacements for small cannons, were added to this inventory (Collin and Wahl 1981, 47). The abris formed a very weak Stop Line behind the main line until 1939, when additional MOM-type blockhouses were added (Truttmann 1979, 287).

The CORF casemates, smaller than the abris, guarded the gaps between the ouvrages. They came in a few basic designs, including single and double casemates. The latter had two exposed faces with firing embrasures. Depending on the location, they had one or two levels, but two floors were the most common. Like the abris, the casemate was able to operate independently. The garrison was normally a platoon of about twenty-five to thirty men with an officer (Bruge 1973, 32). Most of these casemates had a diamond fossé in front of their entrance and embrasures. The concrete thickness in some cases was up to the maximum strength of 3.5 meters. These casemates were similar to those of the infantry casemates of the ouvrages.

Many of the single-type casemates were built in pairs. Both casemates of a pair were given the same name and were distinguished from each other by a cardinal direction; for example, Marckolsheim Nord and Marckolsheim Sud, which also carried the number designations of 34/3 and 35/3.[1] Underground galleries linked many of these casemates to one another (Mary 1980, interview; Truttmann 1979, 257). The early CORF casemates had two to three cloches of the GFM and JM type. Casemates built later, as part of the New Fronts program in the mid-1930s, included in some cases searchlights and mixed-arms cloches. A few had unusual armament for interval casemates such as a turret of mixed arms with a 50-mm mortar and crenels for 81-mm mortars (Mary 1980, 48). Normal armament for these casemates consisted of anti-tank guns, 50-mm mortars in cloches, JM, and FM. Each casemate had its own communication equipment, which was used to call supporting fire, to direct the fire of the nearby ouvrages, and to report on enemy activities. The main form of communication was through buried telephone lines, which linked the casemates with ouvrages and higher headquarters.

Excluding the SF of the Sarre, there were seventy-eight CORF casemates in the RF of Metz and another seventy-nine in the RF of the Lauter (Mary 1980, 48). The Rhine Defenses, which were mistakenly considered part of the Maginot Line, held 128 casemates and abris. These CORF casemates, built mostly before 1930, are considered substandard. Four types of the casemate were built along the Rhine. Since the water table was high in this area, danger from flooding was very real. Thus, the casemates consisted only of a single floor and included some added protection against rising water levels. In addition, most of the Rhine casemates also included a cloche.

The Rhine casemates had several serious flaws. Truttmann points out that the Achilles heel of these casemates was that too few of their weapons faced the river. Furthermore, their concrete protection consisted of no more than protection 1 or 1.75 meters. Finally, most of the Rhine casemates were poorly armed. Many of them mounted a Hotchkiss 13.2-mm Mle 1930 machine gun instead of a 37-mm or 47-mm anti-tank gun. This weapon was adopted for use against light armor and shipping in zones where tank attacks were not expected. Ninety-eight pieces were in service in 1940 in the Rhine casemates and some casemates in the densely overgrown terrain of the Lower Vosges (Truttmann August 1982, correspondence).

Behind the Rhine line stretched a second line of bunker-like abris followed by a third line of double casemates, similar to those on the river, known as the "Village Line." The firing embrasures of the Rhine casemates were more vulnerable than the other types because they had no protective fossés under their firing embrasures (Truttmann 1979, 74, 262-264). This made it possible for enemy assault troops to reach the crenel without facing a final major obstacle.

After the dissolution of CORF, the STG built other distinctive one-level casemates mounting the standard array of weapons. A number of these STG casemates mounted a cloche. Some were single and others were double. A few mounted a 75-mm gun, a more powerful weapon than the 47-mm anti-tank guns of the CORF casemates. A number of STG casemates were built in the SF of the Sarre and the Maginot Extension.

Observatories were also a common feature of the Maginot line. They were usually located in the main line of ouvrages, in commanding locations. Their function was to keep track of enemy movement that could not be observed from the forts or casemates and relay the information to the ouvrages. Although these positions were vital for the Maginot Line, the CORF only built eleven in the RF of Metz and two in the RF of the Lauter (Mary 1980, 59-62). In 1937 President Daladier, fearing that the Germans would storm and take the Maginot Line by surprise, issued orders to extend the fortifications to the North Sea (Hohnadel and Truttmann 1986, 6). The observatories that were built later did not meet CORF specifications as they were more hastily assembled. Some were endowed with old cloches from the last war, including the Pamart models, resembling an elephant head. In other cases, the body of an old FT 17 Renault tank was placed in concrete and turned into a bunker and its turret, sunk into the ground, became the weapons and/or observation position. A number of these old tanks were used on the Sarre sector (Mary 1980, 52).

Observatories of the CORF type varied in shape and size. Some had a single level, others had two. Generally, they were equipped with a GFM and a periscope cloche. The observatory of La Ferme du Bois du Four was typical. It was designed to hold a crew of fourteen men, including an officer. Like other CORF positions, it was intended to operate independently and for this purpose, it comprised all the facilities found in the other organs of the Maginot Line, such as the air filters, communications equipment, and so on. These positions were too small to maintain their own usine. A protective fossé with a single crenel covered its entrance. Although it was vulnerable to an assault from the rear, it could rely for support on the artillery of neighboring ouvrages.

Another type of fortification used to reinforce the Maginot Line and other positions was the blockhouse, built mostly by soldiers lacking construction experience or skills. Many specimens of various sizes and types, most quite unique, were built during the first year of the war. They were located where they could cover the remaining gaps in the defenses. Some of these block-houses stood in groups, unlike the casemates and abris, which tended to cluster around ouvrages. Within the same cluster of blockhouses there appears to be some degree of uniformity.

The army had planned to build eighty large blockhouses consisting of two groups of mixed arms: JM and 25-mm guns. These constructions, with protection 1 only, held a garrison of about twenty men. There were plans to build some of these blockhouses to strengthen the Rhine defenses, but none were actually erected in that area (Bruge 1973, 84).

At least twenty-four special CORF blockhouses, based on 1931 plans, formed the main defenses of the SF of the Vosges between Bitche and Lembach. According to the 1939 CORF terminology, the "blockhouse" was an infantry facility smaller than an interval casemate, usually not equipped with a generator for producing electrical power. However, it had a ventilation and filter system. Instead of the twin machine guns, it included only light machine guns in embrasures and cloche. The type plans were drawn up by the technical notice of March 13, 1931 (Truttmann August 1982, correspondence). Some had one or two cloches and many included a protective fossé for their weapons crenels. Some of these may have mounted 13.2-mm Hotchkiss anti-tank machine guns. The effectiveness of these positions is questionable since the area they defended in the Vosges was overrun by the Germans in 1940.

Later blockhouses and casemates built by the army were not as elaborate as the CORF works. Some had armored doors, but no individual power supply: few were as self-sufficient as the CORF casemates. A few blockhouses consisted of two levels, most had only one level, some had no firing crenels and served as mere abris for a very small number of men, others still had no back wall. Blockhouses built into the ends of buildings turned those structures into fortified houses. The smallest variety of blockhouse, built by MOM, met higher standards than those constructed by regular field units. Because of their small size, they did not include cloches nor features such as a fossé. Many other blockhouses built by army units had a concrete thickness usually averaging about one meter or less; they varied in quality according to the skill of the troops that built it. Most of these positions were rather primitive with walls so thin that they became vulnerable to small arms in some cases. The small blockhouses mushroomed early in the war in the SF of the Sarre and other lightly defended areas of northeast France.

The smaller works such as casemates and abris designed by CORF to back up the Maginot Line's ouvrages, and other works in forward position, proved to be effective positions. The greatest weakness appeared to be the mixed variety of works built by the MOM and field units in the form of many nonstandard blockhouses. In some cases the positioning of some of these positions also turned out not to be very advantageous.

NOTE

1. The numbers do not appear to be based on a standard system, especially since the numbers 155 and 156 are also used for these two positions on military maps.

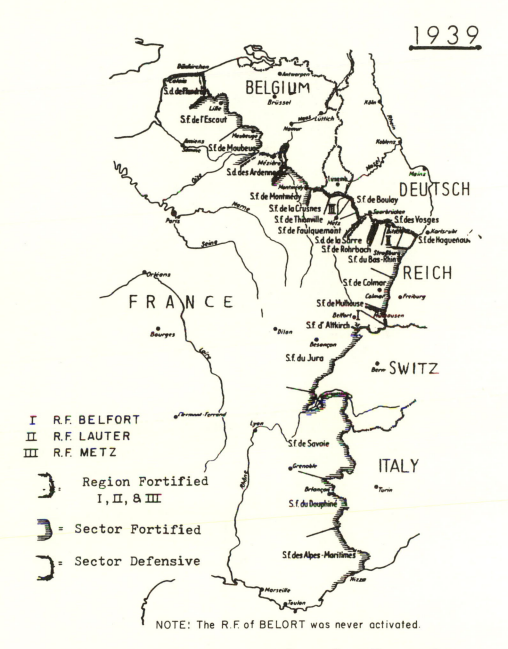

Figure 1. German Map of French Fortified Sectors

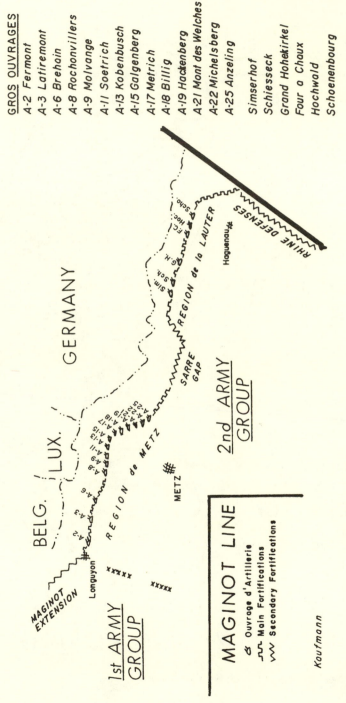

Figure 2. Artillery Ouvrage of the Maginot Line Proper

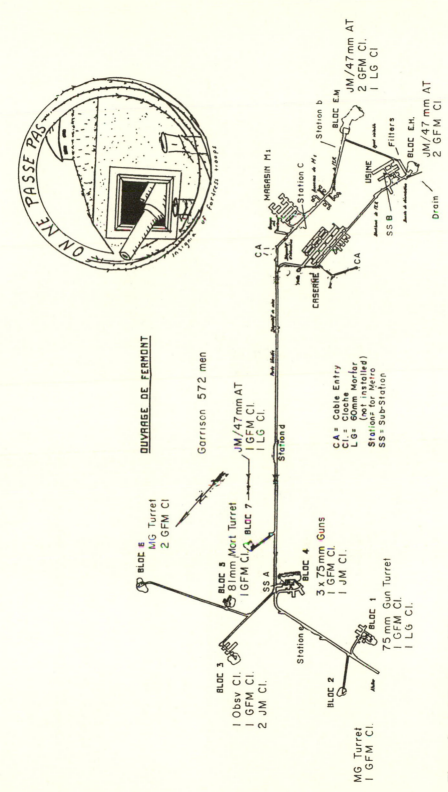

Figure 3. A-2 Ouvrage of Fermont

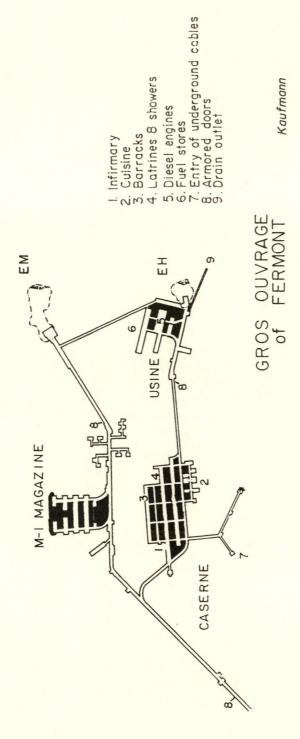

1. Infirmary
2. Cuisine
3. Barracks
4. Latrines & showers
5. Diesel engines
6. Fuel stores
7. Entry of underground cables
8. Armored doors
9. Drain outlet

GROS OUVRAGE
of FERMONT

Kaufmann

Figure 4. Support Area of Fermont

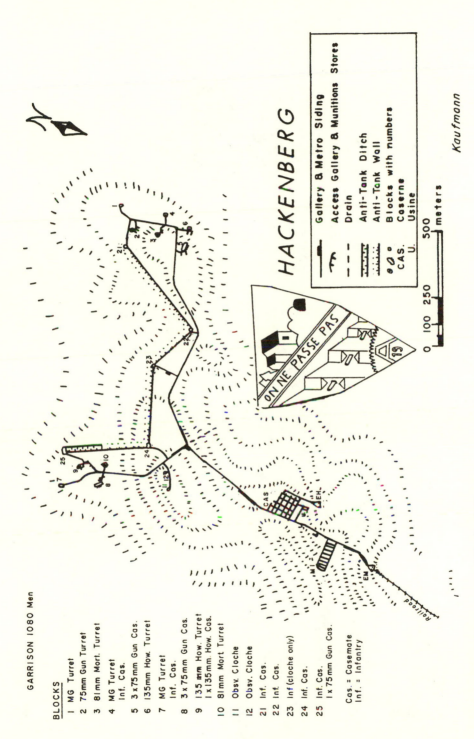

GARRISON 1080 Men

BLOCKS
1 MG Turret
2 75mm Gun Turret
3 81mm Mort. Turret
4 MG Turret
   Inf. Cas.
5 3 x 75mm Gun Cas.
6 135mm How. Turret
7 MG Turret
   Inf. Cas.
8 3 x 75mm Gun Cas.
9 135 mm How. Turret
   1 x 135mm. How. Cas.
10 81mm Mort Turret
11 Obsv. Cloche
12 Obsv. Cloche
21 Inf. Cas.
22 Inf. Cas.
23 Inf (cloche only)
24 Inf. Cas.
25 Inf. Cas.
   1 x 75mm Gun Cas.

Cas. = Casemate
Inf. = Infantry

HACKENBERG

——— Gallery & Metro Siding
—— Access Gallery & Munitions Stores
– – – Drain
⌐⌐⌐ Anti-Tank Ditch
······ Anti-Tank Wall
●●● Blocks with numbers
CAS. Caserne
U. Usine

0   100   250   500
          meters

Kaufmann

Figure 5. A-19 Ouvrage of Hackenberg

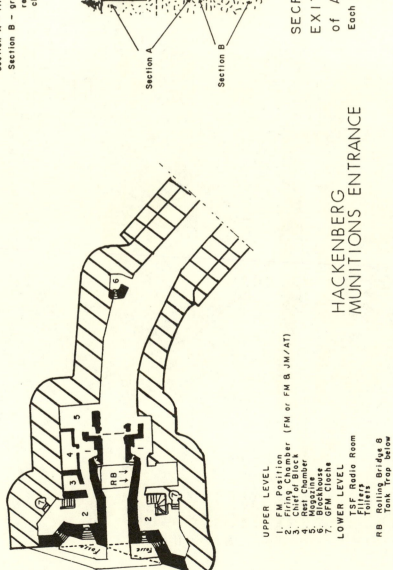

Section A – filled with gravel.
Section B – gravel from Section A was released into this empty chamber so exit could be used.

Secret Escape Hatch covered with earth

Trap Door

Main Gallery

Section A

Section B

SECRET EMERGENCY
EXIT of the Ouvrage
of ANZELING
Each Gros Ouvrage had one.

Kaufmann

UPPER LEVEL
1. FM Position
2. Firing Chamber (FM or FM & JM/AT)
3. Chief of Block
4. Rest Chamber
5. Magazine
6. Blockhouse
7. GFM Cloche

LOWER LEVEL
TSF Radio Room
Filters
Toilets

RB Rolling Bridge 8
Tank Trap below

HACKENBERG
MUNITIONS ENTRANCE

Figure 6. EM of Hackenberg and Secret Exit of Anzeling

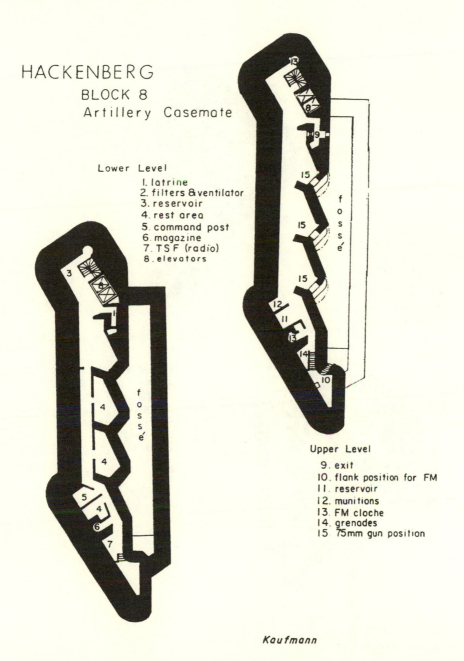

HACKENBERG
BLOCK 8
Artillery Casemate

Lower Level
1. latrine
2. filters & ventilator
3. reservoir
4. rest area
5. command post
6. magazine
7. TSF (radio)
8. elevators

Upper Level
9. exit
10. flank position for FM
11. reservoir
12. munitions
13. FM cloche
14. grenades
15. 75mm gun position

Kaufmann

Figure 7. Hackenberg: Block 9 of Western Combat Group

HACKENBERG
BLOCK 9
Artillery casemate and turret

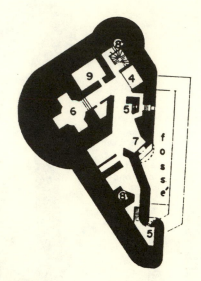

Lower Level
1. rest area
2. stores
3. resrvoir
4. elevator

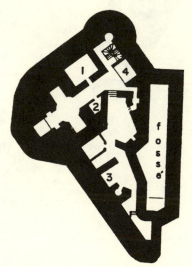

Upper Level
5. FM position
6. control level of
   135mm howitzer turret
7. 135mm howiter position
8. GFM cloche
9. shells
10. exit

Kaufmann

Figure 8. Block 9 of Western Combat Group

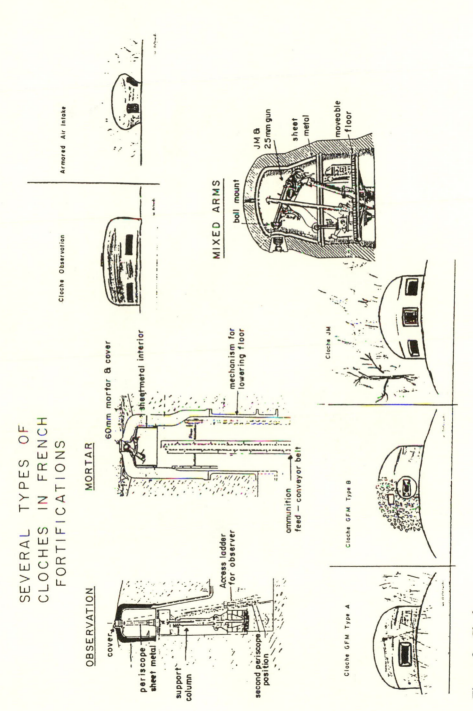

SEVERAL TYPES OF CLOCHES IN FRENCH FORTIFICATIONS

OBSERVATION

cover

periscope
sheet metal

support column

Acess ladder for observer

second periscope position

MORTAR

60mm mortar & cover

sheet metal interior

mechanism for lowering floor

ammunition feed – conveyor belt

Cloche Observation

Armored Air Intake

MIXED ARMS

boll mount

JM &
25mm gun

sheet metal

moveable floor

Cloche JM

Cloche GFM Type B

Cloche GFM Type A

Figure 9. Cloches

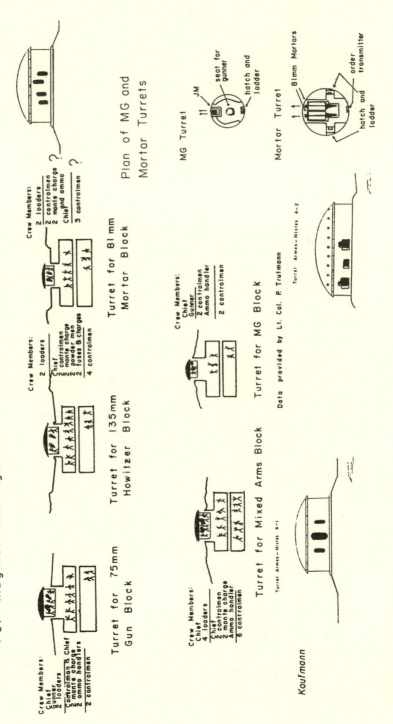

Figure 10. Turrets

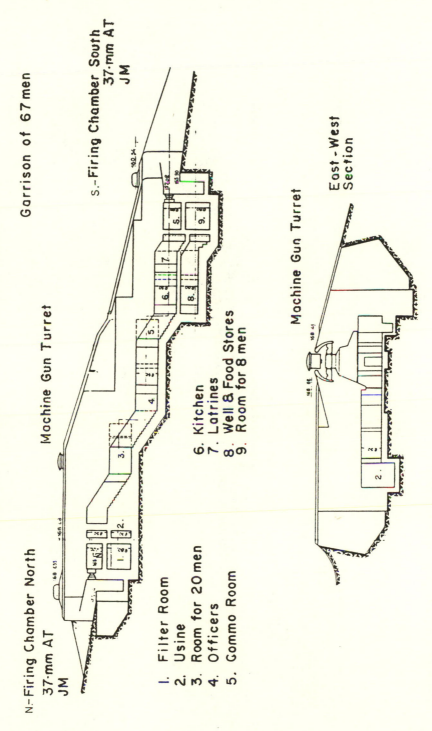

PETIT OUVRAGE SENTZICH

Garrison of 67 men

Machine Gun Turret

N.-Firing Chamber North
37-mm AT
JM

S.-Firing Chamber South
37-mm AT
JM

1. Filter Room
2. Usine
3. Room for 20 men
4. Officers
5. Commo Room

6. Kitchen
7. Latrines
8. Well & Food Stores
9. Room for 8 men

Machine Gun Turret

East - West
Section

Figure 11. Monolithic Ouvrage of Sentzich

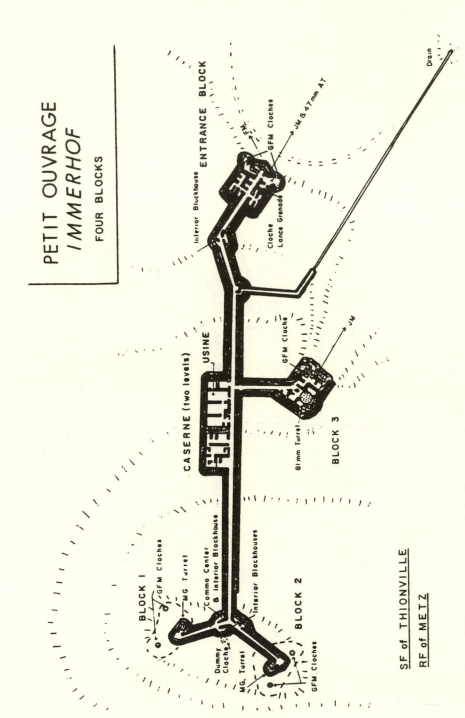

Figure 12. Multi-Block Petit Ouvrage

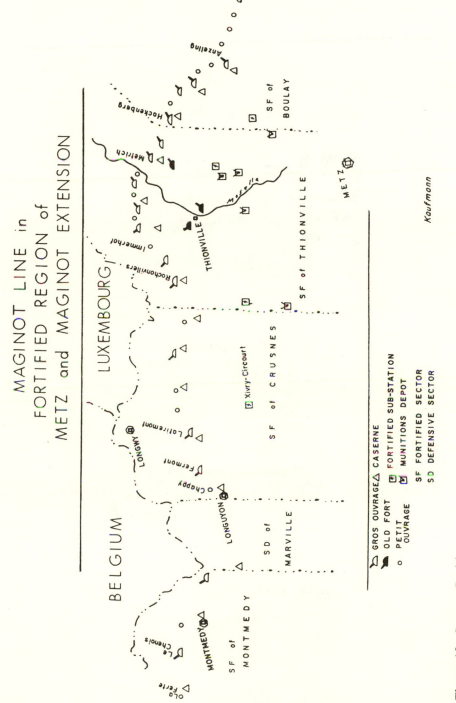

Figure 13. Support Positions

FORTIFIED HOUSES

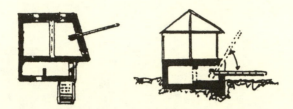

Frame structure over bunker

Bunkers at both ends of building

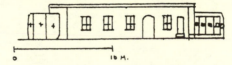

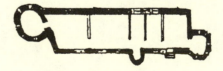

Figure 14. Border Positions

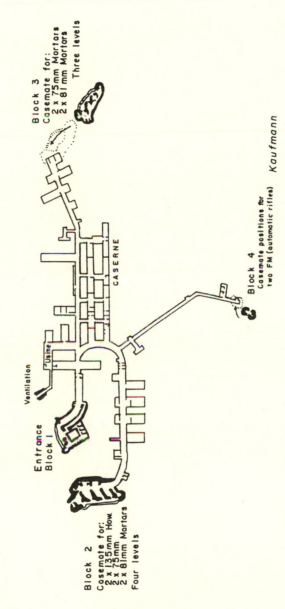

OUVRAGE of SAINTE AGNES

in MARITIME ALPS

Block 3
Casemate for:
2 x 75mm Mortars
2 x 81 mm Mortars
Three levels

Entrance
Block I

Ventilation

Usine

CASERNE

Block 4
Casemate positions for
two FM (automatic rifles)   Kaufmann

Block 2
Casemate for:
2 x 135 mm How.
2 x 75mm Mortars
2 x 81mm Mortars
Four levels

Figure 15. Alpine Ouvrage

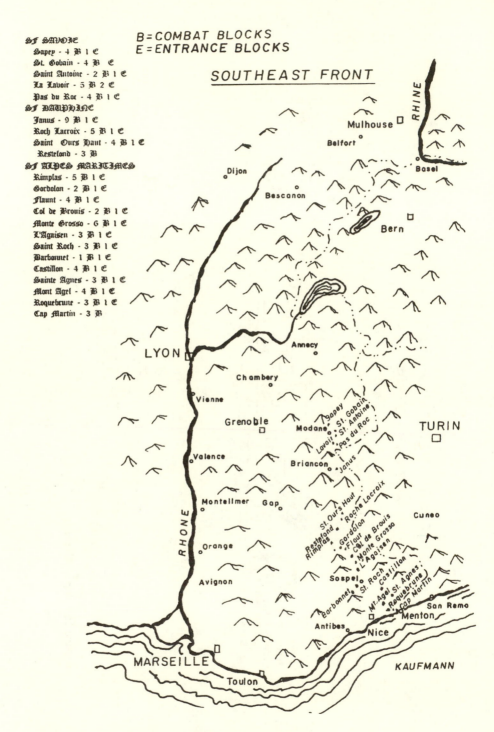

Figure 16. Gros Ouvrages of the Little Maginot Line

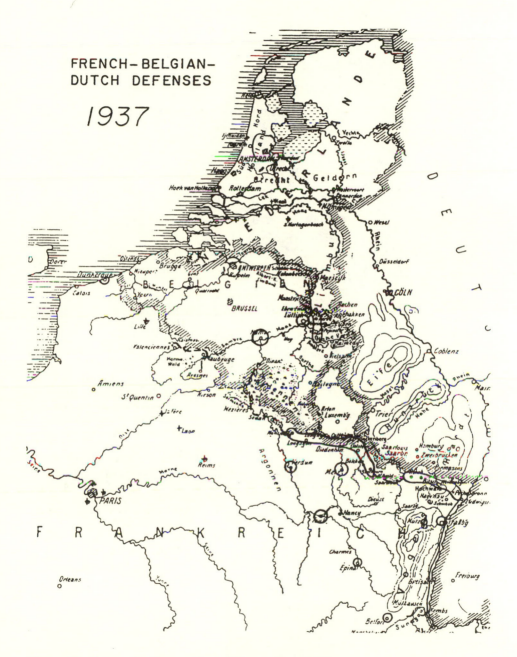

Figure 17. German Intelligence Map of Western Front 1937

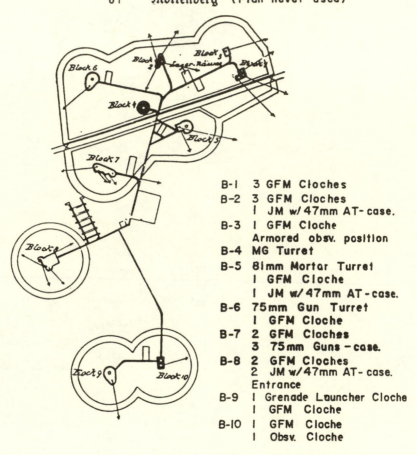

1937 GERMAN PLAN
of   Mottenberg (Plan never used)

B-1   3 GFM Cloches
B-2   3 GFM Cloches
      1 JM w/ 47mm AT-case.
B-3   1 GFM Cloche
      Armored obsv. position
B-4   MG Turret
B-5   81mm Mortar Turret
      1 GFM Cloche
      1 JM w/ 47mm AT-case.
B-6   75mm Gun Turret
      1 GFM Cloche
B-7   2 GFM Cloches
      3 75mm Guns - case.
B-8   2 GFM Cloches
      2 JM w/ 47mm AT-case.
      Entrance
B-9   1 Grenade Launcher Cloche
      1 GFM Cloche
B-10 1 GFM Cloche
      1 Obsv. Cloche

Figure 18. 1937 German Intelligence Plan: Projected Fort

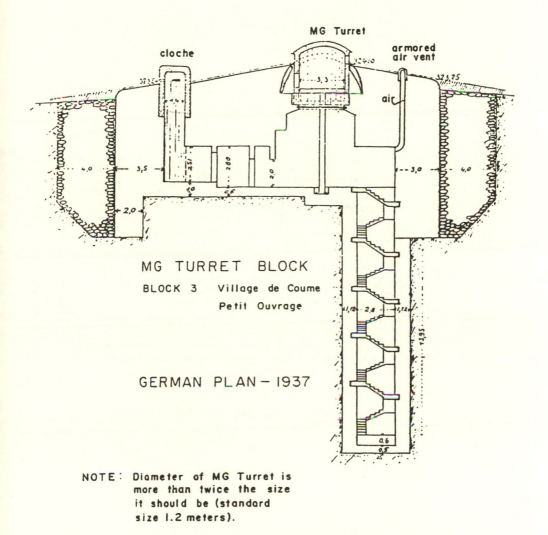

Figure 19. 1937 German Intelligence of an MG Turret Block, Cross-Section

BLOCK I of OUVRAGE of METRICH

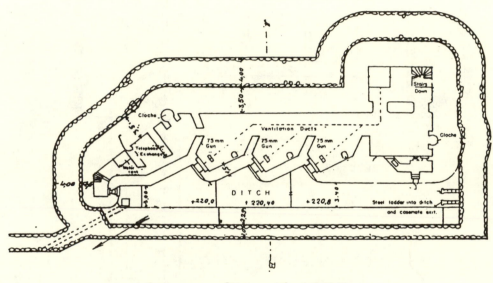

German Plan of 1937

Figure 20. 1937 German Intelligence Plan: Artillery Casemate

FRENCH MAGINOT LINE ABRI

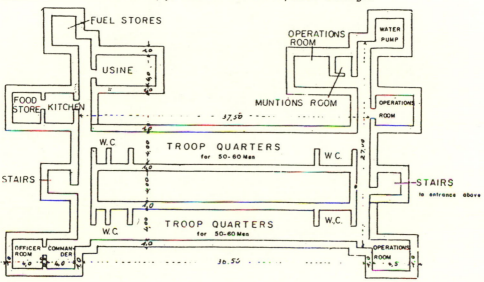

German Plan— 1937

Figure 21. 1937 German Intelligence Plan: Cavern-Type Abri

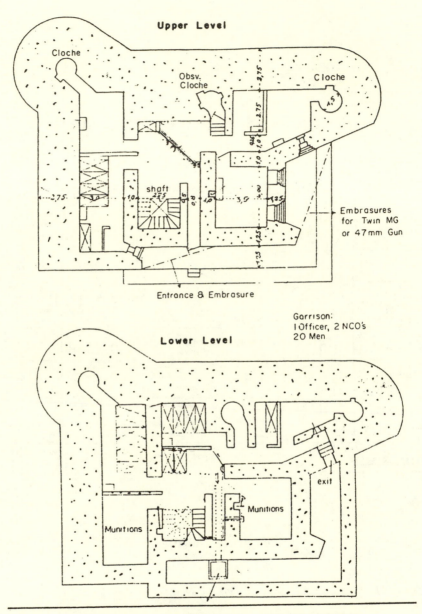

Upper Level

Cloche

Obsv.
Cloche

Cloche

shaft

Embrasures
for Twin MG
or 47mm Gun

Entrance & Embrasure

Garrison:
1 Officer, 2 NCO's
20 Men

Lower Level

exit

Munitions

Munitions

FRENCH INTERVAL CASEMATE
of MAGINOT LINE — German Plan 1937

Figure 22. 1937 German Intelligence Plan: Casemate

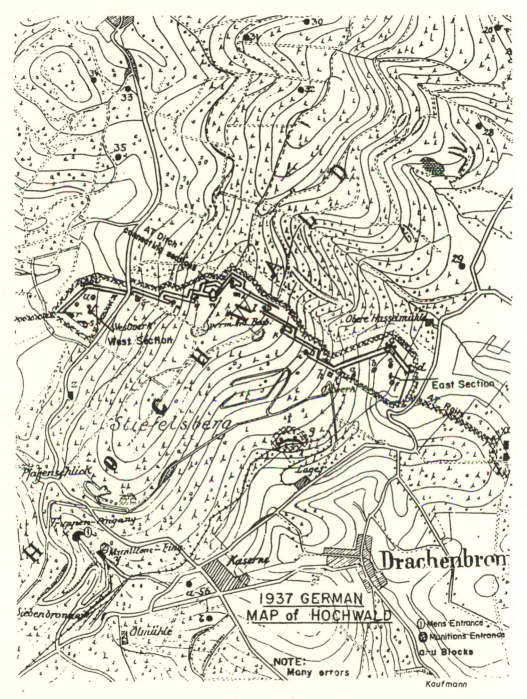

Figure 23. 1937 German Intelligence Map: Ouvrage of Hochwald

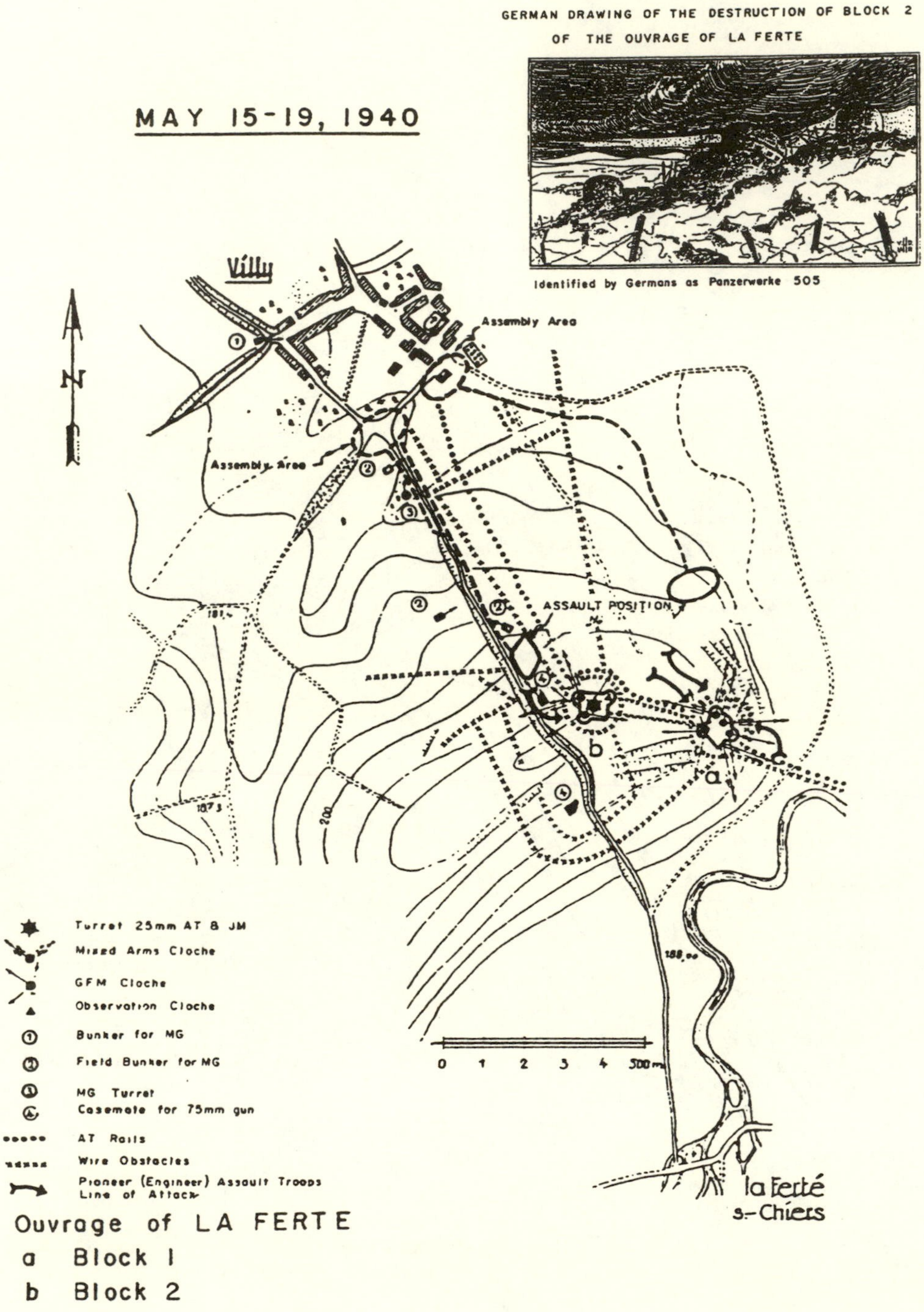
GERMAN DRAWING OF THE DESTRUCTION OF BLOCK 2
OF THE OUVRAGE OF LA FERTE
Identified by Germans as Panzerwerke 505
MAY 15-19, 1940
Villy
N
Assembly Area
Assembly Area
ASSAULT POSITION
b
a
200
0 1 2 3 4 500m
la Ferté
s.-Chiers
Turret 25mm AT & JM
Mixed Arms Cloche
GFM Cloche
Observation Cloche
Bunker for MG
Field Bunker for MG
MG Turret
Casemate for 75mm gun
AT Rails
Wire Obstacles
Pioneer (Engineer) Assault Troops Line of Attack
Ouvrage of LA FERTE
a Block 1
b Block 2

Figure 24. German Map of Attack on Ouvrage of La Ferté

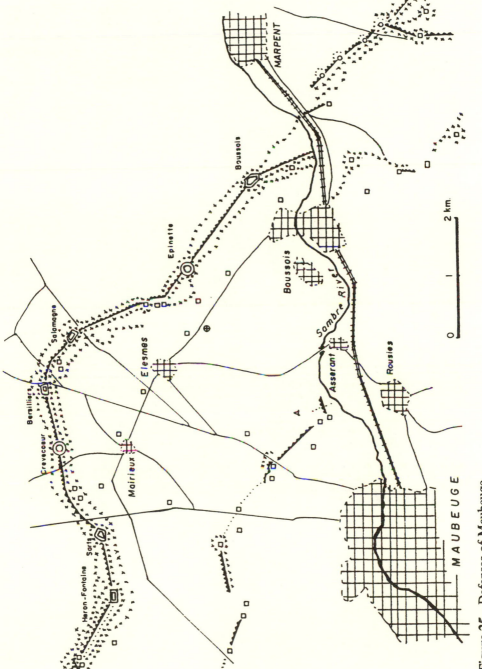

Figure 25. Defenses of Maubeuge

6

SUPPORTING POSITIONS

The vital support positions were located behind the Maginot Line, and in some cases right inside it. The two old German forts of Guentrange and Koenigsmacker in the old Thionville ring were included in the support line. In addition, heavy railway guns could be stationed on spurs specially built off the main rail lines. However, many support facilities had nothing to do with artillery support but were instead centers for logistics and administration, which included munitions depots, electrical power substations and casernes (military camps).

Fort Louis, one of the pre-World War I forts on the Rhine, served as the terminus of the SF of Haguenau and the Maginot Line Proper. It is here that the Rhine Defenses began. Only a few casemates of the Rhine Defenses were located further down the river from Fort Louis. The Rhine fortifications passed through the city of Strasbourg, already ringed by a dozen German forts built late in the nineteenth century. These old forts, that had little in common with the modern German Feste of the Thionville area, had little military value. A few of them, such as Fort Joffre and Fort Uhrich, mounted artillery batteries in 1939, and Fort Ducrot with a couple of sections of 75-mm guns in casemates served as the site of an army corps headquarters. The old Feste of the Mutzig area was used by the French Fifth Army as a headquarters (État-Major de L'Armeé de Terre 1967, v 3, 771). Just like the German Feste at Metz, none of these forts, were intended for an active supporting role in the Maginot Line and those the army reactivated served mainly for use by the field army.

The German Feste in the Thionville sector, on the other hand, provided active support to a major section of the Maginot Line in the RF of Metz. In 1935 Fort Guentrange's two four-gun turret batteries and Fort Koenigsmacker's one four-gun turret battery were rearmed with long-range 105-mm guns, which could cover all the ouvrages of the SF of Thionville (Truttmann 1977, 2). These old German forts had a number of modern features that made them an asset rather than a liability to the Maginot Line. For instance, they consisted of blocks dispersed on a hill dominating the area. The blocks were linked to each other by a tunnel, much like a Maginot ouvrage. The Maginot fortifications included many of the features of these Feste.

However, the Thionville Feste also had a number of antiquated and undesirable characteristics that turned them into a liability in the main line. For instance, unlike the new French ouvrages, the artillery blocks usually held four single-gun turrets rather than one. In addition, the caserne and other supporting positions were not located deep below the ground. Instead, they were housed in large structures with massive facades facing towards the rear, which, it was thought when they were built, would make them immune from direct enemy fire. Furthermore, the moat that surrounded the forts was large and defended by coffres. Finally, the shelters for the troops and the fighting positions were located on the surface, and were as vulnerable as those used in World War I trenches.

The German Feste of Metz was further behind the line and played a smaller role than the forts of Thionville. These forts did not serve the Maginot Line although some were armed. Fort Jeanne d'Arc, for example, served as a headquarters for the French Third Army in 1939. Generally speaking, however, the army found no need to refurbish the Metz forts because they were too far behind the main line to render effective fire support. The Metz ring did not see action until 1944, when the Germans used them against the Allies. Fort Driant, the most impressive of these forts, became a major German bastion. With five artillery blocks—three with 100-mm guns and two with 150-mm guns—it was larger than the forts of Thionville. The French had done little after the Great War with its weapons or those of the other Metz forts. It was in September 1944 that the Germans made an effort to refurbish the guns of equipment of these neglected forts. These forts proved capable of stemming the tide of the Allied advance in 1944 (Cole 1950, 154, 263-269; Kemp 1981a, 37-38). The Allies also found Fort Koenigsmacker at Thionville a major obstacle to their progress in 1944. These forts demonstrated that the old Feste could be quite formidable. The most serious drawback to the Metz ring was that it had been designed to repel an enemy advancing from the west. Thus, the strongest of the Feste were built on the western side of the line, and the weakest infantry forts on the eastern side. This may be why the French did not make a greater effort to incorporate them into the Maginot Line.

A number of other World War I era forts returned to service as supporting positions in both the Northeast and Southeast Fronts. In a few instances the old turrets were refurbished and readied for action. Such was the case with the Mougin turrets of Fort Suchet, adjacent to and part of the Maginot ouvrage of Barbonnet. The majority of the old forts, however, were used for command and logistical support.

The Maginot Line was to receive artillery support not only from these older forts in the rear area, but also from field artillery units and heavy artillery batteries mounted on rail wagons. The heavy rail guns allowed for long-range artillery fire that the Maginot forts were not capable of achieving.

Each of the sectors of the Maginot Line had its own organic field artillery, which usually included various models of 155-mm L and 155-mm C guns with ranges from 10,000 to 17,000 meters. These guns could be used only to support the ouvrages under attack, unless they were moved up into the line to shoot in the direction of the border (Fitzsimons 1978, 2014). Only the super-heavy guns of the rail artillery, with their long ranges, were capable of supplying defensive and offensive support. These included cannons of 305-mm (27,000 meter range), 320-mm (24,000 meter range), 340-mm (37,000 meter range), 400-mm (15,000 meter range), and 520-mm (24,000 meter range) (Fitzsimons 1978, 2128). This type of artillery was ideally suited for the needs of fortified lines. In addition, the heavy guns and the smaller field artillery pieces were less vulnerable to ground assault because they were mobile. Their main disadvantage was that they remained exposed to air attack. Because heavy artillery was not placed in the ouvrages, the forts were spared the huge logistical burden of maintaining this type of weapon.

Roads and .60 gauge military rail lines also came into service to ensure logistical support for the ouvrages. Some railroad sidings could be used for the rail guns, but many were of the narrower .60 gauge and too small. These narrow-gauge lines linked the supply depots adjacent to the French National Railroad lines to the ouvrages. Some ouvrage entrances accommodated military trucks, others the rail cars from the narrow-gauge track, whereas a few could receive both.

The well-protected substations that supplied the ouvrages with electrical power were strategically located at points that allowed them to service several forts. There were five of these substations in RF of Metz and only two in the RF of Lauter. One of the substations of the RF of the Lauter was not even fortified (Wahl 1982, interview). In general, they were located about ten kilometers behind the line of ouvrages and connected to an unfortified substation on the national grid. These positions looked like concrete fortifications, but they had no protection other than their walls and the troops assigned to defend them. Each station received high voltage from the civilian power grid and stepped it down from 65,000 volts to either 17,500 or 10,200 volts before transmitting it on to the ouvrages. The current had to be stepped down because the underground cables could not carry as high a voltage as aerial lines. There are claims that the power lines between the substations and the ouvrages were entirely subterranean, but Truttmann, who has made a thorough study of the subject, found that the lines normally departed the substation as aerial lines and then went underground within a few kilometers of the ouvrages (Truttmann 1979, plan 7; Truttmann 1988, interview).

In the RF of Metz, the substation of Xivry-Circourt sent electrical power to the ouvrages of Fermont, Latiremont and Bréhain. Some of the petits ouvrages in the sector were to be connected through underground cables to nearby gros ouvrages to take advantage of their power supply. However, the project was never completed. Aerial lines linked Xivry-Circourt to the substation of Lommerange, which was connected, in turn, to the national grid. A link between Lommerange and Bréhain was planned, but the underground section was not completed. However, this substation supported Rochonvillers and Molvange. The substation of Reinange had a heavy load since it supplied electricity to Soetrich, Kobenbusch, Galgenberg, Metrich, Billig and Hackenberg. The substation of Bettelainville supplied Hackenberg, Mont des Welsches, Michelsberg, and Anzeling. Another substation at Fouligny was intended to furnish power to some petits ouvrages that were too far away to be tied into a gros ouvrages. As a matter of fact, few, if any, of the petits ouvrages of the RF of Metz received their power from neighboring gros ouvrages. In the RF of Lauter, the substation of Goetzenbruck tied into the gros ouvrages of Simserhof, Schiesseck and Grand Hohékirkel. The remaining ouvrages of Four à Chaux, Hochwald and Schoenenbourg, received their electricity from the unfortified substation of Mertzwiller, near Haguenau, about twenty kilometers distant. Mertzwiller apparently was not a special military substation, but it was able to step down the voltage to the required 2,200 volts (Collin and Wahl 1981, 22). In this sector too, links to the petits ouvrages were not available. However, it must be remembered that it was not until 1936 that the army finally received the funds to hook up the ouvrages with the national grid. The work, begun in 1938, was still incomplete by 1940. At this time radiators were installed to heat the ouvrages. This system, which required hot water, could only function with an external power supply (Truttmann 1979, 350, 356).

By the time the war began, few of the underground links between ouvrages, large or small, were completed. The connection between Fermont and Latiremont was one of the few to be operational. It is commonly believed that the ouvrages connected to an outside power source relied on it only in peace time, reverting to their own engines during war time. In fact, the military substations were fortified so that they could continue to supply power to the ouvrages as long as possible. It appears also that the underground supply was not designed for peace time use. Most ouvrages, including the small ones and those in the Alps, had a direct aerial connection to the national grid solely for peace time use. A small surface structure near the fort housed a transformer to reduce the voltage to 440 volts (or 220 volts in the Alps). The ouvrages did not have transformers in their usines until after 1938 when work began on the underground lines and the substations. It was also at this time that the *Génie* created either special galleries or used drainage tunnels for the underground power lines (Truttmann 1979, 350-356).

The munitions depots played an integral part in logistical support for the Maginot Line. Seven major depots supported the artillery ouvrages of the Maginot Line Proper: Mance, St. Hubert, Reinanage, Rurange, and Chailly in the RF of Metz; Montbrann and Neubourg in the RF of Lauter. These depots were usually located a little further to the rear than the substations. They were often adjacent to the main railroad and connected to the ouvrages by military rail lines or by road.

The surface caserne or military camp was essential to the Maginot Line, especially in peace time when it was impractical to maintain garrisons in the ouvrages for extended periods of time. It was also logistically and administratively more economical to keep the fortress troops in regular military camps. Most of these bases were located well behind the main line. Their primary function was to give the garrisons of the ouvrages more comfortable quarters and working areas in time of peace. It also facilitated training, which included a variety of activities from classroom instruction to firing infantry weapons on special ranges. There were about fifteen of these camps and munitions depots in RF of Metz, about a dozen camps and smaller munitions depots in the RF of Lauter, and four camps in the Maginot Extension. Since few of these large camps were situated near the ouvrages, smaller temporary casernes were built near the forts themselves. These so-called *casernes legères* or light camps provided quarters for a security force and could quickly be pulled down when war began and the troops moved underground. In the Alps, the camps for the garrisons of the Maginot Line had to be placed wherever the terrain permitted.

Additional casernes and service areas could be found further behind the Maginot Line on an axis running from Verdun to Strasbourg. Last but not least, were the engineer depots, located also to the rear. They provided the Maginot Line with such things as technical support and material, construction and repair supplies, and so on. They were as essential to the smooth operation of the Maginot Line as were the quartermaster and ordnance services.

Thus the supporting positions, although not as impressive as the fighting positions of the Maginot Line itself, played a key role in making the whole system of fortifications function smoothly. These facilities required a sizable amount of funds for their construction, maintenance and operation. Without them the army would have found it difficult not only to maintain the operation of the ouvrages, but also to keep their crews trained and ready for action.

7

THE RHINE DEFENSES, NEW FRONTS, AND ALPINE FRONT

In addition to the Maginot Line Proper, the Maginot scheme of defenses included other major projects, such as the Rhine Defenses, the New Fronts, and the Maginot Line in the Alps, or the Little Maginot Line. The Rhine Defenses are probably the least impressive because they consisted mostly of small fortifications no larger than casemates. The New Fronts were created when the mission of the Maginot Line was altered early in the 1930s. Indeed, at this point the military started thinking of the Maginot Line as an active defensive unit rather than a delaying mechanism that would buy time for mobilization. It quickly became evident that there were serious weak points in the line. Thus, the New Fronts were created to extend the Maginot Line in the northeast and to partially close the Sarre Gap. The creation of these New Fronts marks perhaps the beginning of the so-called "Maginot Mentality," that is, the idea that it was possible to achieve victory by relying on concrete defenses. Finally, the Maginot Line in the Alps had a slow start, because of the Depression and mushrooming building expenses. However, in the early 1930s Mussolini's Ethiopian adventure and the formation of the Axis gave an added impetus to the construction effort in the Alps.

THE RHINE DEFENSES

The Rhine defensive sector, which was not part of the Maginot Line Proper, was originally designed as light defenses and relied on the mighty river for protection. Instead of ouvrages, 128 CORF casemates and abris and an unspecified number of blockhouses distributed among three lines of defenses formed the defenses of the Rhine SFs. The first line, built into the bank of the Rhine, consisted of blockhouses reinforced at strategic points—such as river bends and especially bridging sites—by casemates or abris. A so-called "Village Line" extended from the Ried forest to the River Ill. Sandwiched between these two, the second line secured key points at bridges and roads (Truttmann 1979, 74-75; *Memorial of the Maginot Line* 1983, 1-2).

Most of the CORF casemates in this area consisted of a single level and conformed to several patterns, as previously noted.   The largest casemates were located in the village line. The blockhouses, which were not designed by CORF, were very small, accommodating only three to four soldiers. They were found in all three lines. The second line depended on the forest for its security in many places. In a few places, groups of field fortifications sketched a fourth line. Such was the case of the SF of Colmar, where short stretches of defensive positions were built near the Ill River (*Memorial of the Maginot Line* 1983, 2).

According the Truttmann (1979, 74), the main weakness of the Rhine Defenses was that the casemates were too distant from each other for effective mutual support. In addition, the "Village Line" was blinded by the Ried forest and was not able to defend the river line efficiently when the Germans attacked in June 1940.

The SF of the Rhine, with thirty-four casemates, extended from Seltz to a point south of the old ring of forts of Strasbourg. The SF of Colmar, with another forty-three casemates, continued from south of Strasbourg to Blodelsheim. The SF of Mulhouse, with sixteen casemates, defended the vicinity of the city of Mulhouse. Finally, the SF of Haute Alsace, with only seven casemates and more than forty blockhouses, stretched from Sierentz to Folgensbourg and ran parallel to the Swiss border. This is the only sector that did not depend on the Rhine for protection, relying instead on the numerous blockhouses that formed a line from the southeast of Blotzheim to the south, along the Swiss border. Its mission was to seal off a German penetration from that quarter.

The presence of the Rhine made continuous lines of anti-tank obstacles and ditches superfluous. Unfortunately, down river, past the point where the Rhine enters Germany, there are no other natural obstacles to protect France. The area between Fort Louis and the gros ouvrages of the Maginot Line Proper near Haguenau was only lightly fortified since the petits ouvrages that had been planned were never realized. This did not seem to be a major problem to the planners, however, who counted on the Rhine to effectively stop the enemy, and who felt that these SFs required fewer field troops and garrisons than the Maginot Line Proper. Even if the enemy succeeded in crossing the mighty river, he would not be able to advance very far in French territory without encountering the Vosges mountains, which could be easily defended.

THE NEW FRONTS

Between early 1935 and late 1936, the French military became acutely aware of many vulnerable gaps in their frontier fortifications, created mostly by the changing political situation. The frontier facing the German Saar region was only lightly defended. The frontier with Belgium was largely unfortified between Longuyon and the North Sea because the original plans had counted on that country's allied status. The French realized that it would be foolish to think that they could quickly occupy the Saar in the event the Germans began a war. French intelligence sources in the late 1920s were also fully aware that the people of the Saar would never vote for integration with France. Eventually, over ninety percent of the Saar population voted for unification with Germany in the plebiscite of January 1935. A few months later, in March 1936, the Germans boldly marched into the demilitarized Rhineland. In October 1936 the new Belgian king broke off his alliance with France, declaring neutrality.

Perceiving the threat on the eastern borders, late in October 1936 the new war minister, Daladier, urged for a build up of fortifications in the northeast. He wanted more casemates, but had no interest in new forts (Hohnadel and Truttmann 1988, 6; Gunsburg 1979, 41). The planning and some construction of the New Fronts had been under way since 1934. A second, and perhaps more compelling reason for extending the fortifications between Bitche and the Sarre, was probably that by the 1930s the French High Command had given up any serious thoughts of a major French offensive between the RFs of the Maginot Line Proper, opting for greater reliance on fortifications (Kaufmann and Kaufmann 1993, 30). Thus, an attempt was made to extend the Maginot Line further along the Belgian border from its terminus at Longuyon. The result was the construction of New Fronts, which included the Maginot Extension.

The New Fronts benefited from the experience acquired in building the Old Fronts, but they suffered from new financial limitations. The shortage of funds was caused by Mussolini's invasion of Ethiopia in the fall of 1935 and the subsequent creation of the Axis a year later, which diverted the attention of the French military to the Southeastern Front.

Maubeuge became a major bastion in the north, beyond the range of the Maginot Line and the Maginot Extension. Beyond it the major industrial center of Lille was left unprotected because it was too close to the border to defend efficiently.

Work began on two new petits ouvrages and additional casemates on the left flank of the RF of Lauter, extending the defenses to a point overlooking the Sarre Gap. Both of these new ouvrages were given only three combat blocks but mounted the new mixed-arms turrets with two JM sets and 25-mm anti-tank gun. They also included several mixed-arms cloches, but lacked artillery and were beyond the effective range of the nearest gros ouvrage of the Maginot Line Proper. The petit ouvrage of Rohrbach also received a new mixed-arms turret and cloche (Mary 1980, 16, 266-267). The left flank of the RF of the Lauter was just as weak as the right flank of the RF of Metz and could not be effectively held without sufficient artillery support.

The Maginot Extension, the best known of the New Fronts, included the SF of Montmédy and the weakly defended sub-sector of Marville. The Marville sector had no ouvrages and included about twenty-five STG type casemates as well as numerous blockhouses (Mary 1980, 66). It lacked larger fortifications because the area was well endowed with natural obstacles and not considered a likely avenue of enemy advance. It also linked the SF of Montmédy to the Maginot Line Proper. When the war began this sub-sector was removed from the SF of Montmédy and attached to the SF of La Crusnes of the Maginot Line Proper (Truttmann 1979, Plan 65).

The remainder of SF of Montmédy, on the other hand, had some ouvrages and CORF casemates. Two gros and two petits ouvrages with a dozen casemates and some smaller fortifications were erected in this sector. Unfortunately, the four ouvrages were well beyond the range of the guns of the Maginot Line Proper. In addition, the two gros ouvrages were so widely separated that they could just barely cover the petits ouvrages between them, and could not support each other. They each mounted only a single turret of 75-mm guns and had no other artillery weapons. Thus, these fortifications were not able to form as effective a barrier as those of the Maginot Line Proper.

Between the ouvrage of La Ferté, the western terminus of the extension located near the village of Villy, and the vicinity of Maubeuge lay the SD of the Ardennes, which relied on natural obstacles and smaller fortifications, such as small blockhouses, for defense. Before the war, the and Military Region, covering the area between Montmédy and the SF Maubeuge, was under the command of General André Corp, who would defend it unsuccessfully against the German onslaught. Between 1937 and 1938, after the completion of the initial work, Corp received no funds for improvements. The situation for the adjacent SFs was not much better. Bruge (1973, 31, 34) mentions in his history of the Maginot Line that an appropriation of only 140,000,000 francs had been made as early as 1934 for the Maginot Extension, which was almost as inadequate as the 112,000,000 francs allotted for SF of Maubeuge. However, according to his calculations, this sum was barely enough to fund the construction and outfitting of four ouvrages. Claudel (1974, 34), on the other hand, estimates that a petit ouvrage cost about 10,000,000 francs, and a gros ouvrage of smaller proportions, 70,000,000 francs or less. Thus the sum allocated to Corp was woefully inadequate, especially for the construction of defenses to link the SD Ardennes with the SF of Montmédy and SF of Maubeuge. Work in his sector did not resume until 1939 after General Gaston Prételat, the head of the fortifications commission, pointed out that the defenses of the northeast were inadequate (Draper 1944, 8).

Beyond the SD of Ardennes, four additional fortified sectors extended to the North Sea. The first was the SF of Maubeuge where four old forts, Fort Sarts, Fort Bersillies, Fort Salmagne, and Fort Boussois, were selected as sites for petits ouvrages. This would be the most heavily defended sector north of the Maginot Extension, guarding a traditional invasion route. Although work on some of the ouvrages there did not begin until 1936, the planning had been well under way even before Belgium declared neutrality in October. The second fortified sector in the Flanders region was the SF of Escaut, where one new petit ouvrage was built to cover the gap between Lille and Maubeuge. The third and fourth can hardly be qualified with the term of "fortified sector." The SD of Lille encompassed only light defenses and Lille, located so close to the border, was too difficult to defend properly. The SD of Flanders, which extended to the sea, also consisted only of light fortifications. The army upgraded both of these two sectors to SFs on March 16, 1940, and January 20, 1940, respectively (État-Major de L'Armeé de Terre, Service Historique 1967, v 3, 563, 575). The army divisions and engineer units in these sectors had done nothing more than create additional field works.

Even though the four sectors covering the border from Maubeuge to the sea were part of the New Fronts funding and the Maginot program, they had little in common with the Maginot defensive scheme. They were even less integrated than the fortifications of the Maginot Extension, and received less consideration.

Theodore Draper (1944, 4-5), who analyzed the causes of France's collapse during the war, claims that the Superior War Council was willing to battle the Germans in Belgium or behind the Somme, but was reluctant to put the industrial regions at risk by fighting in it. According to Draper, the Minister of National Defense, F. Pietr, requested 240,000,000 francs—twice the amount allotted for the Maginot Extension—for the development of the fortifications north of Montmédy. However, the council turned down his request in 1932 because it felt that there was no need to extend the fortified front beyond Montmédy. Pietr's successor, Pétain, convinced that Belgium must be used as a forward defense line, decided that minor fortifications would be sufficient to block the exits from the Ardennes. After Belgium declared neutrality in 1936, the French government, no longer concerned about Belgian sensibilities, forged ahead with plans for the defense of its northern border.

Of the positions created on the New Fronts, the Petit Ouvrage of La Ferté, located at the end of the Maginot Extension, would become the first Maginot fort to fall to the enemy. This ouvrage was only supported by the single 75-mm gun turret (1905 model) of the gros ouvrage of Le Chesnois. The defenses erected on its northern and western flanks had little staying power, leaving La Ferté dangling on a relatively tenuous position overlooking the Chiers River.

The smallest ouvrage of the Maginot Extension, La Ferté consisted of only two blocks linked by a gallery about 30 meters below the surface. Like the other ouvrages, it contained complete facilities for a garrison of about a hundred men.

Block 1, overlooking the Chiers River, consisted of four cloches: two of mixed-arms and two GFM. The former had a JM with a 25-mm gun sandwiched in between. These cloches had a limited field of fire extending over a small part of the unfortified region beyond the Maginot Extension. The two GFM cloches provided good all-around coverage, but at the same time they presented prominent targets for enemy gunners. This block also had one firing chamber for a pair of JM with one 47-mm anti-tank gun mounted on the standard monorail behind one of the JMs. Only the GFM cloches covered the approach from the access road leading into the ouvrage from the rear.

The most effective position of the ouvrage was Block 2, which consisted of a turret of mixed arms and three cloches: one GFM, one mixed arms, and one for observation. The turret commanded the whole of the ouvrage with its two 25-mm guns, each with its JM. Today, the remains of the weapons still lie on the floor of the turret, which was displaced from its mounting during the German assault.

Each block of La Ferté has an emergency exit and is encircled by an additional ring of barbed wire and anti-tank rails to this day. Two small casemates, probably of the STG type, protected the approaches to the ouvrage. Casemate East commanded the main road and the approach to the access road. Casemate West, situated to take maximum advantage of the terrain, covered the main road from the other direction with its 75-mm gun. The only other approach to La Ferté was from the steeper slopes of the hill into which the ouvrage had been built.

The gros ouvrage of Le Chesnois not only covered La Ferté with its only 75-mm gun turret, but was also responsible for supporting the four interval casemates between them, the petit ouvrage of Thonnelle, and four interval casemates located on its other flank. Clearly, if more than one position required support at the same time, Le Chesnois would be overwhelmed. The mixed-arms turret of this ouvrage was located among some hills where it was better concealed than La Ferté, whose position was quite vulnerable, especially without the proper artillery support.

THE ALPINE FRONT

The Alpine Defenses ran from the Swiss border to the Mediterranean, protecting an area almost equal to that of the Maginot Line Proper and the Rhine Defenses combined. Although the front in the Alps had more gaps between sections than the main line, the mountain barrier made it much less vulnerable than the Sarre Gap. In addition, the Swiss border and the Mediterranean Sea provided rather secure flanks compared to the almost undefended Ardennes on the flank of the main line.

The Alps alone form a formidable barrier. When the heavy fortifications were added to its mountain passes, they became virtually impregnable. The terrain sometimes permitted ouvrages to be built in dominant places allowing the forts to create a web of interlocking fires much more complex than that of the Maginot Line Proper since it involved a greater number of positions.

The Maginot Line of the Alps was divided into three fortified sectors. The SF of Savoy included five gros ouvrages and five petits ouvrages, which defended the access routes to the Arc Valley in the vicinity of Modane and the northern route from Chambéry to Italy, along the valley of the Isère. Further south, the SF of Dauphiné, guarded the major roads in and around Briançon with its four gros ouvrages and twelve petits ouvrages. Finally, the largest sector, the SF of the Maritime Alps, secured the southern invasion routes through the Alps and Nice with its fourteen gros ouvrages and seventeen petits ouvrages. The last gros ouvrage of this sector stood over the sea at Cap Saint Martin, putting the city of Menton right in the front lines.

The greatest concentration of forts was in the SF of the Maritime Alps where the ouvrages formed an almost continuous line from the vicinity of St. Etienne-de-Tinée to the city of Menton,   especially on the coast near Menton. The border was defended by a line of concrete *avant-postes* to the east of Menton and by a series of artillery and petits ouvrages to the west.

The Alpine fortifications were not built according to the blueprints of the Maginot Line Proper. Instead, they tended to be unique since they were designed to take maximum advantage of the mountainous terrain. Among non-French historians, the Maginot Line of the Alps is known as the *Little Maginot Line*, a term that seems to dissociate it from the rest of the Maginot defenses. In fact, the Alpine forts were most definitely part of the Maginot scheme and were perhaps stronger than most ouvrages in the Maginot Line Proper. Their locations alone, often breathtakingly spectacular, give them a formidable defensive advantage. However, the rugged terrain did not permit the construction of a continuous line of interlocking fires.

Such is especially the case of the SF of Savoy, where the main defensive positions were concentrated over access routes, forming clusters of positions rather than a continuous line. Near the city of Modane, the ouvrages, located a mere ten kilometers from the Italian border, blocked the approaches from the east. Only one secondary road wound its way south to the border where it turned into a mule track in Italy. The Mont Cenis Tunnel linking the two countries to the south of Modane was easily closed off. Three gros ouvrages effectively sealed off the secondary road above the tunnel, which passed through very rugged terrain. For an Italian offensive to succeed, therefore, it would be necessary first to reduce these forts, an operation requiring the heaviest siege artillery, which maneuvered with great difficulty in this type of terrain.

The route of advance towards Modane from the east, through the Arc Valley, went through the pass of Mont Cenis, which could not be fully defended since it belonged in part to Italy. Thus, the main defensive line was placed nearer Modane, about forty kilometers from Mont Cenis. However, the area was not left totally undefended. An invasion force that overran the defenses at the mountain pass would run afoul of the old forts of the Arc, which were still in working order. If these failed to stop it, two Maginot ouvrages overlooking the approaches to Modane would put up a spirited defense. These, in turn, would be supported by a third fort, St. Gobain, perched on a hill in the valley beneath them. It was also flanked by two casemates which stood on each side of the valley, just above it.

Except for the fact that it lacks positions for 75-mm guns, the ouvrage of St. Gobain is in many respects a typical Alpine fortification. Like most artillery forts in the southeast, it was designed for a relatively small garrison of 150 men. Its layout was more compact than that of the ouvrages of the Maginot Line Proper, but its firepower was equal and its weapons were more heavily concentrated in the combat blocks. Like the majority of the Alpine ouvrages, St. Gobain had no gun turrets because they are unnecessary or impractical in the mountainous terrain. Actually, there are few defensive locations in the Alps where turrets can have a 360-degree radius. Thus, only four Alpine ouvrages have turrets of any type: three in the SF of the Maritime Alps and one in the SF of the Dauphiné Alps (Mary 1980, 280-320).

Artillery casemates provided a more economical alternatives to turrets, especially since their field of fire was restricted by the topography. Since many of the artillery casemates did not cover the flanks, but faced the enemy, they were reinforced with extra armor and stronger concrete protection.

St. Gobain's facilities were similar to those in the forts of the Maginot Line Proper, but smaller because they were designed for a smaller garrison. Like most Alpine ouvrages, St. Gobain was equipped with three diesel engines. Also like most gros ouvrages of the area, St. Gobain consisted of a small number of blocks, four to be precise. The entrance was kept secure by a special armored drawbridge spanning the diamond fossé, an obvious variation of the rolling bridge prevailing in the forts of the Maginot Line Proper. The facade of the entrance block was covered by a crenel for a JM and an anti-tank gun. However, instead of two cloches, there was only one GFM cloche above.

Immediately behind the entrance block lay the caserne, the usines, and all the other facilities of the ouvrage. No long galleries separated the interior support sections of the ouvrage from the combat and the entrance blocks. In fact, the two areas were not distinctly separated from each other. St. Gobain was similar to many petits ouvrages of the Maginot Line Proper in these respects. Its blocks were built in close proximity because the cost of digging long galleries in the mountainous terrain was prohibitive. Thus an Alpine ouvrage was typically built in a single hill or mountain section. Instead of distance, what separated the blocks was elevation, which was much more considerable than in any on the Northeast Front.

Block 1 of St. Gobain contained two 81-mm mortars mounted in crenels. Mortars were normally situated below the level of the rim of the fossé. However, these crenels were not located in the fossé. This is probably because it faced south, away from the enemy line of advance along the Arc Valley, and, therefore needed no extra protective measures. The exposed facade along the fossé was pierced by an FM crenel for close defense. An unusual aspect of this block is that it had an additional exposed face, which served no significant purpose, but was defended by a small fossé and an FM crenel. It would seem, however, that a cloche might have provided more efficient local protection for this corner of the block. On the other side of block 1 there was a GFM cloche.

Block 2, the second artillery block, also double-faced, occupied the highest elevation of the ouvrage. Both of its facades had important functions. The first, overlooking the Arc Valley, had two embrasures at its lower level for 81-mm mortars that fired through the fossé. This moat masked the weapons crenels from direct enemy artillery fire. The second face had two embrasures that mounted two JMs and 47-mm anti-tank gun. Two cloches rise above the surface of Block 2. The GFM cloche protected most of its surface whereas the JM cloche guarded the area in front of the mortar crenels.

Block 3, situated below Block 2, overlooked the rear of the ouvrage. It had a single crenel and a GFM cloche, which mounted special signaling equipment directed towards the ouvrage of Sapey on top of a nearby mountain. Sapey, like many other Alpine ouvrages, had the same type of signaling embrasure.

Block 4, located at the lowest elevation, overlooked a bridge leading to the site of an electrical plant. It had only two JM crenels. Its armament consisted of two JMs and probably an anti-tank gun. It was surmounted by a single GFM cloche.

The mortars of Block 1 and the machine guns of Block 4 of Saint Gobain combined with those of the Saint Antoine casemate, on the other side of the valley, to seal effectively the road running between them. In addition, the artillery from Sapey and the ouvrage of Saint Antoine (not the casemate) provided additional fires. Saint Antoine and St. Gobain were positioned in such a way that they could give each other mutual support.

The ouvrage of Saint Antoine was perched high above the valley. Its main combat block was able to deliver devastating fire into the Arc Valley with its two 75-mm guns and four 81-mm mortars (Mary 1980, 284). Its other block contained no artillery weapons.

Finally, on a mountain behind Modane was the gros ouvrage of Sapey, which mounted four 75-mm guns in three of its four combat blocks (Truttmann 1979, Plan 83). These well-protected guns were able to join its fires to those of Saint Antoine to seal off the Arc Valley. Together, these three ouvrages created a formidable barrier, which could seriously delay the enemy or even stop him in his tracks.

The three fortified sectors of the Alps were as diverse as the ouvrages that made them up. The SF of Savoy included five gros and five petits ouvrages. The garrisons of the artillery ouvrages averaged about 160 men. Two of these ouvrages had four generators instead of three in the usine. The gros ouvrages in Savoy mounted their artillery in two blocks and had up to six weapons per block, including a mixture of 75-mm and 81-mm mortars. Most had four 81-

mm mortars, except for Sapey. Although 75-mm guns were also common, they were not found in St. Gobain because of the location. The five petits ouvrages had garrisons of about fifty men. Their usines had been designed to hold two diesel engines, which had not been installed at the time the war began. Their main weapon was the JM.

The SF of Dauphiné consisted of four gros and twelve petits ouvrages. In the larger forts, the garrisons averaged about 200 men. The artillery, consisting of 75-mm guns and 81-mm mortars, was concentrated in one to three blocks. The twelve petits ouvrages were similar to those of Savoy with fifty man garrisons, but they were equipped with two diesel engines and their main armament was the ubiquitous JM.

Finally, the SF of the Maritime Alps included fourteen gros and sixteen petits ouvrages. The gros ouvrages typically sheltered about 290 men. Only Monte Grosso, one of the largest in this sector, mounted four engines instead of the standard three for the Alps. The artillery, usually concentrated in two or three blocks, generally consisted of two to four 81-mm mortars for every two 75-mm guns mounted. Three of these artillery ouvrages included gun turrets. Of these, Mont Agel had as many as two 75-mm gun turrets. The only 135-mm howitzer in the Alps was mounted in a turret of fort Mont Grosso. The sixteen petits ouvrages, like others in the Alps, relied on JMs and had garrisons of fifty men. Here, too, the two diesel engines for the usines were not installed.

When the war began, many of the Alpine ouvrages were still incomplete because the terrain, although ideal for defensive purposes, was difficult to build on. The excavation of the galleries and preparation of the blocks required greater effort and, therefore, greater costs in the Alps than in the Northeastern Front. Added to this was the cost of transportation of the crews and building materials since the forts were erected in hard-to-reach locations. To make matters even slower, the Alpine fortifications did not have top priority because Germany was considered a greater threat than Italy for most of the 1930s.

In addition to the ouvrages, the Alpine positions included many concrete multi-block *avant-postes*, very different from those found on the Northeastern Front. In the mid-1930s the High Command decided that leaving the territory between the border and the line of ouvrages undefended was a mistake. Thus, it was decided to add twenty-five forward positions within sight of the border. Seventeen *avant-postes* were built in the SF of the Maritime Alps between 1935 and 1938. Their construction was supervised by the *Génie* of the XIV and XV Army Corps (CA) from 1935-1938, but the actual labor was supplied by reserve Alpine troops or MOM (Rocolle 1990a, 98-107; Truttmann August 1982, correspondence). Many of these *avant-postes* had rather thin walls and lacked roofs. Shallow underground galleries led to the various blocks, which had either firing embrasures or, in many cases, open firing positions. Some *avant-postes* even had an observation cloche, and housed machine guns and other infantry weapons in most of their blocks. They were usually on commanding terrain and constituted formidable delaying positions that would not be easily routed.

The combination of rugged terrain, strategically placed ouvrages and *avantpostes* and interlocking fires in key areas rendered the Maginot Line in the Alps formidable. The SF of the Maritime Alps illustrates this effectively. Its two sub-sectors of Sospel and Corniches, which ran from a point north of the town of Sospel to the city of Menton, formed a continuous line with interlocking fires covering virtually all the important points between fortifications. This north-south line of fortifications was anchored in the north by the artillery ouvrage of Col de Brouis with only two combat blocks for 81-mm mortars and an entrance. A few kilometers east of this fort lay the *avant-poste* of Croix de Cougoule, consisting of a few small bunkers and concrete-lined positions for light weapons and observation. It formed part of the line of Alpine *avantpostes*, which ran all the way to the sea. Croix de Cougoule, located well above the valley floor, was difficult to assault and virtually immune to light weapons. Its panoramic view allowed its observers to direct the artillery fire of Fort Monte Grosso with deadly accuracy.

The gros ouvrage of Monte Grosso itself was perched atop a mountain of the same name. Its six combat and one entrance blocks could only be accessed from the town of Sospel, by means of a long road that wound through the valley behind it. It was often isolated by winter snows and spring landslides which blocked the high mountain passes. Its entrance block led directly to its usine and caserne, which were located mostly below the reverse slope of the mountain. Although it housed only 370 men, this ouvrage had more firepower than most gros ouvrages of the Maginot Line Proper. Block 3 mounted two 75-mm guns in a casemate and covered the left flank and the ouvrage of Col de Brouis. This block also included small-arms positions and cloches for the close defense of the northern slope of the mountain. A second block, Block 2, was planned, but not built. It would have mounted two 75-mm mortars to cover the right flank. Block 4, just above the caserne area, mounted four 81-mm mortars in casemates. Two fired across the northern flank of the forward slope; the remaining two fired towards the southern flank of the forward slope. Block 5 had one of the few 75-mm gun turrets in the Alps and a single GFM cloche. This powerful gun turret could fire to the north and forward, beyond the Italian border, easily dominating all the terrain around Fort Col de Brouis as well as the *avant-poste* to the east of it and one petit ouvrage about ten kilometers to the north. This same turret could also deliver supporting fires to every position between Monte Grosso and Sospel and almost as far south as Ste. Agnès. Turret and blocks alike were virtually invisible from most of the front line *avant-postes*. Forward of Block 5 was Block 6 with the only turret for 135-mm howitzers in the Alps. It covered Col de Brouis, the border, as well as Sospel to the south. On the forward slope of Monte Grosso was Block 7 with its three cloches: one GFM, one for JM and a third for observation. In addition, the facade of this block sported a flanking embrasure for a JM. Block 8, a little further north, had a similar flanking crenel for a JM and two cloches: one GFM and one observation.

Fort Monte Grosso, like many Alpine ouvrages, had no anti-tank guns because there were no likely avenues of approach for such vehicles. On the other hand, the ouvrage of Col du Brouis, being more accessible, was assigned a 47-mm anti-tank gun for one of its blocks. Adjacent to the town of Sospel, on top of the overlooking mountain to the north, was the artillery fort of L'Agaisen, which housed an impressive array of firepower in its three combat blocks. Block 2 included two embrasures for two 75-mm mortars and below them, firing through the fossé, two 81-mm mortars that could cover the entrance block. Block 2 also had several defensive cloches. Block 3 relied mostly on its two GFM cloches to direct the fires of its 75-mm gun turret and its two 81-mm mortars in a casemate. It provided covering fires for Monte Grosso. Block 4, located beyond Block 2, was a smaller infantry block with an observation cloche. This type of mutual fire support arrangement continued down to the coast.

One artillery ouvrage, St. Roch, located on the main road at the outskirts of Sospel, consisted of three combat blocks. The largest block contained most of the artillery: one 75-mm gun, four 81-mm mortars in casemates, and a JM. The other two combat blocks only included observation cloches, one of which could only be reached from the main gallery after a long climb. This was not a rare feature in the Alps.

Near St. Roch was the ouvrage of Barbonnet built adjacent to and into the older 1870s fort of Suchet. The old fort mounted two old Mougin turrets with 155-mm guns, which could reach as far as the ouvrage of Col du Brouis to the northeast and the ouvrage of Ste. Agnès in the south. The artillery of the old fort provided support for Barbonnet's two 75-mm guns and two 81-mm mortars in casemates. With only an entrance block and one combat block, Barbonnet was one of the smallest gros ouvrages, but it held a garrison of about 310 men. Its personnel manned not only the new blocks, but also the two old Mougin turrets of Fort Suchet. The ancient 155-mm guns gave support to almost half of the SF of the Maritime Alps (Cima and Cima 1988, 8; Truttmann 1979, Plan 85).

On the southern end of the line, the ouvrage of Mont Agel is perched on one of the highest summits in the area and can be seen from many kilometers away. Like Barbonnet, St. Agel was built into an older fort. It had three entrances (one of them for a cable car) and four blocks. Two of these blocks mounted 75-mm guns, which swept an arc along the coast, across the Franco-Italian border, and as far north as Sospel (Mary 1980, 317).

The ouvrage of Ste. Agnès with its entrance and three combat blocks was named for the medieval mountaintop village near which it was built. The village was located slightly downhill behind the fort, and near the top of the mountain were the ruins of a medieval castle. Ste. Agnès' observation cloche was located in a small block on the east side of the mountain. Its artillery block, Block 3, was on the north side of the mountain. It housed two 75-mm guns and two 81-mm mortars, which fired northward on the left flank. Block 2, the largest combat block of any Maginot works, sat on the south side. It held two 135-howitzers, two 75-mm guns, two 81-mm mortars, and four cloches in a multi-level block. Ste. Agnès offered a clear view of several other ouvrages, of the city of Menton, and of the Italian border. No other part of the Maginot fortifications was as formidable as that running from Sospel to the sea.

The Rhine Defenses relied too heavily on the Rhine and other natural obstacles to be effective without sufficient interval troops and reserves. Still, the great river made massive defenses there unnecessary. However, these fortifications are not truly representative of what history refers to as the Maginot Line. The New Fronts, built upon the experiences of the earlier Maginot fortifications, received some significant modifications. The increasing construction costs and lack of time resulted in the defenses of the New Fronts being too far apart and not as fully developed as they should have been to be as effective as the main line. The Maginot Line of the Alps also suffered from the same spiraling costs and a late start on construction of a number of its positions. In this case, the Alpine position, although not complete, demonstrated in 1940 that it was the strongest of all the Maginot positions and required less field units to support it.

8

THE FRENCH ARMY AND FORTRESS TROOPS

Before World War I, fortress duty was relegated to lower category troops, which included older men and those no longer physically fit for strenuous field duty. When the Maginot Line began to go up, the High Command decided to upgrade the quality of the fortification troops because they would be in the front lines from the very beginning of a conflict. The army designed the new ouvrages for independent operations, meaning the garrisons had to expect to be cut off and continue fighting in the tradition of Fort Vaux. This was too much to ask for from second-rate soldiers.

As a result, in 1933 the army planned to organize thirty new units known as "fortress battalions." As the ouvrages were completed, an army directive of May 1934 ordered the creation of these units to immediately be formed to garrison each of them, and 14,000 men were drawn to create the first of these battalions and "fortress regiments." In 1933 the High Command also designated the Fortified sectors and defensive sectors (Bruge 1973, 33). Each of the ouvrages was assigned to an SF, and the new fortress units became part of the defensive organization that controlled that sector (Truttmann 1979, 437). In 1934 forty-five of the fortress battalions were needed for the Fortified Sectors and the Defensive Sectors. By 1937, the number had increased to fifty-seven (Rocolle 1990a, 111; Hohnadel and Truttmann 1988, 7). In September 1939, after mobilization, all the Fortified and Defensive sectors from the North Sea to the Mediterranean included fifty-four fortress infantry regiments totalling 153 fortress battalions and over 200,000 men ready for battle. By 1940 the forces of the Maginot Front had expanded to over twenty-five regiments of fortress infantry (Truttmann 1979, 445; État-Major, 1967, 629-763 v 3).

The inter-war period had witnessed a drastic reduction in size of the French army. In fact, this was a motivating factor for the creation of a line of fortifications. The French High Command, despite the Versailles Treaty, had continued to fear a resurgence of German military power. Unable to keep a large standing army, it decided that the best way to prepare for war was to build fortifications that would delay the enemy at the border for at least eight days, long enough to allow France to mobilize (Truttmann 1979, 437).

However, all efforts were not concentrated on the Maginot Line alone. The French army also continued to develop tanks during the 1930s, but its leaders failed to create a large and effective armored force, a fact for which they were severely criticized. Until the 1930s, the advocates of a strong armored force had not succeeded in convincing those in power that armored formations would be able to operate effectively in all terrains. Most of the French military leaders continued to think of the tank as merely an infantry support weapon. In the 1930s, they could not see any advantage to developing fast breakthrough forces. They reasoned that such forces would be halted by the major barrier of the Rhine, and, if they succeeded in crossing it, they would be stopped by the hilly and mountainous terrain behind the Rhineland. None of this appeared to be good tank territory. In the meantime, the Germans discovered that tracked vehicles were capable of more than just crossing trenches and that they could maneuver in difficult terrain. However, as the Germans developed tank unit tactics, the French stagnated, concentrating all efforts on the defense of their borders and the creation of a more traditional army.

Between the wars the French regular army was deployed across the country in eighteen Military Areas. It consisted of twenty infantry divisions, five cavalry divisions, and five tank brigades. Across the Mediterranean, the French defended North Africa and the Middle East with five regiments of the Foreign Legion, twenty-one infantry regiments, and three tank battalions of old Renault FT tanks. Five more regiments occupied the other French African colonies and another five regiments of infantry with four tank companies of Renault FT tanks were stationed in Indochina (Tarnstrom 1983, 2-5). The number of men in these units began to shrink by the 1930s. The length of compulsory military service was reduced to one year between 1928 and 1935, only to be raised again two years later (Dear 1995, 399). This situation forced the army to concentrate most of its best personnel in specialized key units, which included fortress units. The creation of a few modern mechanized divisions during the latter part of the decade diverted additional first-rate troops.

Generally, the men selected to serve in the fortress units came from the area under the jurisdiction of the Fortified Regions. This policy was especially advantageous for the reserve personnel because it could respond quickly during mobilization. In addition, elite troops were selected for the Maginot defenses. Their mission was considered very important, because they would have to cover the frontier while the army mobilized behind them (Truttmann 1979, 437). Although the mission of these fortress troops to simply delay the enemy for a week had changed by 1939, the quality of the troops given the assignment had not declined.

The Fortified Regions were organized like army corps, but had additional service organizations. The key organic elements in RF Lauter included a battalion of sapers-miners, a railroad battalion, a specialized company of electricians (engineers), communications companies, and other units for maintaining logistical and support functions. A three-squadron reconnaissance group and aviation units were also assigned to this RF. RF Metz was similarly organized, but had two additional motorized reconnaissance groups (État-Major 1967, 543 and 581 v 1; Truttmann 1979, 438).

Each of the Fortified sectors under the jurisdiction of the Fortified Regions included a fortress brigade, which directed the activities of its sector. About a half dozen of these brigades maintained the positions of the Maginot Line Proper. The Fortified Sectors outside the jurisdiction of Fortified Regions had similar formations and organizations.

The fortress brigades were assigned about ten kilometers of front. In peace time they included an active fortress infantry regiment and an artillery regiment. Theoretically, these brigades would able to respond quickly to a German surprise attack while awaiting the reserves to join them. During mobilization, the fortress infantry regiment was to become three regiments as the reserves were called up. Each of these new regiments would then be assigned to a subsector of the Fortified Sector to which it belonged. The artillery regiment would expanded in a similar way upon mobilization (Truttmann 1979, 439-440).

The SF of Thionville illustrates the expansion of the fortress brigade in war time. The infantry regiment became the 167th RIF (*Régiment d'infanterie de forteresse* or Fortress Infantry Regiment), the 168th RIF and the 169th RIF. The 167th RIF garrisoned the ouvrages of Galgenberg, Sentzich, Metrich and Billig; the 168th RIF, Immerhof, Soetrich, Karre, Kobenbusch and Oberheid; and the 169th, Rochonvillers and Molvange. All three regiments also had to man the interval casemates. Attached to the infantry was the 3rd Battalion of the 460th Engineer Regiment (*Régiment de pionniers*). The artillery regiment became the 70th RAF (*Régiment d'artillerie de forteresse* or Fortress Artillery Regiment), supporting the fortifications. The 151st RAP (*Régiment d'artillerie de position* or Artillery Regiment, fixed or non-mobile) was in charge of the artillery of the ouvrages of Rochonvillers, Molvange, Immerhof, Soetrich, Metrich, Billig, and two batteries of 155-mm guns outside of the forts. In addition, three independent batteries occupied the gun positions of two of the restored German forts near Thionville (two batteries in Fort Guenterange and one in Fort Koenigsmacker). The artillery also comprised service units, including an artillery park and munitions section. Further supporting formations comprised the 203rd Engineer Battalion, two signal companies (one telegraph and one radio), other technical units, and even aviation units (État-Major 1967, 653 v 3; Mary 1980, 233-243).

The number and type of units per Fortified Sector varied slightly. The Fortified Sectors outside the jurisdiction of a Fortified Region, and the Defensive Sectors within the RFs usually had similar brigade formations, but less artillery and sometimes fewer troops. The exception were those sectors that expanded into Fortress Divisions early in 1940. Such was the case of the SF of Maubeuge, which became the 101st DIF (*Division d'infanterie de forteresse* or Fortress Infantry Division); the SD of the Ardennes, which changed into the 102nd DIF; the SF of the Lower Rhine, which transformed into the 103rd DIF; the SF of Colmar, which converted into the 104th DIF; and the SF of Mulhouse, which metamorphosed into the 105th RIF. The Alpine sectors of the Maginot Line in peacetime were manned by demi-brigades of Alpine fortress infantry whose artillery and support units were similar to those of the Maginot Line Proper. The SFs of Savoy and Dauphiné had two of these demi-brigades and one and two artillery regiments respectively, while the larger SF of the Maritime Alps had three demi-brigades and three artillery regiments (État-Major 1967, 601-813, 897-911 v 3).

The organization of the Southeastern Front, or Alpine Sector, was similar to that of the Northeast Front in the sense that the units assigned to its Fortified Sectors were also supposed to expand by tripling their number. However, the demi-brigades differed from the rest of the Maginot Line because they contained Alpine troops, such as skiers. In addition, the artillery regiments in the Alps included specialized mountain units.

Instead of placing the Fortified Sectors under the command of an RF, the High Command put two corps—the XIV and the XV—in charge of logistical and other supporting operations. The XV CA (*Corps d'Armée* or Army Corps) controlled the SF of the Maritime Alps. Instead of managing a railroad for the ouvrages, the *Génie* of the Alpine regions furnished cable-car units for those forts that were equipped with that type of entrance. In all other respects, the engineer units were identical to the Fortified Regions of the Northeast (État-Major 1967, 295, 307 v 1; Truttmann 1977, 443 v 1).

The front was reorganized in early 1940, after the outbreak of the war. The Fortified Regions became "Fortress Army Corps" (CAF) and a few Fortified Sectors became Fortress Infantry Divisions (DIF). RF Metz became the XLII CAF, taking over all the support units of the old RF, the infantry, and artillery regiments assigned to the Fortified sectors in the region. Likewise, the XLIII CAF formed from the units of the RF of La Lauter (État-Major 1967, 609, 621 v 1).

Truttmann (1979, 445) notes that this last-minute reorganization led to a great deal of confusion at mobilization time. However, the change was necessary to coordinate operations more effectively. Unfortunately, the fortress units lacked the transportation elements of typical formations and were sometimes expected to carry out functions they were not able to perform. Thus, despite being well supplied with automatic weapons and machine guns, the fortress units remained static.

The fortress regiments had a unique organization. One fortress infantry regiment consisted of over 3,000 men and included three machine gun battalions, each containing a company with mortars and anti-tank guns. By comparison, a typical infantry battalion consisted instead of three companies of light troops, with fewer mortars and 25-mm anti-tank guns, and one machine gun company. In addition to their standard organization, the fortress battalions also included "ouvrage companies," which manned the fortifications (Truttmann 1979, 440; Bruge, 1973, 33).

In the Fortified Regions, the units of the *Génie* comprised sappers, electricians, railroad personnel, and signal units for radio and telephone communications. The 1st Engineer Regiment was stationed in the RF of Lauter, the 2nd, in the RF of Metz, and the 4th, in the Alps. Some of the more specialized troops were detached from other formations. For instance, the railway engineers came from the 15th Engineer Regiment and the signalmen from the 18th Engineer Regiment (Mary 1980, 159).

The Mobile Republican Guard, professional soldiers of the Gendarmerie, occupied the advance line or *avant-postes* and was expected to sound the alarm at the first signs of an attack. These units, formed into platoons, were stationed near the border on the Northeastern Front (Hohnadel and Truttmann 1988, 7; Truttmann August 4, 1982, correspondence).

In the French literature, the garrisons of the ouvrages are referred to as "crews" because they were organized on the same pattern as the navy. About one third of the men came from the infantry, another third were artillery men, and the remainder came from engineer units. The infantrymen mostly manned the infantry blocks, whereas the artillerymen served the casemates and turrets, mounting 81-mm mortars, 135-mm howitzers and 75-mm guns. The various types of engineers were in charge of most of the supporting and logistical functions within the ouvrage, such as operating the usine, handling communications, and so on. After many problems surfaced during the 1936 mobilization in response to the German occupation of the Rhineland, the army sent some officers from the ouvrages to observe and train with naval units in order to learn how handle men from different services working together in the same unit (Bruge 1973, 33).

As a result, the ouvrages were run like ships, according to a system that included alerts and watches. Condition A was the normal watch during the occupation of the ouvrage; Condition B constituted an alert. In both cases, the garrison operated under four watches: the lookout watch of four hours for observers on duty, the picket watch of four hours for personnel at rest or assigned to the blocks, the reserve watch of eight hours for those at rest, and a standby watch of twenty-four hours for those on call. Condition C was general quarters with all positions fully manned (*The Simserhof Fort* 1988, 6).

There seems to be some confusion as to how the garrison was organized for duty. Apparently, teams were formed for specific duties. In some cases, these teams operated in two to four shifts, depending on their mission. Other teams had no shifts. The teams took turns preparing for the different types of actions: watch, alert and combat readiness (Truttmann 1979, 446-447).

After the war began, many of the troops found that they did not like rotating between the combat blocks and the caserne for their shifts because they had to haul their belongings back and forth between the two areas. They could not leave their things in the caserne area, which was built to hold only one third of the garrison at a time. In addition, the enlisted men found the caserne unwelcoming because they had no mess hall and had to dine in the gallery, at tables that were actually shelves that opened off the gallery wall. Only the officers enjoyed the luxury of eating in a mess all. In addition, the caserne itself was a cheerless place, with few luxuries and few decorations. As a result, the enlisted men felt more comfortable eating and living in the rest area of their assigned combat blocks, and the majority tended to set themselves up permanently there and had little communication with the rest of the ouvrage (Mary 1980, 161).

The organization of the infantry units occupying the interval casemates was similar to that of the ouvrages. Some of these troops had to receive specialized training in communications, electricians, etc., because no engineer troops were assigned to their positions. In general, only two electricians of the *Génie* were stationed in the abris. However, at least dozen technicians served in those abris serving as command posts (Truttmann 1979, 446-447).

During peace time, the garrisons of the forts usually occupied the barracks or *casernement* to the rear of the main line, which could be considered a small military base with all the necessary facilities, including family quarters. Adjacent to most of the ouvrages were smaller wooden barracks, occupied by fewer soldiers who provided security for the mostly unoccupied fortifications. During mobilization these smaller barracks could be quickly destroyed as the men moved into their forts. A large percentage of the garrison of the ouvrages consisted of reservists, many of them local residents, so that, according to army estimates, every position would be fully manned within a week (Mary 1980, 159).

Unlike most army units, the personnel of the ouvrages and interval casemates was not able to train with most of its weapons. Indeed, the artillery and most of the infantry weapons of the forts could not be tested without endangering the civilians living in the immediate vicinity and the private property in the area. In addition, the supposedly secret location of the ouvrages would be uncovered the minute they fired their guns.

However, the fortress troops needed a place to train if they were to be efficient when war came. Special training centers had to be set up where specialists could refine the necessary skills to operate the technical equipment of the ouvrages and the combat troops could train with weapons. Thus, most of the barracking areas or *casernements* were equipped with a firing range, which included positions similar to those found in casemates, where the crews of the ouvrages could train with the infantry weapons, including machine guns and anti-tank guns. The training for the heavier weapons took place annually at the military camp of Bitche, where the ouvrage of Grand Hohekirkel was situated right on the firing range. At Bitche the troops could also use 81-mm mortars. On the Southeast Front, training casemates for the infantry were built near the ouvrages of Rimplas and Agaisen, and a firing range for the 81-mm mortars was sat up at Mont Agel (Truttmann 1979, 449).

To facilitate direction and observation of artillery fire, the command post had a large map an panoramic photos of the area surrounding the ouvrage. The artillery observers who fed the data to the command post required special training. In 1937 the observers in cloches received photographs and diagrams to make target identification quicker and more accurate. Normally, one observer, usually an officer, would report the target with a rough designation of its location whereas another observer, an NCO, in a nearby cloche would locate the target and work out its exact coordinates (Kemp 1981b, 66, 71). Using permanent observation positions, through repeated exercises these men became adept at quickly pinpointing possible and sending back data on them.

Other observers also were responsible for directing the fort's defensive infantry weapons against approaching enemy units. These men needed technical training in target acquisition to swiftly put the ouvrage's machine guns and anti-tank guns on target.

One of the most valid criticisms aimed at the Maginot Line is that these fortifications absorbed a large proportion of the French army's best troops. The field army was denied a large number of first-rate men, who went to the Maginot Line where men with technical skills or training were in high demand and where service carried a certain cachet. The problem with this situation was that these soldiers would occupy their positions and remain in a static position throughout the war, never taking part in the type of offensive actions that might bring the final victory.

However, despite the commitment of so many excellent troops to the defense, the French still managed to mobilize an army ninety-four divisions, which included seven motorized, three light-mechanized and three heavy-armored divisions (Dear 1995, 401). Many of the best divisions occupied the front between the Maginot Extension and the North Sea where the main German thrust was expected. The French army even had more tanks than the German. Even though a good number of the French tanks were obsolete, several excellent models were capable of matching most of the German armor. Over fifty percent—thirty-three out of sixty divisions—of the French field army's infantry was made up of reservist divisions (Dear 1995, 401). These included the second-rate divisions of limited value categorized as A and B types. Category A included a cadre consisting of about twenty percent regular army troops, whereas the B category had a much smaller cadre consisting of reservists over the age of twenty-eight, including some elderly men over the age of forty (Horne 1969, 177; *Die Französische Kriegswehrmacht 1939* 1939, 74-75).

Although over a third of the army's divisions were assigned to the Maginot Line and the frontier with Germany, or were placed in reserve behind it, it consisted mostly of second-rate divisions. By the third day of the campaign, about twenty of over thirty divisions assigned to these sectors belonged to the A and B type.   Unfortunately, about a half dozen of these divisions covered most of the frontier with Belgium, facing the Ardennes, from a point south of Sedan to Namur.   Of course, this became the point where the Germans launched their decisive breakthrough.   In the midst of the confusion of the first days of battle, one division of fortress troops, the 102nd DIF, demonstrated the outstanding quality of its troops.   Unfortunately, all on its own, it could not stem the tide.

The French army, a formidable force on paper, theoretically should have been able to match the Germans.   Unfortunately, other factors, such as training, morale, methodology, leadership and blind luck, played against the French, allowing victory to slip through their fingers.   The Germans did not really owe their triumph to overwhelming numbers or much better equipment. Nonetheless, the elite troops of the fortress units were not totally wasted. During the month of May 1940, they made it practically impossible for the Germans to launch a major diversionary attack along the Franco-German border as they had done in Northern Belgium and the Netherlands.   Nevertheless, the French proved unable to bring their forces into the critical sector.

9

REPORTERS AND SPIES

What has transformed the Maginot Line into a myth even before it was finished is the misinformation fed to the public by the media and the intentional deception fed to the media by the French military establishment. Truths, half-truths and lies have been deeply interwoven over the years to create an image of the Maginot Line that borders at times on the fantastic. German intelligence contributed in some measure to the growth of the myth by supplying selected information from the data it was able to garner from its own sources.

THE MEDIA

In the 1930s and long after the war, rumors abounded about the Germans having information about the Maginot Line. The leaks were attributed to ethnic Germans hired as laborers and spies, but it was never clear how much the Germans were supposed to know about the fortifications. According to some, the data available to the Reich extended only to the kind of details that could be gleaned by peering through high-powered binoculars. This theory seems to be indirectly confirmed by General Erwin Rommel, who proclaimed that his divisions had overrun the Maginot Line after he broke through the Ardennes (Hart 1953, 20, 34). Other high-ranking Germans seemed to believe the French heavy fortifications ran all the way to the North Sea, which indicates a lack of knowledge on the subject.

Many German officials seemed to believe in the propaganda on the Maginot Line that French authorities allowed to flourish. Indeed, the East Wall, built to protect Germany against Poland in the 1930s, seems to have been inspired by the fictitious Maginot Line, complete with a tunnel complex that linked the ouvrages to each other. The East Wall project was eventually abandoned when Hitler declared it a waste of money and time and when it was discovered that the Maginot Line was not really as sophisticated as it was believed at first.

It has been suggested that French military officials deliberately allowed a certain amount of accurate information about the Maginot Line to be leaked out to give credence to the exaggerations of the media. For example, they released photos artfully retouched by censors. And, shortly before the war, they invited selected journalists to visit a few of the forts. Thus, a mystique grew around the Maginot Line, mixing fact with fiction.

The February 1929 issue of the British *Contemporary Review* published an interview with Minister of War, Paul Painlevé, in which he not only expressed his concern for the safety of France after the planned evacuation of the Rhineland in 1935, but also described his conception of a fortified border. Apparently, his idea of building a large number of concrete forts in the endangered areas had not met with a great deal of enthusiasm on the part of most military leaders, who did not believe in the efficacy of such defenses. Painlevé further pointed out the failures and triumphs of Verdun and explained two essential lessons learned there for the construction of a fort: "Firstly, to provide adequate shelter for those troops who are suddenly exposed to attack; secondly, that the artillery defending a fort must not be situated within the fort itself" (Heathcote 1929, 156-157). These two key ideas would later be incorporated into the design of the Maginot forts. From this point on, as the actual work began, the descriptions became more confused and entangled with exaggeration.

In April of 1930, as work began on the Maginot Line, American journalist George Adam (1930, 265-270) published an article in the *Century*, entitled "The Bristling Parapet of Peace." His details were vague, but he claimed that the French would rely mainly on flooding large areas for their defenses, that the new fortifications would only be armed with machine guns and light, quick-firing artillery, and that the French would rely on the Belgians' ability to defend their own borders. Other American sources, such as the *New York Times* (February 18, 1930, 2), had reported months earlier that France planned to flood the frontier between Dunkirk and Lille in the event of a war, but Adam identified with more precision the fortified districts of Metz and Thionville. However, he also incorrectly mentioned Nancy and Toul as the main areas of concentration for the defensive installations.

Adam's (1930) description of the future Maginot Line is a curious mixture of fancy and fact. These fortified sectors, he claimed, would be "bristling with guns, seamed by trenches honeycombed by gas-proof underground road" (269). It would also include "huge subterranean caverns" (269), where the garrison would be safe from the heaviest type of bombardment and from gas warfare. Electrical subways and elevators would move troops and light and heavy artillery underground. These depictions conjure images of many kilometers of tunnels, deep under the bowels of the earth, a gross exaggeration of the facts. Adams correctly said that the positions on the Rhine would be "heavily-armored machine-gun nests" (269), but then mentioned that they would be linked by underground passages. He also correctly identified the fortifications of the Alps and its strongest sector in the Maritime Alps.

In November 1930 André Maginot gave an interview to the press where he clearly stated that the new defenses would consist of a series of large and small forts within machine gun range of each other (*New York Times* November 24, 1930, 2).

In 1931 several articles about the Maginot Line further enlightened and sometimes confused the public. The first, which appeared in the *Literary Digest* on June 20, 1931, compared the new French fortifications to the old Roman walls or the ramparts of a medieval town. This wall, it claimed, stretched from the North Sea to the Swiss border. Even though it presented a highly imaginative view of the Maginot Line, this article caught the public's imagination, even that of some German soldiers, until 1940 (*The Literary Digest* June 20, 1931, 14).

On October 10, 1931, when the building was well under way, the American *Saturday Evening Post* published Wythe Williams' "The Great Chinese Wall of France," which deals more with "mobile parks" than Maginot ouvrages. These parks, wrote Williams, consisted of "a large amount of barbed-wire entanglements and much material for digging trenches and building machine-gun emplacements" (Williams 1931, 140), which could be quickly moved by rail or truck and double the defensive strength of any given area within days. Unlike his contemporaries, Williams wrote a fairly realistic account of the Maginot defenses but remained rather vague. For instance, he claimed that the "mobile parks" would include materials for all types of positions, from small machine gun bunkers to gigantic concrete forts. The bunkers, Williams explained, were designed for twelve-men garrisons and had a "periscope tower," which housed a gun (an apparent reference to the cloche). According to him, the forts had miles of subterranean passages, a barracks area, magazines, and a power source and were supposed to protect each other's flanks. Williams also correctly identified the forts of Hackenberg and Hochwald as the two largest.

Like many others, Williams (1931, 138-141) expressed the belief that the Maginot Line was to extend from Dunkirk to the Swiss border. In addition, he mentioned defensive positions between Mont Blanc and Nice. The Rhine and the border with Belgium, and the Italian Alpine front, he claimed, would only be defended by "pillboxes." Although Williams' information is relatively accurate, one finds it difficult to form a picture of the Maginot fortifications.

Also, in October 1931, another, slightly more fanciful description of the Maginot forts, titled "French Fortification," appeared in the American magazine *New Outlook*. According to this article, the French defenses would cover about 300 kilometers and include four lines. The first line would consist of two-level, reinforced concrete "pillbox" forts built into the ground, about a kilometer apart, complete with machine guns, telephone, electrical lights, and a twelve-men garrison. This is possibly a depiction of the line of *avant-postes*; however, they were not so fancily built or equipped. The second line, the article reported, would consist of large forts that were supposed to mount heavy artillery. The third line would comprise even larger forts like the ouvrages of Hackenberg and Hochwald. The article gives no descriptions or details about the nature of the forts in either line. Finally, the fourth line would encompass large troop shelters. This may well be a reference to the abris, which were actually located in the line of ouvrages and not behind it (*New Outlook* October 1931, 329-330). Except for exaggerating the number of lines and the size and quality of the *avant-postes*, this article gives a rather reasonable view of the Maginot Line.

In December 1932, the British *Daily Telegraph* reported that the French were not really building forts in the traditional sense of the word, but "a permanent elaboration of the deep trench systems of the war" (Rowe 1961, 81). After this article came out, both British and American reporters continued to refer to the Maginot Line as a "trench system," a term that is misleading.

On May 16, 1933, the British *Daily Express* printed a series of articles that claimed that the chain of subterranean forts ran from the English Channel to the Vosges and that their garrisons, consisting of corps-size units, were supplied for a year at a time. The forts, it was claimed, were invisible, even from the air. In one of the later articles, the reporter asserted that he had travelled by road from the North Sea to the Mediterranean, seldom failing to see a fort, even in places such as the Belgian border where they did not, in fact, exist (Rowe 1961, 82-83).

Other articles in 1933 gave even less detail. The *New York Times* called the Maginot Line a 125-mile "Trench and Casemate System" extending from the Rhine to Luxembourg (*New York Times* August 28, 1933, 1). Later, *Newsweek* and the European press announced the motto of the Maginot Line: "*Ils ne passeront pas*" or "They shall not pass," borrowed from Pétain's statement at Verdun in 1916.

Instead of shedding light on the French fortifications, this article only succeeded in further muddying the waters. The first line of defenses, it claimed, consisted of 200 miles of twelve-men bunkers fully equipped and linked to each other and to the rear by deep trenches. On September 9, *Newsweek* (1933, 10-11) took up again the subject of three lines of fortifications, hidden forts, big guns and troop shelters. In October the completion of the border fortifications was announced in a French newspaper, *Le Jour* (Phillip 1933, 4). At about the same time, the *New York Times* noted that the Swiss and the Belgians were strengthening their defenses, thus securing the French flanks (Callender 1933, 12-13).

On November 5, 1933, Harold Callender's article for the *New York Times* (1933, 4-5), "The Bristling Line that Divides Europe," came complete with photos showing a gallery, an entrance block, an anti-tank ditch, and a map correctly placing the main defenses between Longuyon and the Rhine and the lighter works running from Longuyon to Dunkirk and along the Rhine, with no new forts in those areas.[1] Callender noted that the central gallery, located thirty meters below the surface, was served by a railway, which led to the subterranean munitions and storage areas. He also mentioned a ventilation system for gas protection, electrical power and special surface barracks near the forts for peace time use. Finally, he made a rather vague reference to an anti-tank ditch.

In his article Callender (1933, 4-5) also applied the term *cloche* to the bell-shaped steel chambers for observation, but had no name for the interval casemates, calling them simply "concrete machine-gun nests." Further, he did not refer to turrets, but stated that the guns rise, fire, and drop into a shaft for reloading. He too was aware of the ouvrages of Hochwald and Hackenberg, since he referred to them by name in his article. Despite a few inaccuracies, Callender's information is probably the most accurate of its time. To a knowledgeable reader, his information is largely reliable, but an uninformed reader in the 1930s would have found it difficult to conjure up an image of the Maginot Line.

In December 1933 the foreign editor of *Paris Soir* claimed that the strength of the French fortifications had been greatly exaggerated and that their Belgian and Swiss flanks were vulnerable (Sauerwein 1933, IV-12).

In 1934 the British *Daily Herald* was informed by its Paris office that, according to rumors, the new French forts were shoddily built and that their concrete was already cracking (Rowe 1961, 85). In 1935 the British news media continued to propagate the myth of a continuous line of fortifications stretching from Dunkirk to Basel, on the Swiss border. In September the name of Maginot Line first appeared in the press (Rowe 1961, 90).

In April 1935 in a column of the *New York Times*, P.J. Phillip (1933, 4) wrote that the Maginot Line consisted of three lines: a line of "pillboxes" followed by the main line of resistance about eight kilometers to the rear and a "Ligne d'Arrêt," or Stop Line. He claimed the third line was still incomplete, but included some unspecified heavy fortifications. It is possible that the latter are actually some of older forts that were being rearmed. However, Phillip did not give enough details to permit a positive identification of these positions.

Later that year the *Literary Digest* ran another report, "France's Mighty Wall Against Germany", stating that it covered about 240 kilometers from the Belgian to the Swiss border. The fortifications were attributed 300 gun turrets, that is, more than twice their actual number in 1939. The article also mentioned "railroads which stretched for miles under the surface linking main bases far behind the lines with advanced forts." In addition, an accompanying map showed the main line running through Verdun, Metz, Toul, Épinal and Belfort, with the strongest section between Bitche and the Swiss frontier. According to the article, the Maginot Line included five major forts and one small fort. The large forts were purported to be in the vicinity of the actual forts of Rochonvillers, Hackenberg, Hochwald, Bitche and Strasbourg and the small one, between Strasbourg and Switzerland (*Literary Digest* September 7, 1935, 13).

In 1936 and during the crisis caused by the German reoccupation of the Rhineland in 1936, a French employee of the British *Daily Mail* was recalled to duty and served in the Maginot Line. When he was released from duty, he was allowed to publish an article on the Maginot fort in his newspaper. Here he gave a general and vague description of the underground corridors and turrets (Rowe 1961, 90-91).

Until this point, the information circulated by the media was such a mixture of fact, fiction and distortion of the truth that no one outside the circle of planners and builders could come up with a reasonably accurate picture of the whole complex. In October 1936 the most detailed and accurate account of the Maginot Line appeared in the media. It was an article written by Thomas Johnson (1936, 14-15) titled "Underground Fortresses Guard France from Invasion" and printed in *Popular Science Monthly*. The illustration accompanying the article appears to be a revision of a drawing first used in the British media in *The Illustrated London News* during the fall of 1933 (Gilbert 1989, 37, 97). The 1933 blueprint shows an accurate detail of an M-1 magazine, a relatively reasonable layout of an ouvrage, and dome-shaped combat blocks listed as casemates. The 1936 drawing gives a slightly different perspective, leaving out some details while adding others. For example, the entrance block is depicted with its weapons embrasures set up for cross fires, its tank trap labeled as an "Elephant Pit," and the anti-tank rails and wire entanglements surrounding it. The picture also includes an inaccurate blueprint of a command post linked to an observation cloche. As in the 1933 drawing, the combat blocks are identified as casemates, but this time they are armored and shaped like cloches large enough to hold a dozen men. Johnson's description is also accompanied by photos of what appears to be a block with a GFM cloche at the edge of a village and of the interior of a firing chamber of a 135-mm howitzer. However, the weapon has been blacked out from the picture by a censor. A photo of a Munitions Entrance is also shown, curiously with no visible cloche. A map of the French border shows a line of "pillboxes" extending from the North Sea to the end of the Maginot Line. The Maginot Line Proper is placed in the correct area, but is purported to include the Rhine Defenses, which are shown to have only lighter fortifications. The Alpine defenses are mentioned as "sunken concrete forts and guns." Johnson noted that flooding was to be used along the Belgian frontier, especially in the Sarre Gap, and that the Ardennes would be mined.[2] He identified some of the basic features of the ouvrages, claiming that their rapid-firing guns would cover great distances. He also stated the forts would mount guns varying in size and caliber from 75-mm to 400-mm. Other small inaccuracies have slipped into his article. For instance, he claimed that the elevator shafts of the combat blocks, which he calls "towers," reach depths of up to ninety meters! He also mentioned concrete trenches, anti-aircraft defenses, artificial trees used as observation posts, searchlights, light cannons in galleries, and miles and miles of underground galleries. On the other hand, he accurately listed other characteristics such as the interior defenses, armored doors, *monte-charges*, and the communication system, including order transmitters. Johnson did not appear to know the difference between a turret and a cloche, but this is understandable since the English language makes no distinction between these two features (Johnson 1936, 14-15).

On March 21, months before Johnson's article appeared in the *Popular Science Monthly*, the British *Daily Express* printed a drawing that left an impression on the public imagination that no amount of accurate facts would dislodge. It showed a supposed cross-section of the Maginot Line about a hundred meters and seven levels deep, with combat blocks near the surface. On the lowest level were found the magazines and just above that, the subway linked all the forts to each other. The other levels accommodated a hospital, supply rooms, another ammunition magazine, the headquarters, the garrison area, and a power plant. The combat blocks of this fantastic underground city were mostly rotating turrets mounting heavy artillery. They were linked to the lower parts of the fort not only by a stairway, but also by an elevator that carried the ammunition from below (Rowe 1961, 91; Mallory and Ottar 1973, 92).

Later in the same month news reports, announcing that the Maginot Line could hold up to 100,000 men and that its forts were linked to each other by subways, added credence to the drawing of the *Daily Express* (*New York Times* March 13, 1936, 12). Also at the end of March, General von Metzch of the German army heavily derided the Maginot defenses, putting in question their effectiveness (*New York Times* March 29, 1936, 28). Major General Sir Charles Gwyn of the British army (April 19, 1936, 35) fired a response in the *London Morning Post*, claiming that the belts of fortifications covering the whole eastern frontier of France and the Franco-Italian border were indeed impregnable. Gwyn also insisted that the Ardennes were easily defended, but offered no concrete evidence to contradict von Metzch's comments.

By 1937 it was difficult to separate fact from fiction and even the noted military writer for the *New York Times*, Hanson Baldwin (1937, 9), could do little to turn the tide of misinformation. In the spring of 1937 Baldwin wrote that the new anti-tank defenses in the Maginot Line consisted of rails planted upright with mines and anti-tank guns in between. The French, he added, had tested these defenses against their own tanks.

As the year 1938 began, the *Literary Digest* (January 29, 1938, 17-18) played up the Maginot myth by touting that "one million Frenchmen can live underground for three months in comparative comfort." It is true that the forts were able to hold out for three months, but the number of men was not only grossly exaggerated but also unlikely. What general would want to lock up so many of his men? This article, based on reports from *Le Soir*, claimed that the fortifications consisted of about 14,000 pillboxes, all of the "rotating type" with no surface exits. The article failed to explain how the three-men crew reached their combat stations. Some vague allusion to guns that disappeared below the surface was accompanied by a photo of a pillbox with a three-gun casemate for 75-mm guns. Finally, the article ended with the bizarre claim that over forty kilometers behind the "Maginot Line there is located well underground a secret chamber. If an enemy should capture or occupy considerable portions of the Maginot Line . . . the pressing of a single button will blow up . . . the entire 600 miles of fortifications" (*Literary Digest* January 29, 1938, 17-18).

The Munich Crisis of 1938 brought a new flurry of reports, each more preposterous the other. One of these was published in the fall of 1938 by Robert Leurquin, who informed his readers that the guns of the Maginot forts were long-range weapons capable of covering also the rear of the forts. After visiting over thirty casemates, he stated that each represented a unique variation on a standard pattern. He painted a reasonable picture of the facilities in the ouvrages, but seemed to be confused about some of the details. None of his comments matched the accompanying diagram, which was an even more fanciful version of the 1936 *Daily Express* drawing. Now the Maginot Line not only had a subway linking the various forts, but also underground hangars for aircraft, garages for tanks, and anti-aircraft gun emplacements on the surface. Furthermore, the forts were endowed with a mysterious infrared ray weapon or machine. Leurquin also described with reasonable accuracy the gas defense system, the ball-mounted guns, the panoramic telescopes, the buried telephone lines, the interior defenses, and the method for setting up anti-tank rails at varying heights with booby traps, which are easily overlooked in the context of his more extravagant claims (Leurquin 1938, IV-3).

All this misinformation made it almost impossible to separate fact from fiction. During the war the first reasonably intelligent and accurate report came from war correspondent Dorothy Thompson (1940, 51-52), who was invited to visit an ouvrage in 1940, just before the German attack. In her article she revealed that the fort had a concealed opening and was built into a great wooded hill. She compared the whole complex to a great subterranean battleship, a simile used by many military leaders and historians of the Maginot Line. She noted that the fortress troops were first-class soldiers. She then went on to describe the command post with its maps, manuals, telephones, and order transmitters. She was also taken into a turret block after descending into the main gallery via an elevator and walking a good distance. After observing the movement of ammunition cases on overhead monorails, she climbed into the confined quarters of a gun turret and witnessed the automatic feeding of the 75-mm guns and the firing of the weapons. Although she did not disclose the identity of the fort, the proximity of the Germans indicates that she must have been in the RF of Lauter, most likely at Hochwald.

The misinformation circulating before the war confused the general public regarding the Maginot Line throughout the 1930s and 1940s. It was not until the 1970s that the secrets of the Maginot fortifications were revealed to the public.

GERMAN INTELLIGENCE

Of the above articles, only one is of special interest: the one that published General von Metzch's critique of the Maginot Line in March 1936. According to von Metzch, the much-touted French defenses could be overrun at several points and taken from the rear where its guns could not fire. The general also added that the air-pressure system used to protect the forts from gas attack would magnify the explosion of grenades and kill everyone inside. Neither statement is correct and with regard to the latter he does not explain how the grenades would be delivered inside an ouvrage. The most interesting statement he made was: "We know it well [the Maginot Line] but we do not find it worthy of imitation" (*New York Times* March 29, 1936, 28).

It is doubtful that von Metzch actually knew much about the Maginot Line and probable that he was trying to unnerve Germany's opponents. However, archival evidence now indicates that the Germans were indeed well acquainted with the composition of the French fortifications even though they tried to build a match for the imaginary Maginot Line in their own East Wall.

The sources for German intelligence are not known with any certainty. As we have seen, information from the media was of limited value. German agents might have interviewed any of the thousands of ethnic Germans or other foreigners who worked on the Maginot Line and who, for patriotic reasons or bribes, might have disclosed information on the fortifications. Another possible source was the thousands of crew members, active or reserve, who could have been blackmailed, bribed, seduced, or tricked into revealing details about the forts in which they served. Most people living in the vicinity of the fortifications are convinced to this day that by the time the war began, the Germans knew as much about the Maginot Line as the French army itself! The only thing missing, until recently, was the proof.

The takeover of the Czech fortifications in the fall of 1938 after the Munich Crisis provided the Germans with a great deal of information on the Maginot Line because the Czech defenses had been built in consultation with French military engineers. The Czech fortifications offered a good testing ground for assault methods against fortifications. In addition, the general layout and pattern of the Czech ouvrages, which was very similar to the French forts, gave the Germans some idea of what they could expect to find in the Maginot Line. However, since the Czechs had introduced important modifications to the basic French designs, they did not yield all the secrets of the Maginot Line. It appears, nonetheless, that the Germans had known those secrets long before the takeover of the Czech defenses.

In 1932 the French newspaper *Le Matin* announced that a number of German firms had been contracted to work on the Northeastern Front, but in actuality these turned out to be Alsatian. At first it was believed that the leaks had come from the construction companies working on the defenses. However, the leaks had sprung at a lower level. On the Northeastern Front, many agents of the Reich found employment with the construction firms, which employed many ethnic Germans. On the Southeastern Front, on the other hand, Italian spies could easily have blended in with their compatriots, who constituted a substantial portion of the work force (Rowe 1961, 81). A year earlier, on April 23, 1931, there had already been reports of spying. For instance, the *New York Times* trumpeted: "Five Held by France in German Spy Plot." The article explained that only 5,000 of 8,500 workers on the fortifications were actually French while 143 were German (April 23, 1931, 3). In August 1933 the French arrested an engineer as he tried to cross the border into Germany. He reportedly carried plans of the Metz and Boulay sectors (*New York Times*, August 29, 1933, 1). By 1935 the Germans had in their possession detailed specifications on the Maginot Line. This information was of the highest quality, taken from actual blueprints, rather than derived from sketches obtained through observation and interviews with workers. Included with the plans and diagrams in German possession, was even a nonexistent ouvrage from an early plan that had been discarded (Truttmann 1988, interview).

Today the German intelligence documents concerning the French fortifications appear to be incomplete. In the late 1970s, J.Y. Mary, while researching in the German archives for his book on the Maginot Line, found three documents on the French fortifications: *Grosses Orientierungsheft Frankreich* of April 1, 1936, *Die französische Grenzbefestigung im Abschnitt Mosel-Kanalküste* of November 10, 1939, and *Die französische Grenzbefestigung im Abschnitt Mosel-Kanalküste* updated on March 15, 1940. According to Mary, the last two documents reveal detailed and relatively accurate information on the Maginot Line and include photographs taken with telephoto lenses and plans. The first, on the other hand, contained little of importance (Mary 1979, 210-211).

In reality the first volume of *Grosses Orientierungsheft Frankreich*, compiled between 1935 and 1936, presents a relatively good description of the development of the Maginot fortifications. Unlike the newspapers, it contains astonishingly accurate information. It clearly shows that German intelligence was able to follow construction developments easily and accurately. The gap between the two RFs of the Maginot Line is identified and the use of *"parcs mobiles"* is duly recorded. The document also notes the increase in building activity on the front after the return of the Saar to Germany in 1935, the creation of the New Fronts beyond Longwy and along the Belgian border, and the barring of the gaps on either side of Maubeuge. It also records the creation of a new Fortified Sector at Maubeuge (Valenciennes-Maubeuge-Avesnes) and a line between the Forest of Raismes and Normal, and the work along the Swiss frontier at places like Pontarliers and around the Belfort Gap. It does not even overlook the Alps. The main Alpine positions are not only identified, but also accurately marked along the line Menton-Sospel-Nice (near Nice a couple of ouvrages were built), and in the areas of Barcelonnette, Briançon, and Modane. Finally, the document concludes that the French military would complete the main fortified front and anti-tank barrier sometime before the end of 1936.

The *Grosses Orientierungsheft Frankreich* also shows that the Germans were familiar with the Fortified Regions and Sectors, most of which are correctly identified. Only a few sectors on the Swiss border are left unmentioned. The document also includes a discussion of the role of the ouvrages in the Maginot Line, of the so-called "Fortress Zone" consisting of an unbroken chain of infantry and artillery fire, of the less critical areas defended by petits ouvrages, casemates, and blockhouses filling the intervals between the larger works. It discusses the ouvrages' use of flanking fire, their mutual support for close defense, and their all-around defense capabilities. Neither is the disposition of fortress troops secret. The document reports that the ouvrages were only watched by guards and that most of their garrisons were stationed in nearby camps. However, it expresses the view that a surprise attack would not succeed.

The fortifications along the Rhine did not escape the notice of German intelligence either. The document notes that they consisted mainly of blockhouses on the river and a line of casemates two to five kilometers behind it. However, the reports incorrectly indicate that the old forts of Strasbourg and Mutzig were modernized. The lightly defended area between the Rhine and the RF of Lauter and the Sarre Gap with its machine-gun bunkers and dams for inundating the area were also well known to the Germans. The area between the Meuse and Maubeuge and the regions of Mezieres and Givet are reported to be still unfortified because of French reliance on the difficult terrain for defense. The coastal sector in Flanders is also described as unfortified.

The organization for French fortress troops is given, indicating a knowledge that they were well equipped with machine guns. The report indicates that these fortress regiments consisted of elite troops who had been given their own uniforms and special insignia. The active regiments had only a third of their troops and were to triple in size with the mobilization of reservists. The document also covers the fortress brigade organization and credits each Fortified Sector with a brigade of three infantry regiments of three to four battalions each and one or two artillery regiments. This estimate is apparently based on full mobilization and the intended creation of new regiments. The intelligence also clarifies the difference between the light caserne near the ouvrage and the large security caserne where the garrison resided; it also indicates the mobile guard's duties.

The German intelligence officers also identified virtually all the weapons used in the fortifications, including the new French light machine gun, the twin-machine gun set (JM), the 47-mm anti-tank gun, the special mixed-arms combination of a 25-mm gun and a JM in turrets and cloches, the 50-mm mortar (with a note that no details were available), the 81-mm fortress mortar, the 135-mm fortress howitzer, and two types of 75-mm fortress cannon. In the case of the 75-mm gun and the 135-mm howitzer, the Germans appear to have transposed their range.

The *Grosses Orientierungsheft Frankreich* is not error-free, however. For instance, it reports that each block of an ouvrage was manned by twenty-five to thirty men, but estimates the entire garrison of the average ouvrage at only 150 to 300 men, and the crew of the larger forts at only 600 men. German intelligence also came to the conclusion that the forts' artillery would need aircraft support for reconnaissance and observation. It suspected, therefore, that there might be underground hangars near the front to protect them. The Germans also feared that the French long-range artillery could be a threat to the German war industry because it was within striking range of the key industrial towns of the Rhineland. This contingency, however, had not been contemplated by the French.

Although the first volume of the 1936 *Grosses Orientierungsheft Frankreich* gives a thorough overview of the Maginot Line, it does not go into great detail. Most of its information could have been obtained without a great deal of difficulty. The second volume, on the other hand, includes detailed illustrations. One of the maps covers France's Northeast Front and the Low Countries, indicating the fortified areas. For example, the RF of Lauter and the RF of Metz are clearly marked as areas of heavy defenses whereas the Sarre Gap is shown as lightly defended. The only error is that the area between Longuyon and Montmédy is shown to have heavy defenses. A more detailed map clearly lays out the extent of the Maginot Line Proper, ending it in the vicinity of Longuyon. Whoever drew the map also attempted to show the location of the ouvrages and casemates. The old fortress rings of Verdun, Metz, Mutzig and Strasbourg are included as if they were active positions. Another map of the Southeastern Front indicates the heavily fortified sectors of the Alps, but makes no distinction between the old and new works. A map of part of the SF of Thionville shows the location of several ouvrages, supporting positions, such as munitions depots, new roads and bridges built to service the Maginot Line, and the .60-gauge railroads laid down for the railway guns and to service the forts. A map of the SF of Rohrbach reveals in even greater detail the location of the positions within that sector, including the individual blocks of ouvrages.

Finally, the second volume of *Grosses Orientierungsheft Frankreich* includes a list, compiled in mid-1936, of all the fortifications in the SF of Rohrbach. Virtually every ouvrage with its individual blocks, every casemate, every abri, and every blockhouse is identified. The armament of the ouvrages did not escape detection either. The cloche for lance grenades, a 60-mm mortar, which was not mentioned in the first volume, is listed in the second. The weapons mounted in turrets and cloches are correctly indicated. Only the information concerning weapons mounted in the other positions is not always accurate. Almost no mention was made of the 37-mm anti-tank guns in the ouvrages, except in one instance, which indicates that the Germans were not sure which weapons were deployed in casemate positions.

What effect this information had on German planning can only be speculated. When the Rhineland was occupied in March 1936, German intelligence could only warn the High Command that no offensive would be practical against the French because all branches of the Wehrmacht were too small to hope to breach the Maginot Line. The German occupation force, which consisted of only a few battalion-size units, was ordered not to fight for the Rhineland, but withdraw if the French appeared. Although their army of less than a dozen regular divisions was too small to contemplate a major campaign, the Germans did everything they could to convince the French of the contrary. If Hitler had decided to order his troops not to withdraw before an attack, the French might have a difficult time pushing the Germans out of the Rhineland, which was not that difficult to defend. A possible reason why Hitler decided not take a stand is that German intelligence suspected, as already mentioned, that the French had moved a large number of heavy artillery pieces behind the Maginot Line, putting their industrial centers in grave jeopardy. At the time, the Germans did not have the capability to eliminate such weapons if they were placed behind a fortified barrier. Thus, thanks to the Maginot Line, the French found themselves for the first time in a position to put the Germans in check; however, they failed to take advantage of it.

The next important document concerning intelligence is the *Grosses Orientierungsheft Frankreich* issued in July 1937. This work contains enough detail to give the German command a full working knowledge of the French fortifications. Terms such as "great works" and "heavy defenses" are now complemented by reasonably accurate illustrations. Some small terrain maps showing selected areas include the locations of several ouvrages for reference. Plans of the gros ouvrage of Simserhof are enclosed together with a chart giving details on its weapons. The positions of the blocks, the location of the subterranean galleries, the usine, the caserne, the M-1, and the command post are correctly shown. Block 1 with its machine gun turret and GFM cloche, casemated 135-mm howitzer, and JM/47-mm anti-tank gun combination is correctly identified on both chart and plan. Likewise, Block 2 with its 81-mm mortar turret, GFM cloche, and observation cloche is accurately described. However, the description of Block 3 contains a slight error. Its mortar turret and two GFM cloches are correctly listed, but instead of the 37-mm gun that was actually there, the drawing shows a 47-mm weapon. Block 4, similarly equipped as Block 1, is also shown to have a 47-mm instead of a 37-mm anti-tank gun. The artillery blocks, Block 5 and 6, which had identical armament, are both correctly marked with their three 75-mm guns, two GFM cloches, observation cloche and lance grenade (mortar) cloche. Block 7, with its 135-mm howitzer turret and its two GFM cloches and Block 8, with its 75-mm gun turret and two GFM cloches are also accurately represented. Even the information on the two entrance blocks is exact, including the fact that the EH had two embrasures for a JM/47-mm anti-tank gun combination rather than a single one, and a lance grenade cloche, which was absent from the EM.

The details included in the plan of the underground are too accurate to have been draw from memory; it must have come directly from French sources. The report on Simserhof even went as far as to list which weapons were for flanking fire and which were meant for all-around fire and close defense. In addition, the blocks are correctly numbered, according to a system that was not established until after 1931 (Truttmann 1979, 457). The document estimates the garrison at 26 officers and 928 men, whereas the actual war time crew consisted of 28 officers and 792 men, not a significant difference. This estimate is of special interest because the earlier document places the largest garrisons at only about 600 men. Another significant item is the fact that the Germans did not seem to realize that the 37-mm guns could not be replaced by the newer 47-mm weapons in those positions whose embrasures were too small. This indicates that most of this intelligence information may not have been obtained during the early phases of construction, but much later.

The *Grosses Orientierungsheft Frankreich* also contains the layout for another ouvrage: the Mottemberg, which is shown to have ten blocks, including one with an 81-mm mortar turret, another with a 75-mm gun turret and a 75-mm gun casemate. Mottemberg was actually a three-block petit ouvrage. At first this might appear to be a "plant" supplied by the French to mislead the Germans, but a closer examination reveals two important facts. First of all, the small sketch of the blocks accurately depicts blocks of those types. In addition, the entrance, which seems to be too close to the combat blocks, is labeled with as Block 8 instead of the term EH, EM or mixed entrance that was used in the 1930s. Only the entrances of the petits ouvrages were sometimes labeled with a block number, usually when they were also meant to serve as combat blocks. It appears, therefore, that this plan is an original design, which, according to Truttmann, may well have been derived from one of the early plans that were not actually realized (Truttmann 1988, interview). It also appears that this plan did not fall into German hands until the mid-1930s since it shows three of the blocks with the combination JM/47-mm anti-tank gun rather than a 37-mm anti-tank gun.

The third plan included in the *Grosses Orientierungsheft Frankreich* is one of the petit ouvrage of the village of Coume. It, too, shows an accurate layout of the underground works, including the caserne and the usine. The weapons and cloche for each block are accurately marked. The only things that differ from the ouvrage that was actually built are an observation cloche on Block 1, which does not exist, and an observation cloche, which is, in fact, a GFM cloche on Block 3. It must be noted that turret blocks with a single cloche, such as Block 3, were usually equipped with a GFM cloche for close defense. The JM/47-mm embrasure of Block 1 and the single-JM embrasure are correctly noted. A plan of the underground works includes the locations of the mine chamber for destruction of the corridor and the interior armored doors as well as the dimensions of the various rooms. In the case of the mine chamber, this was a feature found in all the ouvrages along the main galleries. It usually consisted of a niche on the gallery wall closed by a metal cover. If necessary, explosives could be placed in it and detonated to seal the gallery.

The last diagram included in the *Grosses Orientierungsheft Frankreich* is that of the great fortification of Hochwald. However, its blocks are represented as small circles on a contour map, which also shows the line of anti-tank obstacles, the anti-tank ditch linking the two groups of combat blocks, and the military railroad. Except for the EM and EH, no block is shown in detail. The document lists the various blocks of the east and western combat groups of the fort with their weapons. Virtually every combat block is identified, but is labeled with letters rather than numerals. It is possible that this plan was obtained before the French engineers adopted a uniform numbering system early in the 1930s. However, mention of the 47-mm guns and the large garrison indicates that the data must have been added in the mid-1930s.

The list of weapons for Hochwald is not error-free. In particular, one error is repeated in that casemates with two 75-mm guns and two JM/47-mm anti-tank gun combinations, Block 3 and Block 16, are shown to have four 75-mm guns each and no machine gun/anti-tank gun combination. In addition, Block 13's 135-mm howitzer casemate is incorrectly marked as a turret position. These errors probably crept in because the Germans had obtained data from an earlier plan, which was later modified. The garrison size is estimated at 3,000 men, which is three times larger than it actually was. Thus, the German intelligence turned Hochwald into a stronger position than it actually was.

Despite the limited number of plans, and the very limited information on Hochwald, this material gave the Germans enough data to assess the relative composition and strength of most ouvrages, a task which they ably accomplished in the *Grosses Orientierungsheft Frankreich*.

The actual structural details of the combat block and entrances, which did not appear in the 1936 document, were included in the 1937 document. The plan of Block 3 of Simserhof—a combination casemate and turret block—is shown complete with measurements listing its 3.5 meter thick walls and the thinner 1.5 meter outer wall of the weapons chambers. The air vents and firing crenels are also recorded. In addition, a profile drawing gives a good view of the block. Only one of the embrasures with the JM-the one that included a 37-mm gun—is too small. Furthermore, no distinction is made between the shape of the crenels of the observation cloche and those of the GFM cloche. This indicates that the Germans did not have detailed knowledge of the various cloches or the firing embrasures in the casemates.

A plan of Block 1 of the gros ouvrage of Metrich, an artillery casemate, is accurate, down to the measurements of the 1.5 meter thick walls of the firing chambers facing the rear. Two additional drawings also depict the emergency exit through the fossé. One is a good profile drawing of the face of the casemate. The other is a cross-section of the lower level showing the emergency exit into the fossé, the standard 3.5 meter thick roof of the block, and the surrounding rock work. The drawing shows only one lift when in reality most casemates of this type had two of these ammunition lifts.

A plan and section of Block 3 of Village de Coume illustrates a machine gun turret block. All the measurements appear to be correct and the profile indicates how a cloche, turret and the forward armor were set in a block. Not even the armored air vent of turret blocks is omitted. The only problem is in the measurements of the machine gun turret, which had a diameter of 1.2 meters but is shown in the drawing as measuring 3.3 meters. This was the size of a 75-mm gun turret, the largest used in the Maginot Line. As in an earlier drawing, the crenels for the GFM cloche are also smaller and narrower than the real ones.

The *Grosses Orientierungsheft Frankreich* also includes two plans for munitions entrances. One accurately depicts the EM of Simserhof, the location of its weapons, cloche, armored doors and interior blockhouses. Only the 47-mm anti-tank gun is missing from the JM combination embrasures. A second EM drawing shows a similar layout, but unlike Simserhof, which has a level entrance, this EM includes a lift that descends to the main gallery. The rolling bridge covering the tank trap is correctly represented. Sectional drawings give a better view of the EM of Simserhof and shows how the rock work over the roof allows a reduction of concrete where the block enters the hill.

Other detailed drawings include cross-sections of the galleries with their cable shelves, their gutters, their drains located beneath the floor along one of the walls, their embrasures for light weapons, their concrete anti-ricochet devices, and the tube for disposing of expended machine gun shells casings into the fossé. There is also a plan of a position for the 81-mm mortar on the lower level of a casemate firing through the fossé. However, the mounting of this weapon is inaccurate and the casemate wall is less than the regulation 1.5 meter minimum thick.

The illustrations of the GFM and JM cloches are reasonably accurate and even show the access ladder and the movable floor, which could be lowered or raised. However, no distinction is made between the various models. The interior diameter of these cloches is given as 1.2 meters, but that measurement only applied to earlier GFM cloches; the 1934 GFM and JM cloche were 1.3 and 1.39 meters, respectively (Truttmann 1979, 182). Some examples of interior positions are also included. One of the more interesting is that of a set of three interior blockhouses designed to cover different approaches at the fork of the main gallery. This drawing is similar to a position in the ouvrage of Immerhof. Even though the *Grosses Orientierungsheft Frankreich* is not perfect, it provides enough material to plan an assault on an ouvrage.

Another item included in the *Grosses Orientierungsheft Frankreich* is the plan of a two-level CORF casemate. The drawing shows the weapons positions, the cloche, the interior layout, and the emergency exit with the protective firing position behind it, on the lower level. The garrison is estimated at about two dozen men. Another plan of a cavern-type abri demonstrates its capabilities and facilities. The plan of a double Rhine blockhouse with a cloche is very sketchy. The blockhouses for the *Garde Mobile* and the fortified houses are not forgotten. The latter is shown as a bunker covered by a house. There is even a three-dimensional cross-section of a military dam for flooding the Sarre region, and sketches of barriers and obstacles.

Finally, the four types of concrete strength are compared to the German types. Here the intelligence officers were mistaken, however. They estimated that Category 1, which was used on rear walls, was only proof against shell fragments of medium artillery, when it could actually resist hits of 160-mm guns. Category 2 was thought to withstand only a single hit from a 210-mm gun, whereas it was actually designed to withstand 240-mm weapons. Again, the strength of Category 3 was underestimated, as it was believed capable of resisting only a single hit from a 280-mm gun. In reality, it could withstand the fire of a 300-mm gun. Category 4 was purported to resist the heaviest artillery, but it is doubtful the Germans knew it was designed to withstand shells from a 420-mm gun.

A relatively accurate chart of armor thickness in cloches and turrets was also included. The cloches were purported to have between 20 and 40-cm of armor, but averaged 20 to 30-cm. The turrets were credited with the same amount on their roofs. In fact, the turret, depending on its type, had a thickness varying from 28.5 to 35 cm. All these examples, including the measurements, show that the German intelligence had a solid understanding of these positions in the fall of 1937.

When General von Metzch publicly claimed that the Germans knew the French fortifications well, he probably did not know how correct he was. Even without information on every single position, German intelligence was able to identify the location of virtually every ouvrage, most casemates, and other supporting facilities. The information at their disposal permitted them to estimate the composition and strength of most French positions. Armed with that knowledge, the army would have been able to formulate the best plan of attack on the French fortifications.

The question is to what extent all of this intelligence affected the decisions of the German High Command in 1937 and later. There is practically no documented proof to support the answer to this question, but there is significant circumstantial evidence. First, it must be pointed out that no plans were made for a direct assault on the Maginot Line Proper. Second, from 1936 on the Germans built the strongest points of their own West Wall along the French border. The Germans, like the French, evinced little interest in their neighbor at that time. A year later, when Hitler prepared to pounce on Czechoslovakia, he planned some thrusts through the fortified Czech positions. At the time, the major Czech fortifications were still incomplete and had not received their artillery, allowing the Germans to hope that they could overrun them. The intelligence reports of 1937 indicate that, contrary to some news reports, the Germans did not underestimate the strength of the Maginot Line, and, despite their intimate knowledge of these forts—or maybe because of it—

they chose another route to attack France.

If the above hypothesis is correct, the success of Foreign Armies West, German intelligence, may well have caused the German High Command to reconsider the old Schlifflen Plan, which proposed to outflank France in the event of war. This, in turn, leads to two interesting conclusions. In the first place, the Maginot Line fully succeeded in its mission to divert the Germans from the French frontier, thus offering the French the opportunity to free most of their army for operations elsewhere. In the second place, if the Germans had not been cognizant of the strength of the Maginot Line, they might have launched a major assault on Alsace-Lorraine, changing perhaps the whole course of the 1940 campaign. As it turned out, the French failed to capitalize on their advantage. The Germans, on the other hand, greatly profited from the knowledge they had acquired through their intelligence service.

NOTES

1. Vivian Rowe erroneously states in *The Great Wall of France* (1961, 90-91) that the first official photograph was not released until 1936.

2. The term "mined" refers to preparation of demolitions to block routes rather than actual mine fields since at this time the anti-personnel mine had not been developed in any country. Mine fields do not appear until 1939 although anti-tank mines may well have been in use as booby-traps in areas to be "mined."

10

THE MAGINOT LINE AT WAR

By the mid-1930s, there was a substantial shift in the way the French military establishment viewed the Maginot fortifications. No longer seen as a stop-gap measure to buy time for mobilization, the Maginot Line began to take on a more prominent role in the French war plans, eventually creating the "Maginot Mentality." Indeed, after having sunk enormous amounts of money, time and effort into the Maginot Line, the French military leaders became increasingly reluctant to leave its security in order to launch an offensive on Germany. In 1936, in response to the Rhineland Crisis, the French army moved into the Maginot forts. In 1938, at the time of the German occupation of Austria and later during the Munich Crisis, the French again reoccupied the Maginot Line (Rowe 1961, 98). The French High Command, relying on World War I military doctrine, was reluctant to launch an offensive without months of preparation.

Another contributing factor to the growing dependence of the French military on their static defenses was their failure to develop a flexible military doctrine and abandon the policies developed during World War I. In the meanwhile, the Germans experimented with armored forces, leaving the French, who had been pioneers in the field, well behind. They planned to use massed armored formations to spearhead their advance on the North European Plain, either against the Poles or their French and Belgian adversaries. Most members of the French High Command, on the other hand, remained convinced that tanks could only serve as infantry support weapons. Even though they had created the first armored division, they were unable to see these as formations in strictly independent offensive operations.

The reason for this conservatism can in part be attributed to geography, because the French leaders fully expected Belgium to become involved in any future conflict. As a result, their main plans for that area involved rushing into Belgium, relying on its defenses to hold back the Germans. The mechanized formations would speed up the movement of troops to the front lines. The army would need to reorganize after advancing into Belgium, before contemplating an offensive. Furthermore, the terrain on the Franco-German border was considered hostile to mass-armored formations. In addition, the heavily urbanized area of the Rhineland was not deemed good tank country and would be left to the infantry. Finally, the tank force represented a defensive reserve. Thus, the French, perceiving no good theaters of operation for tanks, saw no reason to put first priority on the development of their armored formations in the 1930s.

The French Air Force, another key element for a future war, was plagued by weak leadership and production problems. As a result, by 1939 the French air arm was a rather puny force. In 1939 the only branch of the French army that represented a force to be reckoned with was its infantry, which, unfortunately, was not ready for large-scale offensives. Theodore Draper (1944) described the situation as follows: "A completely static defense behind a fixed line of fortifications was an understandable doctrine and a war of movement was an understandable doctrine. The trouble was that the French generals were incapable of choosing either" (10).

It is doubtful that the absence of the Maginot Line would have significantly altered the French situation. Faced with obvious provocation on the part of the Germans in 1936, and again in 1938, the French military leadership was not able to conceive any alternative to taking up positions in the Maginot Line and waiting for each crisis to pass. If anything, these events clearly marked the onset of the "Maginot Mentality" and the gradual transformation of the original mission of the defenses. The initial goals were not abandoned suddenly. As late as 1937, during a visit to Metz, Winston Churchill was informed by General Henri Giraud, future commander of the French Seventh Army, one of France's most mobile formations, of the "offensive conception of the Maginot Line" (Churchill 1948, 475). Most likely, he was referring to early French plans to launch an offensive on the Rhineland through the Sarre Gap, between the two RFs of the Maginot Line.

THE PHONY WAR, 1939-1940

When war broke out in September 1939, the French rapidly mobilized their army. Thanks to the Little Maginot Line of the Alps, they were able to maintain a minimum of troops on the Southeastern Front to face a possible Italian invasion. On the Northeastern Front, the Maginot Line was fully occupied as the armies behind it completed mobilization. Over fifty divisions took up position in the Northeast Front while the first units of the British Expeditionary Force moved between two French armies on the Belgian front. General Maurice Gamelin, Commander-in-Chief of the French Army, informed his government during the last week of August that he would not be ready for a major offensive for at least two years. In an attempt to honor France's obligation to Poland, French divisions of the Fourth Army, lumbered out of their positions in the Sarre sector, launched a half-hearted assault on the German

West Wall on September 7.   The offensive came to a grinding halt in the German anti-personnel mine fields of the West Wall defended by only a few Germans divisions (Kaufmann and Kaufmann 1993, 95-99).

During those first weeks of the war the Maginot Line, with its elite troops, sat in complete inactivity because its forts, without long-range artillery, were barely within range of the frontier. Located close to the border, the ouvrage of Hochwald was one of the few exceptions. On September 8, one of Hochwald's 75-mm gun turrets supported the advance of a Moroccan formation by shelling the German village of Schweigen. During this action the 75-mm gun of Block 7 bis came loose from its mounting, revealing for the first time the kinks in the largely untested weapons. During the early months of the "Phony War" many of the ouvrages, especially those in the RF of Metz were able to test-fire their weapons for the first time. The fortress troops discovered that most of the old 75-mm ammunition had to be replaced (Bruge 1973, 67-69; Rowe 1961, 116). Fortunately, the French would have a great deal of time to correct these deficiencies before the Germans turned their attention to the ouvrages. Meanwhile, only the supporting artillery of the former Fortified Regions and the Fortified Sectors—which were being converted into corps and divisions, respectively—had long enough ranges to engage the enemy.

In September 1939 the equivalent of about forty French divisions constituting four armies faced two German armies of only about twenty, mostly weak divisions in the West. A French force numerically superior to the German on the Saar Front was unable to make any headway.[1] The problem stemmed in part from the fact that the reserve divisions were still undergoing training and could not be committed (Rowe 1961, 121). By the end of the month, the French contingent retreated behind the Maginot Line. As France licked its wounds and studied the disaster on the Polish front, it started to look upon the Maginot Line as a great shield that would protect it from the onslaught of the victorious German troops which had inflicted such a humiliating defeat on the Poles.

The German strategy for the West had already been decided upon. The Maginot Line, considered impregnable, would have to be bypassed. Instead, the German High Command worked out plans for an attack through Belgium and Luxembourg, possibly involving the Netherlands as well. The French, realizing that the main German thrust would come from the Low Countries, shifted most of their best forces into the First Army Group along the Belgian frontier during the fall of 1939.

The remaining months of 1939 saw a flurry of digging on the Northeastern Front. Many of the reservist formations, instead of getting additional field training, found themselves engaged in construction. Concrete and wooden structures went up on the front of the Maginot Line like mushrooms after a rain. Generally, the new bunkers were not based on military engineer plans and were only intended to bolster the existing defenses. North or northwest of the Maginot Line, along the Belgian border where there were few permanent defenses, the field troops had to build many new positions.

During the Phony War some of the ouvrages occasionally had an opportunity to fire their weapons at the enemy. For the most part the garrisons of the forts suffered from boredom while the troops in the intervals had the weather to complain about. The French government even demobilized some of the reservists during the Phony War because of what it termed "adverse effects on industrial production." Finally, in order to raise morale, it was decided that the best solution would be to allow the fortress troops to take part in patrols, to move older reservists into the ouvrages, and to place some of the younger men in the field (Rowe 1961, 122).

During this period of inactivity, the British rotated individual battalions from their expeditionary force into the RF Metz where they manned the intervals in one of the sectors for periods of up to two weeks (Linklater 1942, 11; Salmond 1953, 5). By April 1940 the British 51st Highland Division moved into position in the old SF of Boulay in the vicinity of the town of Hombourg-Budange between the French 2nd and 42nd Divisions. The division took over the intervals between the ouvrage of Hackenberg and its neighbors. Here the Tommies found a large number of log cabins that the French had erected to shelter themselves from the weather and the enemy. Deciding that these positions offered little protection from heavy infantry weapons and that they did not have enough troops to man them, the British pulled them down (Linklater 1942, 11-14).

As the Phony War dragged on, time lay heavy on the hands of the troops in the ouvrages. Finally, looking for something to do, the commander of Hochwald requested some old 120-mm model 1878 guns. His request was granted, and before long the men of the Hochwald and Schoenenbourg were setting up open positions on top of their ouvrage. Thus, both the eastern and western combat groups of Hochwald were armed and the crews of the 75-mm gun casemates and the 81-mm guns finally got a chance to break the monotony of their days (Rowe 1961, 126).

In the meantime, over thirty French Divisions—twenty of them reservist— were left in the Second Army Group to defend the Maginot Line Proper and the Rhine. In November 1939 General Gamelin further divided the front, creating the Third Army Group to defend the Rhine and the Swiss border. Although this group was assigned part of the Second Army Group's front and divisions, it further drained the man power because it too required its own reserve of divisions (Kaufmann and Kaufmann 1993, 109). The First Army Group mustered over thirty divisions—only about one third of which were reservists—the British Expeditionary Force, and most of France's mechanized units to counter a German offensive through Belgium (Kaufmann and Kaufmann 1993, 174, 205). Thanks to the Maginot Line, which defended the Franco-German border, the French could have released a good ten additional divisions. Thus, the fortifications allowed the Allies to assemble their best units against the Germans, which were expected to come through Belgium.

Without the Maginot Line the German front would have required a higher number of units with fewer reservists.

BLITZKRIEG IN THE WEST 1940

When the Germans went on the offensive on May 10, 1940, only Army Group C, incorporating less than twenty low-quality divisions and no panzer divisions, occupied the Franco-German border area. It had at its disposal heavy siege artillery, of little use to the other army groups. The mission of Army Group C was strictly to maintain its positions. Although the German High Command had briefly considered some limited offensives involving Italian troops on the Upper Rhine, it finally opted for inaction on this front.[2]

The original German plan for the fall of 1939 was to thrust through northern Belgium and the main Belgian position near Liege with nine panzer divisions assigned to Army Group B. The French, who had expected the German offensive to be concentrated in this area, were ready to rush the bulk of the first-class infantry and mechanized divisions of their First and Seventh Army and the British Expeditionary Force to meet the enemy. However, during the winter of 1939-1940 the Germans changed their plans, shifting most of their panzer divisions to Gerd von Rundstedt's Army Group A. Thus, their main thrust would take place through the heavily wooded and supposedly impassable Ardennes in southern Belgium. Three panzer divisions remained with Army Group B to create the main diversion. One of these divisions would spearhead the assault on the Netherlands to secure the right flank and further divert Allied attention. The other two divisions would lead the attack through northern Belgium, bypassing the main Belgian defenses of Liege, with the intention of convincing the French that this was the main thrust. Meanwhile, Army Group A's panzer divisions and supporting infantry formation would move as rapidly as possible through the Ardennes to breach the Allied front on the Meuse. To facilitate the progress of Army Group A, additional German units were to advance through southern Luxembourg, next to Belgian territory, secure the left flank, and keep the French forces pinned in the Maginot Line in the RF of Metz.[3] This last action brought some of the ouvrages of the RF of Metz into action during the early phase of the campaign and succeeded in diverting French attention from the main spearhead, tricking them into believing that a German force was moving against the left flank of the Maginot Line.

On May 10 the panzer divisions leading the main assault moved into the Ardennes, barely noticed by the Allies. The few Belgian units in that sector had been ordered to pull back. Several French mechanized cavalry divisions rushed to meet the oncoming force, but were unable to stand up to the fast-advancing German panzer units. In southern Luxembourg and Belgium the Germans quickly drove the French back into the Maginot Line. Meanwhile, in the critical sector of the Ardennes between Dinant and Sedan, the French mobile units fell back towards General André Corap's Ninth Army, the weakest of the French forces. Several Category A and B reservist divisions and the regulars of the 102nd Fortress Division were in the vicinity of the threatened zone of the Meuse, which was only lightly fortified at the time. Despite the support of the 3rd and 4th North African Divisions and sporadic attacks from the French 1st DCR (Heavy Armored Division), Corap's army was overwhelmed by May 14. In addition, Charles Huntzinger's Second Army, which was supposed to protect its right flank, began to retreat toward its base positions on the Maginot Extension. After breaching the Meuse near Sedan and Dinant, the Germans decided to drive to the sea and outflank the armies of the First Army Group.

Pétain's miscalculation would cost the French dearly as the poor-quality troops in the supposedly impassable Ardennes folded like a house of cards. Between the end of the Maginot Extension, consisting of two gros and two petit ouvrages, and the fortress of Maubeuge, with its four petits ouvrages, the French front was devoid of significant fortifications, leaving the gap between them facing the Ardennes a vulnerable position. Instead of wheeling to the left in order to encircle the French frontier forces as they had done in 1914, the Germans opted to isolate the French First Army Group in the north. As the First Army Group was destroyed and the British Expeditionary Force escaped through Dunkirk, the French attempted to create a defensive line along the Somme towards the Aisne and the Maginot Line. If Army Group C had been strong enough to attack to Maginot Line during the last week of May and force the French back, the entire French front would have collapsed and the campaign would have ended before June 1.

As it was, Army Group C did launch small probing attacks on the RF of Lauter. A tentative infantry assault against the French fortifications, across the Lauter River, on May 14 quickly broke down under a barrage of fire from the turret guns and the 120-mm weapons in open emplacements atop the ouvrages. Later that day, German 280-mm guns pounded for the first time the ouvrage of Schoenenbourg (Gander and Chamberlain 1979, 229).[4] After cratering Schoenenbourg's surface and tearing up its barricades, the German battery was silenced temporarily by the fort's turreted 135-mm howitzers. The next day it moved out of the range of Schoenenbourg's guns and resumed its pounding of the fort's surface. It was joined by a Skoda 420-mm howitzer taken from the Czechs in 1939, and Stuka dive bombers. The latter had bombed the bunkers near Sedan on May 13, without much success, but demoralized the troops there to such an extent that they surrendered (Rowe 1961, 155-156, 161; Hofmann, 53).[5] As the bombardment of Schoenenbourg continued, the old 120-mm guns of the fort responded with gusto.

On May 19 the fort's turret guns succeeded in breaking up a German concentration of troops preparing to launch an assault in the area of Wissembourg and Altenstadt. The next day, the 280-mm German cannons opened fire upon Hochwald's eastern blocks (Rowe 1961, 178-184). Apparently, the goal of these attacks was to pin the attention of the French on the Maginot Line while their other operations proceeded as scheduled. The French belatedly pulled their troops from the fortified sectors held by the Second Army Group and rushed them off to create new defensive positions between the Maginot Line and the North Sea.

As the Germans began to crush the First Army Group, the ouvrages of Maubeuge went into action. After breaking through the Meuse front, the Germans decided to eliminate the French positions anchoring the Maginot Extension on their left flank. To this end, on May 18 the Germans embarked on an attack on the petit ouvrage of La Ferté, at the extreme end of the Maginot Line. The conquest of this small fort was not crucial to the success of the campaign, but it would improve troop morale and score a great propaganda victory. So the Germans decided to exploit this little side show to the hilt. The German 71st Infantry Division deployed its 194th Infantry Regiment in front of La Ferté and the Maginot Extension casemates up to the vicinity of the gros ouvrage of Le Chesnois. Le Chesnois and the remainder of the extension faced the German 15th Infantry Division, whose mission was to monopolize their attention, leaving La Ferté unprotected. Meanwhile, the German 68th Division on the right flank of the 71st moved on the French 3rd North African and 6th Infantry Division in order to prevent them from coming to the rescue of La Ferté. The 71st Division's other two infantry regiments, the 191st and 211th, advanced on Villy and to the west of La Ferté in an attempt to flank it and cut it off. On May 17 nine huge 210-mm Mörsers, built at the end of World War I and confiscated from the Czechs in 1939, arrived from Belgium and opened fire on the two small blocks of La Ferté. These huge mortars, firing 135 kg (300 lb) shells at a maximum range of 10,000 meters, were placed well beyond the range of the guns of La Ferté and Le Chesnois. The latter fort's only 75-mm gun turret barely had the range to cover La Ferté (Gander and Chamberlain 1979, 225).

The 210-mm mortars and five medium howitzer batteries laid down 2,500 rounds on La Ferté between May 17 and May 19, destroying most of its barbed-wire belts and tearing up anti-tank rails. Actually, the 210-mm rounds accounted for most of the damage, plowing furrows of up to 10 meters in length and over 3.5 meters deep. Despite the tremendous punishment they took, La Ferté's two blocks survived gamely (Hofmann, 44).

La Ferté had no artillery beyond the small 25-mm guns in the mixed-arms turret of its Block 2, but two nearby casemates, built on either side of the road passing near the fort, were armed with a 75-mm gun each. However, these two casemates however, were not connected to each other or to La Ferté by underground passages. Like most casemates, they offered only flanking fires because they had no cloche, and depended on La Ferté for close defense. Believing erroneously that the town of Villy had fallen on May 17, the commanders of these two casemates decided to withdraw that night, especially after they discovered that the turret of La Ferté was jammed and could no longer lend them support.

The subsequent order of events remains unclear. Villy and its surrounding fortifications resisted the 71st Infantry Division on May 17, only to fall to the 2nd Battalion of the German 211th Infantry Regiment supported by a company of engineers and artillery in the late afternoon of May 18. In the evening of the same day, the 210-mm and several medium-artillery batteries renewed their barrage against La Ferté while other artillery units held the French field artillery at bay. Le Chesnois' 75-mm guns failed to push back a German combat team from the 171st Engineer Battalion with elements of the 211th Infantry Regiment, which worked its way to the top of the ouvrage using the shell craters as cover (Hofmann, 44, 110-115; Bruge 1973, 218, 224-239).

By 7:00 PM the assault team, advancing under cover of their own artillery and smoke, was within 250 meters of La Ferté. A detachment eliminated an outpost position as the artillery shifted its fire and began firing smoke shells. Meanwhile, 88-mm Flak guns moved to a distance of about two kilometers, at Fromy, and fired on the embrasures of the cloches, which withstood the shells because the distance was too great. However, just before the German artillery gave up, one of the engineer platoons reached Block 2 and eliminated the GFM with a 3 kg (6.5 lb) charge followed by grenades. A 40 kg (88 lb) charge blew up the already disabled mixed-arms turret. The explosion lifted the turret into the air and dropped it back on its base at an angle, destroying much of its machinery as it crashed on its mounting. Further, the embrasure of a cloche was smashed open and the weapon behind it was destroyed with a 6 kg (13 lb) charge. The assailants eliminated the remaining cloche of the block with similar methods. Special 18 kg (40 lb) charges were dropped through the openings created in the armored positions above the block. Soon the interior burst into flames (*Denkschrift* 1941, 194-195; Hofmann, 59, 115-116).

In the meantime, Block 1 continued to fight back vigorously, preventing the enemy platoon from invading its surface. Another barrage from the big German guns brought more craters on the surface of the little fort, allowing the engineers to approach. By midnight the assault group had destroyed three of Block 1's four cloches. On the next day the engineers took out the last cloche and tried to blow open the door, but failed. A 25 kg (54 lb) charge blew open an embrasure, allowing the Germans to place more charges and set the interior on fire. After they finally gained entrance to the ouvrage, the Germans discovered that those members of the 100 men-crew who had not been killed in the combat blocks had moved into the gallery below where they all had died of asphyxia caused by the fumes of the usine whose air-intake system had been damaged. What is noteworthy about the fall of La Ferté is that the ouvrage was taken by combat engineers, whose efforts were much more effective than the artillery's, which inflicted no significant damage except on the vulnerable cloches (Hofmann, 116-117; Rowe 1961, 177-178; Bruge 1973, 224-239).

Today, the GFM cloche of Block 2 still bears the scars of the 88-mm Flak rounds, some of which might have been fired after the battle. This weapon, originally designed as an anti-aircraft gun, became an effective block buster against the exposed positions of the ouvrages thanks to its high-velocity shells, which penetrated both concrete walls and steel cloches. At ranges of a little over 1,000 meters, an 88-mm firing directly at reinforced concrete walls from a 90-degree angle left craters almost a meter deep and completely penetrated walls of only 0.6 meters. Under the same conditions, the 88-mm round penetrated 0.3 meters into a cloche steel wall (Hofmann, 47).[6] Eventually, the 88-mm Flak would become famous as a tank killer, but at La Ferté it failed to make a major contribution.

After seizing their first Maginot ouvrage, the Germans were ecstatic. Identifying La Ferté as Panzerwerk 505, they soon printed propaganda leaflets touting their victory and dropped them on the other fortifications later that month (Bruge 1973, 239; Rowe 1961, 177-178).[7]

It was not until May 28 that the French commander-in-chief released the details of the action at La Ferté. The fall of this tiny fort served as a warning to the garrisons of the other Maginot ouvrages, which were particularly troubled by the idea that assault engineers could use the craters created by heavy artillery to advance on the blocks of an ouvrage. This did not help morale in the forts, especially after earlier warnings to watch for enemy paratroopers. The first directive had been promoted by the German airborne attack on the Belgian fort of Eben Emael on the first day of the campaign although no one had any details on how the Germans actually took the fort at that time. Sentries were sent out to patrol the surface of some ouvrages like Fermont (Rowe 1961, 208-209; Dropsy interview, 1979).

As the German panzer divisions relentlessly advanced toward the sea, several divisions secured both their flanks near the Meuse bridgehead. While the French left flank and the Maginot Extension were under siege, the German 28th Infantry Division and the 5th Panzer Division pushed their right flank towards the Sambre River, engaging the French 101st Fortress Division at Maubeuge. This last position consisted of CORF-type structures and four petits ouvrages built into older forts in 1936 as part of the New Fronts program. Maubeuge, now the new anchor of an Allied defensive front against the Germans advance from northern Belgium, was to stop the Germans from rolling up what was left of the First Army Group. In the meantime, other units attempted unsuccessfully to stop the German drive to the sea and stabilize the front. The successful defense of Maubeuge might have given the Allies the necessary time to regroup, but the fortifications in this area were too small and weak to withstand the enemy. In addition, the poor showing of the allied troops coupled with the fall of La Ferté was taking a serious toll on morale.

On May 18 the Germans laid siege to the petit ouvrage of Le Boussois, located directly east of Maubeuge, north of the river Sambre. This small three-block fort consisted of two blocks with mixed-arms turrets and one block with a mixed-arms cloche. Its 25-mm cannons were no match to the German artillery. After encountering stiff opposition, the Germans succeeded in placing 150-mm guns and 88-mm Flak guns about 1,500 meters behind the ouvrage and opened fire on the exposed facades of Blocks 1 and 3. The next day German troops captured several of the interval casemates. The bombardment continued on May 20. Stuka dive bombers attacked the Boussois for the second day and the two-block ouvrage of Sarts, located north of Maubeuge. During the bombardment, Sarts was also attacked from the rear. The mixed arms turret of its Block 2 was hit and could not be retracted until the evening when it was repaired under cover of darkness (Mary 1980, 190; Hofmann 119-121).

On May 21 German troops attempted unsuccessfully to capture the CORF casemate of Héronfontaine to the west of Sarts. On that day Boussois was bombarded and attacked again by dive bombers with 500 kg (1,100 lb) bombs. The 210-mm howitzers joined in the bombardment, but failed to cause any significant damage to the fort. On May 21, advancing under the cover of their own artillery fire, German assault troops finally reached positions from which they could launch an assault on Boussois, but the mixed-arms turret stopped them in their tracks. After heavy bombardment, on May 22 the garrison of the casemate of Héronfontaine withdrew, exposing Sarts. In the center of the line the two-block ouvrage of Bersillies with a single mixed-arms turret was placed under direct artillery fire from the rear. The two-block ouvrage of Salmagne with similar armament to Bersillies was put under siege. Another aerial assault by Stukas against Boussois cratered the ground and created enough breaches in the surrounding obstacles to allow assault teams to advance that night. As the Germans moved forward, the guns positioned behind the ouvrage fired upon its embrasures, but every time they paused the weapons of Boussois fired a riposte. As the artillery battle raged on, the assault troops reached the fort and set their charges, destroying its embrasures and air vents. The mixed-arms turret and the cloche were put out of action with flame throwers (Hofmann 119-121; *Denkschrift* 1941, 219).

In the meantime, the 49th Infantry Regiment of the 29th Division attacked Fort Salmagne on May 22 under the cover of light howitzers. The artillery laid down smoke to blind the observers as the German soldiers rushed across 500 meters of open terrain, reached the fort's surrounding line of obstacles, and advanced onto the superstructure. The mixed-arms turret of Block 1 was put out of action by a 3 kg (6.5 lb) demolition charge as it came up into its fighting position. Then the engineers proceeded to smash the barrels of the machine guns with hatchets (Hofmann, 121)! Their exposed facades badly battered and their air intakes on the exposed walls disabled, three of the ouvrages surrendered.

Only Sarts continued to resist for an additional day. After its mixed-arms turret was destroyed in another artillery barrage and suffering an attack by German assault teams, it surrendered on May 23. Light howitzer shells were embedded in the fort's turret and cloches, and in one case a shell had penetrated the armor. The damage inflicted by all these shells was surprisingly light.[8] During the attack on the concrete fortifications of Maubeuge, the 28th Artillery Regiment of the 28th Division placed its guns at about 3,000 meters to smash wire infantry obstacles and penetrate the embrasures of the lighter fortifications (Hofmann, 47, 121; *Denkschrift* 1941, 219).

Further to the northwest, in the SF of Escaut, north of the Mormal Forest and southeast of Valenciennes, the petit ouvrage of Eth consisted of only two combat blocks, one of which had a mixed-arms turret. Just to the north of Valenciennes and the Forest of Raismes stood old Fort Maulde with its series of casemates, including two for 75-mm guns and the only casemate built for a 155-mm gun (Truttmann 1979, Plate 62, 69). At the time the forts of Maubeuge were under siege, the 5th Panzer Division engaged the French in fluid action in the Mormal Forest. By May 21 the German panzer divisions reached the coast and were pushing against the western half of the pocket occupied by the First Army Group. Additional German forces attacked from the east. The defenses of Maubeuge collapsed on May 22 as the Germans continued to clear the Mormal Forest. As the situation rapidly deteriorated, the French desperately attempted to mount counterattacks and possibly break out. The fortress troops sheltering in their underground fastness found little to keep up their morale at this point.

The German 84th Infantry Regiment attacked north of Valenciennes and in the vicinity of Fort Maulde on May 20 and 21, quickly reducing the small blockhouses and non-CORF casemates with light howitzers firing special armor-piercing shells at ranges as close as 450 meters. They usually aimed at the embrasures of these positions, demoralizing the French troops, who abandoned their positions (Hofmann, 44). By May 22, the ouvrage of Eth was under attack. The Germans moved a pair of 105-mm guns to a point about 600 meters behind the fort from where they could smash its facade. The casemated artillery pieces of Fort Maulde laid supporting fires on Eth until they too came under attack. The old fort continued to resist until May 25. Without Maulde's support, its blocks shattered and its cloche breached, Eth surrendered on May 26 (Mary 1980, 185). The southern end of the French pocket was rapidly collapsing toward the coast.

By the end of May, the British Expeditionary Force had already been evacuated from Dunkirk but the remnants of the First French Army Group were still embarking on the beaches. Gamelin was replaced by Maxime Weygand, who prepared the so-called Weygand Line running from the North Sea, near the mouth of the Somme, to the Maginot Line. The French frantically shuffled their divisions from one front to another, bringing several units from the Southeastern Front and the Maginot Line as well. The British 51st Division withdrew from the Maginot Line before the end of May, joining the last British divisions on the Continent, near the Somme River. The French deployed about forty infantry divisions and several armored formations on the new Weygand Line. The remaining seventeen divisions—only one of which was a regular division—continued to occupy positions from the northern end of the Maginot Line to the Swiss frontier (Kaufmann and Kaufmann 1993, 265).

The objective of the final German offensive, which began on June 5, was to clear the Somme front and to push on to the lower Seine. Although the Germans succeeded in driving the French back, they continued to encounter resistance. So by June 9, they decided to shift their effort to the center, between the Oise and Meuse Rivers. By June 12 the Weygand Line began to disintegrate. Soon even a few of the old fortresses around Verdun, some of which had been renovated, were brought into action. By June 15 old Fort Choisel, armed with a 75-mm gun turret and a new GFM cloche, was attacked by the 76th Infantry Division (*Denkschrift* 1941, 206-210).

By this time the Maginot Line was about to see serious action. General Prételat, commander of the Second Army Group, had suggested earlier to Weygand that the interval troops and the divisions protecting the Maginot Line should be withdrawn before the army group was isolated (Rowe 1961, 228). It is doubtful, however, that his advice would have been beneficial. The withdrawal of the interval troops and other supporting divisions would have shortened the line somewhat, but would have sacrificed a great deal of territory, hurt the morale, and forced the troops to take positions on a line that was virtually unfortified. On June 6 General Prételat exhorted the fortress troops in his "General Order Number 2":

Until now the enemy has not yet attacked you. The position that you have been assigned to defend was covered by an advanced position on which all the divisions of the French Army have become seasoned this winter. This advanced position has been voluntarily evacuated in order to permit these divisions to join the battle, where many have already covered themselves with glory. It is your turn now to show that you are worthy of the defenders of Verdun. The Maginot Line, entrusted to your guard, must remain inviolate. The garrisons of the ouvrages, interval troops, everyone must constitute a solid block against which the enemy attacks will break. As the proud motto of your insignias says: "ON NE PASSE PAS." (*Lageberichte West*, 1940)

Without a doubt, in the days that followed the fortress troops, abandoned to their fate, fulfilled their duty.

On June 12 General Ritter von Leeb, commander of Army Group C, learning that Weygand had finally authorized the retreat from the sectors facing him, prepared his own offensive. On the same day, Guderian's panzer divisions of Army Group A began to move across the French rear areas, heading toward the Swiss border in order to cut off the French units stationed in the Maginot Line as well as the withdrawing interval troops.

After the experience of La Ferté, the French leadership realized that the ouvrages of the Maginot Extension were not able to stand on their own. The evacuation of these ouvrages began on the night of June 12/13 with the sabotage of Le Chesnois. The the garrisons of Thonnelle and Veslonnes also pulled out.

On June 14 the First German Army launched Operation Tiger, assaulting the Sarre Gap with three corps, which included ten divisions.[9] On May 31, the directive for the second phase of the campaign, Case Red, had alerted

Army Group C to be on twenty-four hours standby notice for an attack on the Maginot Line between St. Avold and Saargemünd and for offensive operations on the Upper Rhine (Jacobsen 1960, 152-158). Between May 31 and June 3, the 258th Infantry Division pushed back the French outpost line on the eastern end of the RF of Metz as a preliminary action to the offensive. The Sarre offensive was to be launched on June 5 to coincide with the larger operations of the other two army groups. However, things did not proceed according to plan because the French *avant-poste* line continued to resist. As a result, the operation was postponed several times. The 258th and 93rd Divisions were to lead the attack with the 79th Division in reserve.

At the time, the Sarre front was only defended by the French 52nd Infantry Division, the 1st Polish Division of XX Army Corps, and three fortress infantry regiments, who had already received orders to evacuate Alsace and Lorraine (Hofmann, 128-129). The water barrier for the Sarre was not as formidable as planned because the weather that year did not bring sufficient rainfall. The heavily outnumbered defenders, facing nine German divisions with little supporting artillery, were flanked by the petits ouvrages of the RFs of Lauter and Metz, which had no artillery. Clearly, the situation they faced was impossible.

The morning of June 14 began with a heavy artillery barrage from nearly one hundred batteries. Dive bombers joined the action. The heavy rail artillery was assigned counter battery missions against the French artillery in the RF of Metz. The fortress troops in their light fortifications stopped the 258th Division's advance and twice destroyed its foot bridges across the Nied, despite little artillery support. Dive-bomber attacks in the late afternoon failed to dislodge the French from their defenses. By 9:00 AM the German 93rd Division began to make some headway north of Cappel where several blockhouses fell, some without a fight. Late in the morning Cappel was taken after heavy fighting. Later that day fortress troops fighting from bunkers stopped the German advance once more. Assault engineers approaching with hollow charges were driven back. Subsequent assault teams took heavy losses trying to reach the bunkers. During the evening the commander of the German First Army was informed that the French units in the area had been ordered to retreat. At 11:00 PM on June 14 the withdrawal was underway, each company leaving one platoon to hold the line. In light of these events, the German commander prepared to renew the assault in the morning at 5:00 AM. On the morning of June 15 the 258th Division was still held in check at the Nied, but only temporarily. The German formations bypassed all the French strong points, tearing the Sarre front wide open by evening. The German commanders began exploiting the situation, eventually succeeding in encircling the Maginot Line (Hofmann, 133-142).

On June 15 the Seventh Army of Army Group C began Operation Bear, the assault on the Upper Rhine. The departure of the bulk of its interval troops with most of their artillery left the casemates and blockhouses of this area practically at their mercy. The casemates on the Rhine, which were designed for flanking fire, were smashed by the 88-mm Flak guns without offering much opposition. Many of the French crews, seeing the hopelessness of their position, simply abandoned their posts, seeking cover elsewhere (Hofmann, 50). The main assault, which took place near Neuf Brisach, involved four infantry divisions from three corps. The Luftwaffe was prevented from giving support by the rain, but many of its aircraft were busy elsewhere.

The XXVII Infantry Corps led the attack with three divisions (the 218th, 221st and 239th Infantry Divisions), artillery reinforcements, anti-aircraft and engineer units. These troops had received no special training, except for the engineers who had taken courses to cope with bridging of the Rhine but had not profited much from them. The XXV Infantry Corps crossed the Rhine with the 557th Infantry Division in rubber rafts at Rhineau, encountering no resistance. This unit was directed to protect the northern flank of XXVII Infantry Corps by advancing to Bruyères via Schlettstadt and Markirch. The 554th Infantry Division of XXXIII Infantry Corps attacked in the direction of Neuf Brisach and was to advance in the direction of Mulhouse in order to secure the southern flank. Many of the French troops, who had been chased from their bunkers, took up new positions and continued to resist. Some crews even reoccupied their damaged installations, especially at Rhineau where the French gunners forced the 557th Division, which had already landed its lead elements, to move its crossing position that evening. The XXVII Infantry Corps had more success, even though the defenders managed to hamper its advance. It took special assault teams from the 218th Infantry Division to take the French fortifications. In the evening the division reached the Rhine-Rhone Canal northwest and west of Mackenheim. The progress of the 221st Infantry Division was blocked at Artzenheim by the casemates and bunkers around Marckolsheim. The town did not fall until June 17. The 239th Infantry Division, which had crossed the Rhine with little difficulty, moved against the main French position near Baltzenheim. Dive bombers disheartened the defenders, who put up little resistance. By the evening of June 16, the 239th Infantry Division reached Urschenheim and crossed the Rhine-Rhone Canal the next day. Despite the hopelessness of their situation, the French troops continued to hinder the Seventh Army's offensive, but the points of resistance became increasingly sporadic. The Germans realized that they owed their victory on this front solely to the withdrawal of the defending fortress division (Hofmann, 144-150).

The ouvrage of Haut Poirier, on the left flank of the RF of Lauter and overlooking the Sarre Gap, found itself surrounded by the German 262nd Infantry Division on June 14. Its four blocks only mounted mixed-arms cloches and one mixed-arms turret, which was not enough to drive off the enemy artillery. Seven German infantry divisions pushed through the Sarre Gap while others fanned out behind the Maginot Line. The 262nd Division was soon joined by the 275th Division, which pushed further east toward the

Vosges. On the German right flank, the 167th Division moved behind the RF of Metz, striking at the rear of the petits ouvrages of the SF of Faulquemont. The 95th Division moved further north, toward the gros ouvrages of the SF of Boulay. Meanwhile, seven German infantry divisions moved around the Maginot Line to the west of Longuyon. The 161st Division moved against the rear of the western end of the line to engage the ouvrages of Chappy and Fermont. In the Vosges, the 215th began its attack against the line of casemates in the large gap between the ouvrages of Grand Hohekirkel and Lembach. The 246th Division continued to demonstrate in front of the eastern terminus of the line. In the absence of the French interval troops and their artillery, the Germans were victorious on virtually all the fronts they attacked.

However, the Maginot ouvrages had their own victories as well. On June 15 the 75-mm gun turret of the gros ouvrage of Fermont devastated a supply column of the 183rd Division as it passed around the line. Fermont and its neighbor, Chappy, were isolated by June 17 when the substation of Xivry-Circourt fell to the enemy, leaving the ouvrages in its sector to cope on their own. That afternoon a battery of 88-mm guns positioned less than two kilometers behind Fermont opened up on the weak rear wall of the three-gun artillery casemate, Block 4. Positioned facing the facade directly, they were out of the firing sectors of the flanking guns of Block 4. The Germans withdrew from this position, not knowing that another round might have penetrated the casemate and detonated the ready ammunition. That evening the crew of Fermont effectuated rapid repairs and the next day the ouvrage engaged in an artillery duel that lasted until June 20 (Maistret 1979, 22).

On June 20, the Germans attacked the other end of the RF of Metz, the weakest part of that region's defenses with only petits ouvrages. The German 167th Division lay siege to the petit ouvrage of Bambesch from the rear. Its neighbor, Kerfent, attempted to support it, but its heaviest weapons position, a turreted machine gun, was not adequate for the job. In the absence of the interval troops in the gaps between forts, it was virtually impossible to prevent the Germans from taking up positions behind the exposed and intentionally vulnerable rear walls of Bambesch's casemate.

Bambesch's three blocks, one of which mounted a machine gun turret, were virtually at the mercy of the German 88-mm Flak guns positioned at the rear of Block 2 on June 21. The casemate's exposed facade was shattered and its GFM cloche penetrated by many rounds. Dodging the bullets of the turreted machine gun, the German troops approached Block 3 and, two hours after the bombardment had begun, the small fort was forced to surrender. The 88s soon went into action against Kerfent, taking aim at the casemate of Block 2 from behind. The small three-block ouvrage of Mottemberg, also with a machine gun turret, attempted to intervene, but to no avail. Shortly, Kerfent surrendered.

Meanwhile, on that same day the monolithic ouvrage of Einseling with a machine gun turret was helped by the five-block petit ouvrage of Laudrefang, the strongest fort in the sector, mounting not only a machine gun turret, but also a casemate with 81-mm mortars. The two-block petit ouvrage of Téting, which included a machine gun turret, was also saved by the intervention of Laudrefang (Mary 1980, 190, 263-264). The Germans were finally check-mated in the SF of Faulquemont. Had the planned additions to these few petits ouvrages been carried out, the Germans would have found the pickings more arduous in this sector. Indeed, most of these petits ouvrages had been designed with the intention of including an 81-mm mortar turret. Plans included 75-mm gun and 135-mm howitzer turrets for Kerfent and Laudrefang (Truttmann 1979, Plan 71).

Also on June 21, on the other side of the Sarre Gap, the German 262nd Division pressed its attack against the ouvrage of Haut Poirier. It moved its 150-mm guns behind the casemate of Block 3 and blasted its weak rear-facing wall, killing three men and forcing the surrender of the ouvrage that day. Meanwhile, other units of the division moved against the next ouvrage in the line, Welschoff. This three-block petit ouvrage was also poorly armed, com-prising only two cloches and a turret of mixed arms, but unlike Haut Poirier, it was within range of Simserhof's artillery turrets. Despite the support of the gros ouvrage, the exposed casemate of Block 1 was smashed from the rear after two days of bombardment and Welschoff had to capitulate on June 24. The German assault on the petit ouvrage of Rohrbach, on the other hand, was successfully repelled by Simserhof's artillery (Mary 1980, 190; *Denkschrift* 1941, 197).

Here too, the Germans found it relatively easy to take these small forts, which had been rendered vulnerable by the withdrawal of the interval troops and supporting artillery. Originally, Haut Poirier had been intended as an artillery ouvrage with 75-mm guns in casemates and turrets. Rohrbach was also supposed to have 75-mm guns to support Haut Poirier. Had the original plans been carried out, these forts could have easily held the Germans off even if they had been isolated (Truttmann 1979, Plan 74).

While the German divisions fanned out after penetrating the Sarre Gap, others tackled several positions on the Maginot Line Proper. On June 21, on the northern end of the Maginot Line, a few 37-mm and 47-mm anti-tank guns, supporting an attack on some small blockhouses near Longuyon, forced the French garrisons to withdraw. These small, already obsolete, anti-tank guns scored few other successes against the fortifications during this campaign. Meanwhile, the Germans laid siege to the rear of the small two-block ouvrage of Chappy, the casemate of Puxieux, and the observatory of Puxieux. Fermont's artillery forced the Germans to give up the effort, drawing their attention to itself. The Germans fired a massive barrage from three 210-mm Mörsers, four 305-mm Mörsers, six batteries of 105-mm guns, and two bat-teries of 88-mm Flak guns. The 305-mm Czech mortars fired a 289 kg (640 lb) shell. The ouvrage was hit, but the damage was minor. Not even a glanc-ing hit from a 305-mm round on the 75-mm gun turret succeeded in inflicting any significant harm.

Latiremont's casemated 75's fire went to the rescue of Fermont, which was saved from an attempted assault. Fermont sustained only one fatal casualty when a German anti-tank gun scored a direct hit on a GFM cloche of the EH. The fort's 81-mm mortar turret silenced the weapon responsible for the casualty (Bruge 1975, 131-39; Maistret 1979, 23; Gander and Chamberlain 1979, 229; Hofmann, 42, 51; *Denkschrift* 1941, 199-200).

A few other ouvrages in the RF of Metz saw limited action. For instance, Bréhain engaged German troops advancing on the casemate of Ravin de Crusnes. On June 22 a German assault on the gros ouvrage of Michelsberg was successfully repelled with the help of Mont des Welches (Mary 1980, 190).

The ouvrages of the RF of Lauter, located nearer to the border, saw more prolonged action than those of Metz. Schoenenbourg and Hochwald, which had received the old 120-mm guns, had been in action since early in the war. On June 4 one of the two guns at Schoenenbourg exploded, causing a few casualties. This did not deter the crews from keeping the remaining guns in action, however. On June 8 more 120-mm guns were delivered to the two ouvrages, and Schoenenbourg's men set up positions for two new pieces. The collapse of the firing platform of the last of Schoenenbourg's original two 120-mm guns on June 13 destroyed the weapon (Rowe 1961; 155, 223-224; Collin and Wahl 1981, 39).

Other forts of the RF of Lauter, like Four-à-Chaux, saw action as early as May 12, when the Germans launched serious probing attacks to divert the French troops in the Maginot positions from the main offensive in the north. Four-à-Chaux's guns even brought down a German Heinkel observation aircraft on June 7 (Rowe 1961, 145, 231).[10] The Germans rolled out their heavy artillery, which had not been considered necessary for the advance through Belgium, against the great forts at the end of the Maginot Line. This drastic action was probably inspired by reasons of propaganda and to boost the morale of the German soldiers.

June 13, a bare week before the petits ouvrages of Haut Poirier, Bambesch and Kerfent would fight for survival, was not a good day for the garrisons of the ouvrages. Their commanders had been informed of the withdrawal of the interval troops and warned to prepare to demolish their ouvrages (Rowe 1961, 248-249). On June 15 Schoenenbourg fired against the German 246th Infantry Division as it assaulted the line of *avant-postes*. Hochwald's eastern artillery blocks and two old 120-mm guns on its western blocks joined in. The Germans failed to break the line of *avant-postes*, which was later evacuated on June 17 (Rowe 1961, 254, 262-263; Bruge 1975, 35).

By then one of Guderian's divisions, the 29th Motorized, had reached Pontarlier on the Swiss border, sealing off the French Second Army Group, which had left the fortress troops completely isolated. The artillery duel between the ouvrages on the east end of the RF of Lauter and the Germans continued. The German units coming from the Sarre settled behind the forts. The German 246th Division renewed its assault on the SF of Haguenau in the vicinity of Ashbach on June 19, engaging the casemates of the main line to the east of Schoenenbourg.

Meanwhile, units of the 215th Division moved through the Vosges between Bitche and Lembach, attacking the line of CORF blockhouses in this lightly defended area with the help of the Luftwaffe. Their progress was finally checked by the ouvrage of Four-à-Chaux. Despite fire support from Four-à-Chaux and Hochwald's western combat block's 75s, the line of interval block-houses fell. The German dive bombers turned their attention to the small ouvrage of Lembach and the larger Four-à-Chaux, scoring twice that day. Block 6 of Four-à-Chaux, an infantry and an observation block, suffered minor damage. Hochwald's guns fired upon the Stukas as they attacked their neighboring ouvrage. In the meantime, the Germans advanced behind the main line as far as Woerth (Rowe 1961, 270-273; Weisbecker 1985, 17).

As the battle raged over Lembach on June 19, a German 420-mm howitzer placed several well-placed rounds on Schoenenbourg, hitting the concrete surface of a combat block and gouging a 70-cm deep crater, which represented the greatest damage inflicted by any heavy-artillery piece with a single round against the Maginot forts. Other shells bored as much as 20 meters deep into the loamy soil surrounding the ouvrage and detonated as close as 5 meters from the underground galleries of the combat blocks. According to the French, the shock was perceived merely as a harmless tremor in the passageway. On June 19 and 20, Stuka dive bombers also dropped 500 kg (1,100 lb) bombs on the fort, placing forty percent on or near the target. In the course of the following days some bombers also dropped 1,000 kg (2,200 lb) bombs. The Luftwaffe continued its attacks on Schoenenbourg until June 22. Schoenenbourg absorbed all this punishment but gamely fulfilled its supporting missions during the bombardment. The big 420-mm howitzer returned to bombard Schoenenbourg on June 21, adding fourteen more rounds that morning to the effects of the air attacks. It continued to pound Schoenenbourg until the very day of the Armistice (Hofmann, 53-54; Collin and Wahl 1981, 40-43; Rowe 1961, 279-284).

Schoenenbourg no doubt underwent the heaviest attacks ever launched against any ouvrage. On the night of June 20/21, after the first day's aerial bombardment, the crew had to clean the soil that had been kicked up into several of the turrets by the projectiles. The only serious damage inflicted was to the fossé of infantry Block 6 where the force of the explosions threw the men sleeping at the lower level from their beds and fissured the walls on June 21. The aerial bombs also caused some minor damages to Blocks 1, 4 and 5, which were quickly repaired (Collin and Wahl 1981, 42; Hofmann, 42, 53-54, *Denkschrift* 1941, 198). Also, on June 21 a 105-mm shell struck the 75-mm turret of Block 3, jamming it in the raised position. However, the damage was minor and quickly repaired in the evening. On June 23 a 420-mm round hit near Block 3's turret, but the only damage was in the gallery where a fissure appeared in the fort's unusual M-1/M-2 magazine.[11]   On June 23 a 420-mm round nearly hit the emplacement of the incomplete and poorly protected lance grenade cloche of Block 5, thus coming close to penetrating the block (Collin and Wahl 1981, 42-43).   Other than this, and the destruction of a small armored air vent on infantry Block 6, the 420-mm shells had little adverse effect on the fort as a whole (Truttmann 1979, 210).

Despite the forts' heroic defense, the enemy was able to continue advancing on both sectors, unimpeded by interval troops. Artillery barrages and air bombardment failed to silence the remaining ouvrages. Even when the first of the petits ouvrages began to fall on the sectors of both RFs adjacent to the Sarre between June 20 and 24, and despite the heavy bombardments directed at it, Schoenenbourg in conjunction with Hochwald continued to break up German attacks in the Haguenau sector (Rowe 1961, 280-285).

When the Armistice took effect on June 25, no gros ouvrage of the Maginot Line Proper had fallen in combat. Some of the forts refused to surrender for several days after the Armistice until they were informed by the French High Command that the campaign was over. One by one, the garrisons reluctantly handed their forts over to the Germans. Most received the honors of war, but also ended up in German POW camps for the duration of the war. The Maginot Line had fulfilled its mission successfully. If France was defeated, it was not because the Maginot forts had failed to serve it well.

NOTES

1. On the entire Western Front, the Germans had eleven regular divisions and thirty-five low quality divisions of reservists. Of this total only about thirty could be committed to combat (Manstein 1982, 35). Seven came from the second draft and twelve from a lower category of the third draft. The fourth draft cconsisted of older Landwehr troops. However, the Germans did not expect a French offensive before the end of the second week of the war (Halder 1988, 12).

2. Italy had yet to be convinced to join Germany in the war. Even if it had made that decision in May, it would not have had time to deploy adequate forces north of Switzerland. As a result, the plan was dropped.

3. Although the RFs and SFs were dissolved by this time, reference is made to them only to clarify location in this text.

4. The 280-mm battery mentioned in the May 14 bombardment of Schoenenbourg may have been either a long or short barreled version of the 280-mm Bruno rail gun with ranges of 22,800 to 28,500 meters, which fired 240 or 302 kg rounds at a rate of one round every five minutes. However, it is not clear which type of weapon was actually used. There is a possibility that they may have been Czech 240-mm howitzers instead (Gander and Chamberlain 1979, 229).

5. The Czech gun, designated as a 420-mm M.17 (t) howitzer by the Germans, had a range of 14,600 meters, and fired a 1,020 kg projectile at a rate of one round every five minutes. It formed a one-gun battery (Number 130). It was paired with Battery 810 to form Artillery Group 800. Battery 810 consisted of one German 355-

mm M.1 howitzer that fired a shell weighing 575 kg at a range of 20,800 meters and a rate of one round every four minutes. Delayed fuses of the 420-mm howitzer allowed its rounds to penetrate the ground and explode closer to the subterranean works of Schoenenberg, inflicting some internal damage and fracturing walls (Prásil 1995, 117-118, Gander and Chamberlain 1979, 208, 230).

6. French crew members claimed that the fire from the 88-mm gun was more demoralizing than that of any other weapon (Hofmann, 47).

7. During the attack on La Ferté, and later on other ouvrages, the German troops had little guidance or preparation on the art of carrying out such an assault. None of the techniques learned with experimentation on the Czech fortifications had filtered down to the field army. The manual "Combat Against Permanent Fortifications" was still in preparation when the war began, but it was never published. None of the material it was to be based on was ever located. The field troops had to make do with small section titled "Attacks Against Positions" in their field manual, which contained little information on assaulting fortifications (Hofmann, 26-27).

8. The Germans claimed after the war that their assault troops actually reached Fort Boussois and Fort Sarts, dropping 1 kg (2.2 lb.) charges down the shaft through the small openings of the armored ventilation dome. The resulting explosion led to the surrender of the two forts (Hofmann, 57). This could only have taken place on the turret blocks of those ouvrages. The other blocks had intakes on the exposed facade, which were supposedly blasted by German artillery. The air intakes on the turret blocks had small openings, normally covered by screens. Thus the German accounts of this action may well be accurate.

9. According to a post war account, the German XXX Corps 93rd and 258th Divisions pulled out of the front line on May 19 to train on the art of laying seiges. On May 28, the corps commander was informed that his divisions would take up positions on the Saar (Sarre) Front and prepare to spearhead a breakthrough of the Maginot positions in that sector. The First Army would engage in operations designed to keep the French pinned to the Maginot Line (Hofmann, 123). It is not known whether any veterans of the attacks on La Ferté took part in training these units, or if any of the staff had access to the intelligence documents on French fortifications of 1937 and 1940. However, many post-war orders of battle show that these divisions were assigned to another corps rather than the XXX Corps. On the other hand, documents from Army Group C, on the other hand, indicate that these two divisions were indeed in XXX Corps (Jacobsen 1960, 246-248). What is noteworthy is that after the breathrough neither of these divisions turned inward to attack the larger fortifications they had been trained to reduce.

10. Later, the 75-mm gun crews of Hochwald and Schoenenbourg discovered that their turret guns could be used against low-flying aircraft, substituting for the antiaircraft weapons the ouvrages did not have.

11. Schoenenbourg was unusual for a gros ouvrage because it had no M-1 magazine. Instead it used a larger type of magazine identified as M-1/M-2 near the artillery blocks, which replaced both M-1 and M-2 magazines.

11

VICTORY IN THE ALPS

As the French armies began to collapse in the face of the German juggernaut in the North, a smaller and more heavily outnumbered French army brought a major Italian offensive to a halt. The key to this success hinged not only on the skill and bravery of French soldiers, but also upon the effectiveness of their fortifications.

The Little Maginot Line on the Southeastern Front was less solid than the Maginot Line Proper in the Northeast and had less depth. Nineteen gros ouvrages covered the three Alpine sectors as opposed to the twenty-two on the Northeastern Front. However, the Alpine forts covered a frontier of about the same length, and had the advantage of being in the mountains. Because of a significant rise in the cost of building fortifications in the 1930s, many of the ouvrages in the Alps were incomplete. Nevertheless, the Alpine forts were outfitted with the same standard equipment as the ones in the Northeast. Extensive belts of anti-tank rails and wire were unnecessary because of the terrain.

The line of Alpine *avant-postes* represented a formidable obstacle, not because of their composition, but because of the terrain. The mission of these forward positions was not simply to sound the alarm, but to engage the enemy near the border for as long as possible. The Alpine petits ouvrages, which mounted mostly small arms, served more as abris than infantry ouvrages.

Unlike the Northeastern Front, there were no exposed flanks or intervals relying on forests, rivers or flooding. Mountains filled the gaps and the flanks of the Southeastern Front. To surround the garrisons of the ouvrages here was not as easy as in the Northeast, and this was the whole backbone of the French defense against Italian aggression.

After mobilization in September 1939, the three sectors of the Alps presented a formidable front to Italy. The SF of Savoy and part of SF of Dauphiné were under the command of XVI Corps, which consisted of one North African and three infantry divisions. The XIV Corps controlled part of the SF of Dauphiné and the northern end of the SF of the Maritime Alps with two infantry divisions. The most heavily fortified part of the SF of the Maritime Alps fell under the jurisdiction of the XV Corps with four divisions and a colonial infantry division.[1]   In addition to these units, there were Alpine fortress and Alpine infantry battalions.

In the fall of 1939, Gamelin began to transfer the Alpine units to the Northeastern Front.   The depleted Sixth Army's mission was simply to observe the frontier with the ski-mounted scout section of the Alpine chasseur and infantry regiments.[2]   By June 1940 the Sixth Army with over half a million had left the Franco-Italian border.   General René Olry took over control of the Southeastern Front with his Alpine Army of about 185,000 men formed into three mountain divisions and a number of Alpine battalions.   The key to the defense of the Alpine Front was the Alpine fortress demi-brigades, similar to the fortress brigades on the Northeastern Front, and two demi-brigades of Alpine chasseurs (Plan and Lefevre 1982, 23-25, 41-47).

The SF of Savoy covered the main passes of Petit St. Bernard, Mont Cenis, and Fréjus.   The *avant-postes*, situated near the border on commanding heights or on the very edge of mountain roads, dominated the terrain.   In many cases they were within the range of the artillery of supporting ouvrages or old forts. Field and fixed artillery also covered the winding roads leading into the valleys to the rear of the *avant-postes* and the approaches to them.

The SF of Dauphiné was similarly organized.   The *avant-postes*, ouvrages or artillery covered the passes of Montgenèvre, Larche, and Restefond.   The strong defenses surrounding the town of Briançon were integrated with the Maginot Line and lent their support to the forward positions commanding the road from Montgenèvre.   Across the border, the Italians had built the large fort of Chaberton on top of the mountain of the same name, overlooking the Italian town of Cesana.   From there, they hoped to dominate the pass of Montgenèvre, its approaches, and the French positions in front of Briançon.

The SF of the Maritime Alps formed a more continuous line of ouvrages beginning south of Restefond and running all the way to the Mediterranean Sea.   The last ouvrage of the line, Cap Martin, was practically adjacent to the beach.   Here the French had erected their strongest positions on the Southeastern Front to protect the approaches to the cities and naval bases of the Riviera.   This was the point where the Italians were expected to attack.

During 1940, the Italians massed two armies—the First and the Fourth, for a total of over twenty divisions—near the Franco-Italian border, and held another army in reserve.   On June 10, 1940, while the Germans pierced the Weygand Line and threatened the remaining French forces in the North, Italy declared war on France.   Several days later, the Italians launched their offensive—mostly small-scale operations—until June 20.   In many places the French civilian population had already been evacuated, and some critical bridges and tunnels destroyed.

The first Italian attack took place in the vicinity of Briançon.   On June 16 the Italian Fourth Army tried to move forward, but was driven back.   About eight kilometers north of Mount Chaberton, the old French fort of Olive engaged in a duel with the Italian fort of Bardonecchia. The next day, Fort Chaberton engaged Fort Olive, silencing it.

Fort Chaberton could be considered the finest of the Italian fortifications. Unfortunately, like so much of the Italian war machine, it did not meet the requirements of modern warfare. Built at the beginning of the century and modernized in the 1930s, it was located on a higher peak than any other European fort. From its mountaintop position at 3,130 meters (10,430 feet), its guns commanded the approaches toward the French town of Briançon, but it was also highly visible. Its creators believed that the towers would be out of the French line of fire, failing to take into account the progress made in the field of artillery. Chaberton mounted eight 149-mm guns with a range of up to 17,000 meters in armored turrets, atop exposed concrete towers, which fired over the crest of the mountain. Its turrets offered minimal protection, serving mostly as shelters against the weather. Chaberton's guns, which formed the 515th Battery, began firing on June 18 on the petit ouvrage of Gondran which, comprised of only three blocks, was situated on an old fort. It mounted only a GFM and a observation cloche and its heaviest armament was nothing more than a JM (Castellano 1984, 24-30; Mary 1980, 291).

On June 19 poor weather conditions hindered Chaberton's ability to support the advancing Italian troops, but early in the morning of June 20 the 515th Battery was able to cover the advance of two Italian divisions. Fort Chaberton next trained its guns on the gros ouvrage of Janus, which was also part of an older fort and included several blocks, one of which mounted two 75-mm guns and another four old 95-mm naval guns. None of Janus' artillery could be aimed at the Chaberton, so the gros ouvrage kept its silence. The Italian fort then switched its fires towards the smaller forts and the field artillery units in the area. The Italians managed to take the village of Montgenèvre, but achieved little else (Plan and Lefevre 1982, 70; Castellano 1984, 60-63).

Some unusual problems developed at Fort Chaberton before it was challenged by the French artillery. Its guns fired so often that they became overheated; hence its gunners were forced to stop shooting to cool down the barrels. Further the hand carts used to carry ammunition and the monte-charges in the turrets, evidently not designed as well as the French models, broke down. As a result, the gun crews and supporting personnel had to hand carry their ammunition from the magazines to the turrets (Castellano 1984, 60-63)!

Soon the French 6th Battery of the 154th Artillery Regiment of four 280-mm mortars positioned itself so it could lob its shells upon the heights of Mount Chaberton. These huge mortars had the capacity of hurling a shell of over 200 kg (450 lb) over a distance of 10,000 meters (Gander and Chamberlain 1979, 229). On June 21 the mortars, with help from the observers of the Janus, pounded the fort of Chaberton despite the cloud of fog that had shrouded the mountain for several days. In the meantime, instead of replying to the French battery, which was out of its line of fire, the Chaberton artillery continued targeting other positions.

When the fog dissipated late in the afternoon, the French were able to observe the devastating effects of their bombardment. Within a short time they hit several of the turret towers with the huge mortar bombs lobbed over the mountains crest. In addition, Chaberton's aerial cable station was hit, effectively cutting off communications with the valley below. Only the radio and the long treacherous road down the icy snow-covered slopes linked the Italian garrison to the valley. The Chaberton's personnel managed to contain a conflagration in one of the magazines. The observatory was not functioning either. As evening shadows lengthened, Chaberton was left with only two functioning gun turrets. The big French mortars had silenced the other six for the duration of the campaign.

On June 22 the French 154th Artillery Regiment's mortar battery failed to finish off Fort Chaberton because a heavy blanket of fog shrouded the mountain again. The French gunners fired a volley of six mortar rounds, one of which seriously damaged a magazine. Chaberton's remaining two guns continued to fire at other targets until they developed mechanical problems, which took them out of action. During the night the Italians repaired the guns, but the next day the fort was again spared by another blanket of fog. Finally, on June 24 the French mortar battery fired a few more rounds but achieved no results before the Armistice of June 25 (Plan and Lefevre 1982, 70-74; Castellano 1984, 63-68).

In the meantime, the Italian had launched another operation about five kilometers to the south of Montgenèvre, at Col de Gimont, but were foiled by the Maginot positions. The battles in the Briançon area pitted 35,000 Italians against a French force of 8,500. The French sustained twenty-six casualties and inflicted almost 700 on their opponent (Plan and Lefevre 1982, 70-77).

Much further to the north, the advance toward Bourg St. Maurice ground to a halt in the face of the cunning and bravery of the French contingent. It was during these affrays that Lieutenant Jean Bulle of the 7th Battalion of Chasseurs Alpins distinguished himself on June 22. While his men lowered him down a precipice with a rope, he fired an FM 24/29 automatic rifle on Italian troops advancing along a ledge, effectively stopping their advance. Along this battle front the Italians assembled over 50,000 men against the defenders' 5,500, but the two Italian divisions failed to make any headway and took almost 800 casualties compared to the sixteen suffered by the French (Plan and Lefevre 1982, 50-58).

The Italian troops failed to penetrate more than several miles towards Bourg St. Maurice. Although it was June, snow still covered the mountains at many points and movement over the terrain remained treacherous. The Italian troops reportedly traversed this harsh terrain in cardboard boots. Some formations like the motorized Trieste Division were not equipped for this type of warfare. Their flimsy little L-3 tanks proved to be of little value. At least, when it came to individual equipment, the heavily outnumbered French had the advantage of better materiel.

The Italians mounted a more serious attack into the Arc Valley, between Bourg St. Maurice and Briançon where the French had already destroyed the bridges and the Modane tunnel. On June 20 to June 21 the Italians success-fully pushed through the pass of Petit Mont Cenis, taking the *avant-postes* and penetrating as far as the valley of the Arc River by June 24. Meanwhile, the main force advancing towards the pass of Mont Cenis was held up by the line of *avant-postes* (Plan and Lefevre 1982, 60-62). This line comprised the posts of La Turra, Mont Froid and Breccia. La Turra, an old masonry fort with a drawbridge, was built in the 1890s. In the 1930s a small caserne, an underground gallery, and two artillery casemates for two 75-mm field pieces that opened on the cliff and commanded the plateau of Mont Cenis had been added to the ensemble. The little fort was incorporated into the outpost line. La Turra was commanded by Lieutenant Proud'hon and manned by less than fifty Chasseurs Alpins and artillery men (Truttmann March 29, 1983, cor-respondence).

While one Italian force outflanked La Turra through the Petit Mont Cenis pass, another group advanced toward Mont Cenis. On June 22, after the little fort suffered heavy bombardment from the guns of the Italian Fort of Paradiso and field artillery for several hours, it was rescued by the fog. The Italians attempted to force their way through the pass, but the French, hauling one of the casemate guns out of the gallery, pointed it down at them. With his two 75-mm guns and four 81-mm mortars, Proud'hon convinced the Italians that they faced a gros ouvrage, forcing them to withdraw. As they retreated, the Italians left a column of about twenty armored vehicles (L-3 tankettes) on the road, which were soon blanketed in snow. The Italians eventually bypassed the position, taking Lanslebourg and moving down the Arc Valley but never reaching the main line of fortifications at Modane. The Italian units advancing into the Arc Valley had to confine themselves to the forests to avoid the heavy French artillery fire (Truttmann March 29, 1983, correspondence; Plan and Lefevre 1982, 61, 63; *La battaglia delle Alpi* 1947, 85).

To the southwest of Petit Mont Cenis and to the south of Modane, elements of the Italian Superga Division pushed their way up the pass at Fréjus after being held in check by the weather and the defenders. On June 24, under the cover of fog, they worked their way up the snow-covered slopes on to the artillery ouvrage of Pas du Roc and the smaller fort of Arrondaz. The four-block Pas du Roc had not been completed, but mounted a pair of 75-mm guns and four 81-mm mortars. Arrondaz, on the other hand, had only two blocks, which were armed with FM and JM (Mary 1980, 286-287). As the Italians invaded their superstructures, the two ouvrages fired at each other, driving the assault force back down the slopes. While one Italian force was pinned down at the Mont Cenis pass, other groups slowly advanced from the pass of Petit Mont Cenis and Fréjus toward their objective: the Arc Valley and the town of

Modane behind its shield of gros ouvrages. But it did not reach its goal by the time of the Armistice. The advanced positions, such as La Turra, were still holding out when the Armistice took effect. The French forces in the sector of the Arc Valley numbered 13,000 men. After all these actions their casualties amounted only to twenty-five men, whereas the Italian force of 40,000 men suffered over 1,100 casualties (Plan and Lefevre 1982, 66, 69).

In the Maritime Alps and a part of the SF of Dauphiné, the Italian First Army faced an even more serious challenge. The first phase of Operation M directed the Italian corps in the vicinity of Maddalena, opposite Larche, to take the mountain passes and occupy Barcelonnette. The second phase optimistically called for an advance on Marseilles as another corps of the army undertook Operation R, advancing up the coast to Menton to seize the Riviera. Between these two corps, a third was to divert the French forces. Realizing the strength of the French defenses and fortifications, the Italians hoped nonetheless that one of their forces would effect a breakthrough. When the fateful hour arrived, the Italian commanders were told to bypass the ouvrages rather than engage them. The main assault was planned for June 23 with a morning artillery barrage and an air attack (*La battaglia delle Alpi* 1947, 67-70, 74).

After June 20 two Italian divisions of the First Army began their advance on the town of Larche from two directions in SF of Dauphiné. They successfully pushed through the pass of Larche, but were hindered by the weather and the easily defended terrain. When they finally encountered the line of *avant-postes*, the Italians faltered again. Some units came within range of the guns of two of the gros ouvrages located further down the valley covering Saint Ours. The two 75-mm turret guns of the ouvrage of Roche Lacroix opened fire on an Italian battery of 240-mm guns that was bombarding the advanced French position at Viraysse and also helped prevent the Italians from reaching the town of Larche, halting them before the line of *avant-postes* (Plan and Lefevre 1982, 92-93).

On June 14, 15, and 16 the Italians started patrolling the environs along the valley of the Roya up to Saorge and other areas further up and down the front. They reached the line of *avant-postes* by June 20. By this time, the Italian troops were tired after having been delayed by poor weather, which prevented artillery support and deteriorated the road conditions. The French garrison of the *avant-poste* of Croix de Cougoule, overlooking the valley of the Roya from its perch, observed the Italian movements. The troops in this position had little to fear, because it was protected by the guns of the ouvrages of Col de Brouis and Monte Grosso (Plan and Lefevre 1982, 108; *La battaglia delle Alpi* 1947, 67-68).

Monte Grosso, the largest ouvrage in the Alps, opened fire on a group of Italian mortars and destroyed them on June 15. On June 20 the fort was pounded by 149-mm Italian guns. The Italians fired over 200 rounds at the fort. Its 75-mm gun turret was hit while in the firing position. However, it was not put out of action and continued to bombard the Italian forces until the

Armistice (Mary 1980, 308; Plan and Lefevre 1982, 112).

The Italians attacked other ouvrages with their heavy artillery on June 20. After launching their attack on the Riviera on June 22 under the cover of fog, they were unable to take the *avant-poste* of Pont Saint-Louis, which dominated the coastal highway. The little outpost, which received support from the ouvrages, refused to surrender, so the Italians bypassed it and moved on to Menton, using the rail tunnel below it. The Coseria Division (XV Corps), with the Cremona Division in support, was given the mission of taking Cap Martin and Roquebrune. The Modena Division (XV Corps), with the support of alpine troops, was to advance on Castillion and take Sospel. The Italian artillery had to be placed along the road leading to the border on June 22 because there was nowhere else to place it. In the morning the 149-mm and 210-mm Italian guns opened fire on the ouvrage of Cap Martin (*La battaglia delle Alpi* 1947, 67, 76-78).

The entrance block of the ouvrage of Cap Martin, situated on the Mediterranean to the west of Menton, lay near the beach whereas its other two blocks stood higher up, at the base of the peninsula where they held a commanding view of the city and its beach front. The two 81-mm mortars of Block 1, the entrance, were directed toward the town while the 75-mm and 81-mm mortars of Blocks 2 and 3 covered Menton and the area behind it. On the morning of June 22, the French artillery pounded the tunnels near the border, hindering Italian movements along the front. The attackers, who made little headway towards the town of Menton, resorted to bringing in reinforcements in the form of Naval Armored Train Number 2. Armed with four turrets with 152-mm guns, it presented a powerful weapon. In the early morning of June 22 the train moved into position, just past the mouth of the tunnel and began to bombard the ouvrages while the Italian infantry moved through Menton. Two hundred rounds were fired at a 155-mm gun battery on Cap Martin. The ouvrages of Roquebrune, Mont Agel and Saint Agnes, all situated on mountains overlooking Menton, joined in duel after locating the train's position. Soon, the train had to withdraw into the tunnel and did not return to the fray until the afternoon. This time, however, two devastating salvos from the 75s of Mont Agel knocked out two of its four turrets and killed its commander even before it could take up position. Once again it retreated into the tunnel. As it was pulling back into the tunnel, it lost another gun (*La battaglia delle Alpi* 1947, 67, 76-78; Plan and Lefevre 1982, 111). The Maginot ouvrages remained in control of the battlefield throughout this day. Even the tiny garrison of Pont Saint-Louis, now behind the front, continued to resist on the coastal highway.

The fighting continued up and down the SF of the Maritime Alps. Except in the Menton area, the Italians failed to breach the line of *avant-postes*. Other ouvrages in the vicinity of Sospel and along the line to the south successfully kept the Italians from the *avant-postes*.

The Italian plans had also included a limited amphibious operation. They gathered a small fleet of motor boats, launches, hired fishing boats, a squadron on MAS boats, a squadron of torpedo boats, and two submarines shortly before the onset of the ground offensive. The plan was to land a force of about fifty men on the beach near Menton and the border and a larger group of 900 men between Cap Martin and Monaco. The first expedition attempted its invasion in the evening of June 22. However, the amphibious operation got off to a bad start. The vessels in the fleet were too diverse to travel in tandem from the shores of Italy so that by the time Menton was sighted the fleet was too widely dispersed to constitute an effective contingent. Also, the engines of many of the boats broke down, leaving their passengers stranded in high seas. In addition, the motor boats were much too noisy to approach the French coast without detection. The plan required that the troops swim ashore, but they were too exhausted by the trip and many had succumbed to seasickness on the rough seas. The operation was postponed until June 24 and later canceled (*La battaglia delle Alpi* 1947, 76-78).

On June 23 the planned air support of Operation M was diverted to Operation R on the coast, where the pilots were ordered to direct their efforts against the French ouvrage of Mont Agel. However, the air command at Turin canceled the aerial attack because of adverse weather conditions. The second naval assault was also canceled for that evening. On that day the Italians finally recognized the strength of the opposition and also discovered that there were more French fortifications than they had expected. They also realized that the French artillery control was extremely efficient and accurate, even when visibility was reduced by fog and other meteorological conditions (*La battaglia delle Alpi* 1947, 81-82, 89-90).

On June 23 the crew of the encircled *avant-poste* of Pont Saint-Louis, essentially cut off from the other ouvrages, refused to surrender.[3] The Italian attacks continued throughout the day on the Maritime Alps. Menton was attacked from the north. At the same time, two additional armored trains, Number 5, with four 152-mm guns, and Number 1, with four 120-mm guns, moved up to the vicinity of Menton and fired 350 rounds on Cap Martin without being spotted and subjected to counter-battery fire (*La battaglia delle Alpi* 1947, 91). One Italian unit advanced into Menton at noon, only to be greeted by Cap Martin's artillery and machine guns. Showing great determination, they advanced right up to the ouvrage in the afternoon. Block 3, a casemate for two 75-mm and two 81-mm mortars, suffered some direct hits including some on its embrasures, but it remained effectively in action, having sustained only minor damage. The Italians reached the surface of the fort, and all attempts to dislodge them failed until, late in the day, the other forts in the vicinity were called to direct their fire on to the ouvrage of Cap Martin. This finally forced the Italians to withdraw. The ouvrage incurred some minor damage from the supporting French 155-mm guns. For some unknown reason, the bravery of this Italian force has not been acknowledged in the official history of the campaign. This was as close as the Italians came to ever taking a gros ouvrage, which was better than their German comrades ever did (Plan and Lefevre 1982, 116-121).

The weather improved on June 24, allowing the Italian command to order an attack on all fronts (*La battaglia delle Alpi* 1947, 92). That evening the Italian forces withdrew behind the Carei River in Menton. The next day reinforcements arrived, but no significant action took place. The Italians claimed that Menton was in their possession in the evening of June 24. By then they had lost 1,000 men of the 80,000 deployed against the 38,000 French troops in the Maritime Alps. As in the other sectors, French losses were minimal, amounting to less than fifty men (Plan and Lefevre 1982, 121).

While the battle was raging in the Alps, the allied armies in the north had been shattered and were retreating to the south. German units raced unimpeded into the Rhone Valley and toward the Swiss border, trapping any units that had escaped the encirclement. Along the Swiss border the French had built few fortifications in the 1940s. Of course, they were facing the Franco-Swiss border, not the interior of the country. At two critical points, Fort Joux and Fort L'Écluse, a couple of old forts, had been partially renovated and occupied. Fort Joux, a medieval castle at Pontarlier, had not been modernized until the 1880s. It commanded the road leading through the valley to Lake Neufchatel in Switzerland. In June 1940 a company of the 23rd Light Infantry Battalion, a "discipline battalion," held the fort against elements of a German infantry division long enough to allow numerous remnants of the Second Army Group to cross into Switzerland. The fort surrendered on June 24, 1940 (Truttmann February 1992, correspondence).

Further south, along the Swiss border, stood the old fort of L'Écluse at the outskirts of the town of Bellegarde, on the road to Lake Geneva. Also originally a medieval castle, it had not been rebuilt and expanded until the latter part of the nineteenth century. The part of the fort adjacent to the road overlooked the valley below, but a larger part was built above the road. In June 1940 a total of 250 men of the 3rd Company of the 179th Alpine Fortress Battalion, some engineers and some artillery men defended the fort under the command of Captain Fabre. Even though their main armament consisted only of a few old 95-mm guns, they resisted until the Armistice. Their struggle was singled out in the media, which incorrectly identified them as members of the Foreign Legion, well known for their determination (Truttmann February 4, 1992, correspondence; *New York Times* June 25, 1940, 2).

The German advance down the Rhone Valley and the fall of Lyon opened the back door to Olry's command. The arrangements for an Armistice prepared on June 22 became effective on June 25. General Olry's army maintained its positions until the Armistice while the Italians desperately tried to gain some type of a victory before it went into effect. The last communiqué of the campaign issued by the French High Command came on the morning of June 25, 1940:

During the evening yesterday Italian attacks continued and were repulsed. Our advanced posts in the regions of the passes. . . resisted all attacks. At no point were our defense positions broken. In advance of our defense line, a counter-attack resulted in our recapturing the western half of Menton. (*New York Times* June 27, 1940, 2)

The Italians took a more sanguine view of events in their official communiqué of the previous day, claiming that despite bad weather conditions and strong enemy fortifications and resistance, "Our offensive could not be held by the enemy and our troops gained notable success. . . The advance of Italian troops is continued on all fronts penetrating into enemy fortifications and threatening him from the rear" (*New York Times* June 25, 1940, 2).

In reality, they had little success, and penetrated no further than five to ten kilometers in a few areas. The French Army in the Alps stood steadfast in the Little Maginot Line. Thus, the Germans saved the day for the Italians by routing the Allies and forcing them to sign the Armistice.

NOTES

1. Eight of these divisions formed part of the reserve and were not at the front.

2. In June 1940, when the campaign began, these ski units effectively delayed and, in some places, even checked the advancing Italian army.

3. The Italian official history claims that the avant-poste surrendered on June 23, but that was not the case. Its few defenders continued to resist even after the armistice, since their means of communications had been cut off and they had no way of knowing that France had capitulated.

CONCLUSION

After the completion of the campaign against France the myth that the Maginot Line was a white elephant—easily outflanked and even penetrated—persisted. At the beginning of 1941 several articles in European magazines had discussed the effectiveness of the Maginot Line and other fortifications. A German artillery general by the name of Ludwig published an article in response to comments made by other military men in different publications. Ludwig pointed out a few key facts that remained forgotten for many years:

During the present war no attack took place against large fortification groups. . . The German attack against the Maginot Line proper southwest of Saarbruecken was naturally not directed against a strong sector, but against a relatively weak barrier consisting of bunkers, obstacles and dams not used in the attack. A strong counter-attack against the German penetration, which one would naturally have expected, did not take place for want of forces (Peyton 1941, 2).

Colonel B.R. Peyton (1945), the American military attaché submitting this report, commented that:

The presumption taken in this article that the real Maginot Line was not attacked is not correct. The Maginot Line was penetrated in the vicinity of Saarbruecken on 14 June, 1940 and west of Freiburg on 15 June, 1940. It is true that some defending troops had been taken from the line to use elsewhere. It is also true that reliance was placed on flooding areas in the neighborhood of Saarbruecken which did not function correctly. It is also true west of Freiburg too much reliance was placed on the Marne River as an obstacle and the Maginot Line itself was weak at this point (5).

Peyton also pointed out that the Maginot Line lacked depth and that the Germans did not use tanks in the assault on fortified positions. With the exception of a few details, Peyton's report correctly describes the events that took place in the Maginot Line. It also shows how the Rhine defenses and the Sarre sector came to represent incorrectly, the whole Maginot Line, contributing to the creation of the Maginot myth.[1]

The Maginot Line Proper proved that it was one of the most effective fortifications of the war. It served the purpose for which it was intended and the Germans finally breached it only after the interval troops had withdrawn.

Even then the Germans launched major preparatory bombardments against the gros ouvrages of Schoenenbourg, Hochwald, and Fermont without weakening their defenses to the point that they could successfully assault them. Furthermore, although the ouvrages of the Alpine Front successfully foiled Italian attempts to advance, they were not bombarded by super-heavy artillery and aircraft to the same extent as the forts of the main line. If the Germans could not successfully silence a major fort with 500 kg and 1000 kg bombs dropped from the air, a 420-mm monster gun, and other heavy artillery under optimal conditions, their chances would have been even slimmer if the Maginot Line had been properly manned. As a matter of fact, the German intelligence reports of 1937 indicate that the French defenses that constituted the main line could be considered almost impregnable at the time.

In addition, it should be noted that a few forts lacked even some of their basic armament. For example, none of the machine gun turrets had the 25-mm anti-tank guns they had been designed for. These would have turned them all into mixed-arms turrets, but the 25-mm guns with shortened barrels did not arrive until June 1940 when it was too late to install them. This might have made a difference for some of the petits ouvrages that fell. The 50-mm mortars for Block 5 and Block 6 of Simserhof never arrived, although they did not prove critical to the defense of the ouvrage. This was not the case for some of the petits ouvrages, however, especially the few that succumbed to assaults by German engineer teams, who used the cover of craters to advance and might have been stopped with these weapons (*The Simserhof Fort* 1988, 2; Rowe 1961, 249).[2]

The Maginot Line formed an area defense rather than a point defense like a fortress ring where some positions proved more successful than others. Fortified lines do not have a very good track record since virtually every one of them was pierced during World War II. The Maginot Line, on the contrary, held out well and was not penetrated until after the interval troops had been withdrawn in June of 1940. Further, in the South, the Little Maginot Line withstood the test of fire admirably well. There can be no hesitation to characterize the Maginot Line as the most successful gun-bearing fortified line of the twentieth century even though the French army was unable to take full advantage of it.

NOTES

1. The error crept into Peyton's report when he decided to pencil in the word "some" between "It is true that" and "defending troops."

2. Vivian Rowe gives June 13 as the date of arrival for these guns, but incorrectly identifies them as 125-mm weapons for the turrets (Rowe 1961, 249).

GLOSSARY

Abri—Shelter for troops

Armes mixtes—Set of mixed arms including a JM and AT gun

AT—Anti-tank

Avant-poste—Advanced post or outpost position

Casemate—Position with an exposed facade mounting weapons

Caponier—Defensive position giving enfilading fires across a moat

Caserne—Garrison area and associated facilities

CEZF—*Commission d'Étude des Zones Fortifiées*—Organization that set up the fortified zones in France

Chasseurs—Light infantry or cavalry formations

Cloche—Bell-shaped, nonrotating turret or cupola

CORF—*Commission d'Organisation des Régions Fortifiées*—Organization that set the building and equipment standards for the Maginot fortifications

EH—*Entrée des hommes*—Men's entrance

EM—*Entrée des munitions*—Munitions entrance

Entrée mixte—Mixed entrance—type of entrance that allows combined access to men and munitions

Episcope—Instrument similar to binoculars, but uses mirrors like a periscope so that the observer's eye level is below the crenel in which the episcope is mounted

Fossé—Ditch or moat. It can be large, like an AT ditch, or small to protect the exposed facade

Génie—French Army Engineers

GFM cloche—*Cloche Guêt-Fusil-Mitrailleur*—Observation and light machine gun cloche

JM—*Jumelage de mitrailleuses*—Twin machine gun set

JM cloche—Cloche mounting only a JM

Maison fortifiée; maison forte—Fortified position disguised as a house. Found in the advance line near the border

MOM—*Main d'oeuvre militaire*—Military manual labor

Monte charge—Small lift used to carry ammunition from one level to another

Ouvrage—Work, or fort. Used in the 1930s to refer to the new type of forts

Gros ouvrage—Large ouvrage or fort, usually artillery

Petit ouvrage—Small ouvrage or fort, usually infantry

Pionniers—Pioneers. Infantry troops assigned to building or digging tasks

RF—*Région fortifiée*—Fortified Region that includes SFs

Sapeurs—Sapper. Term used to refer to the soldiers of the Génie

Sapeur-mineur—Combat engineer

SD—*Secteur défensif*—Defensive Sector, lightly fortified

SF—*Secteur fortifié*—Fortified Sector

STG—*Services Thechniques du Génie*—Technical engineer service

Turret—In this book the term only refers to a rotating armored cupola. Some may eclipse (move up and down). This term can also refer to any tower-like position

Usine—Power plant or generator room

BIBLIOGRAPHY

Bruge, Roger. *Faites sauter la Ligne Maginot!* France: Fayard, 1973.
———*On a livré la Ligne Maginot.* France: Fayard, 1975.
Castellano, Edoardo. *Distruggete lo Chaberton!* Torino: Il Capitello, 1984.
Churchill, Winston S. *The Gathering Storm.* Boston: Houghton Mifflin Company, 1948.
Cima, Bernard and Raymond Cima. *Ouvrage du Barbonnet.* Menton, France: Auto-Edition, 1988.
Claudel, Louis. *La Ligne Maginot: conception-réalisation.* Lausanne, Switzerland: Association Saint Maurice la Recherche de Documents Sur la Forteresse, 1974.
Cole, H. M. *The Lorraine Campaign.* Washington, D.C.: Office of the Chief of Military History, 1950.
Collin, Lt. Col. Georges and Jean-Bernard Wahl. *La Ligne Maginot en Basse Alsace.* France: Association des Amis de la Ligne Maginot d'Alsace, 1981.
Corum, James S. *Roots of Blitzkrieg: Hans von Seeckt and German Military Reform.* Lawrence, Kansas: University Press of Kansas, 1992.
Dear, I.C.B. *The Oxford Companion to World War II.* New York: Oxford University Press, 1995.
Draper, Theodore. *Six Weeks War: France May 10-June 25, 1940.* New York: Viking, 1944.
État-Major de L'Armeé de Terre, Service Historique. *Les grandes unités françaises: guerre 1939-1945.* Paris: Imprimerie Nationale, 1967.
Fitzsimons, Bernard, ed. *Weapons and Warfare.* New York: Columbia House, 1978.
Gamelin, Paul. *La Ligne Maginot: images d'hier et d'aujourd'hui.* Paris: Argout Éditions, 1979.
Gander, Terry and Peter Chamberlain. *Weapons of the Third Reich.* Garden City, NY: Doubleday and Company, Inc., 1979.
Gilbert, Martin. *Marching to War 1933-1939.* New York: Military Heritage Press, 1989.
Goutard, Colonel A. *The Battle of France, 1940.* New York: Ives Washburn, Inc., 1959.
Gunsburg, Jeffery A. *Divided and Conquered: The French High Command and the Defeat of the West, 1940.* Westport, CT: Greenwood, 1979.
Halder, Franz. *The Halder War Diary 1939-1942.* Edited by Charles Burdick and Hans-Adolf Jacobsen. Novato, CA: Presidio, 1988.

Hart, G.H. Liddell, ed. *The Rommel Papers*. New York: Da Capo Press, 1953 (reprint).

Hicks, Major James E. *French Military Weapons 1717-1938*. New Milford, CT: N. Flayderman & Co., 1964.

Hogg, Ian V. *Fortress*. New York: St. Martin's Press, 1977.

Hohnadel, Alain and Michel Truttmann. *Guide de la Ligne Maginot: des Ardennes au Rhin, dans les Alpes*. Bayeux, France: Editions Hemidal, 1988.

Hohnadel, A. and R. Varoqui. *Le fort du Hackenberg*. Veckring, France: AMIFORT, 1986.

Horne, Alistair. *The Price of Glory*. Boston: Little, Brown and Co., 1962.

———*To Lose a Battle: France 1940*. Boston: Little, Brown and Co, 1969.

Hughes, Judith M. *To the Maginot Line*. Cambridge: Harvard Univ. Press, 1981.

Jacobsen, Hans-Adolf. *Dokumente zum Westfeldzug 1940*. Berlin Musterschmidt-Verlag, 1960.

Kaufmann, J.E. and H.W. Kaufmann. *Hitler's Blitzkrieg Campaigns*. Conshohocken, PA: Combined Books, 1993.

Kemp, Anthony. *The Unknown Battle: Metz, 1944*. New York: Stein and Day, 1981a.

———*The Maginot Line*. London: Fredrick Warne, 1981b.

La battaglia delle Alpi Occidentali: giugno 1940. Rome: Ministero Della Diffesa, 1947.

Linklater, Eric. *The Highland Division*. London: His Majesty's Stationary Office, 1942.

Maistret, Georges. *Le gros ouvrage A-2 Fermont de la Ligne Maginot*. France: Association des Amis de l'Ouvrage de Fermont et de la Ligne Maginot, 1978.

Mallory, Keith and Arvid Ottar. *The Architecture of War*. New York: Pantheon Books, 1973.

Manstein, Erich von. *Lost Victories*. Novato, CA: Presidio, 1982.

Mary, J.Y. *La Ligne Maginot*. Cuneo, Italy: SERCAP, 1980.

Memorial of the Maginot Line, Marckolsheim (Alsace). Colmar, France: S.A.E.P., 1983.

Mayer, S.L., ed. *Signal: Years of Triumph 1940-42*. Englewood Cliffs, New Jersey: Prentice Hall, 1978.

1929 World Almanac and Book of Facts. New York: Workman Publishing Co., Inc., 1929 (1971 reprint).

Plan, E. and Eric Lefèvre. *La bataille des Alpes: 10-25 juin 1940*. Paris: Charles-Lavauzelle, 1982.

Prásil, Michal. *Tezká dela Skoda*. Brno-Nachod, Czech: První, 1995.

Rocolle, Col. Pierre. *2000 ans de la fortification française*. Paris: Charles-Lavauzelle, 1974.

———*Les guerres de 1940: les illusions*. Paris: Armand Colin, 1990a.

———*La guerre de 1940: la défaite*. Paris: Armand Colin, 1990b.

Rowe, Vivian. *The Great Wall of France*. New York: Putman and Sons, 1961.

Salmond, J.B. *The History of the 51st Highland Division*. London: William Blackwood and Sons Ld., 1953.

The Simserhof Fort. France: 1988. (Guide booklet)

The Small Fortification of Immerhof. France: Township of Hettange Grande, 1979.

Tarnstrom, Ronald L. *Handbook of Armed Forces: France: Part II*. Lindsborg, KS: Trogen Publications, 1983.

Truttmann, Michel. *Le fort de Guentrange*. France: Impriemerie Henz, 1977.

Truttmann, LTC Philippe. *La fortification française de 1940: sa place dans l'évolution des systèmes fortifiés d'Europe Occidentale de 1880 a 1945*. University of Metz: Doctoral Thesis, 1979.

Weisbecker, A. *Ligne Maginot: ouvrage du Four à Chaux*. Lembach, France: Syndicat d'Initiative de Lembach et Environs, 1985.

DOCUMENTS

Denkschrift: über die französische, Landesbestigung. Berlin: Oberkommando des Heeres, 1941.

Die Französische Kriegswehrmacht 1939. Berlin: Oberkommando des Heeres, April 30, 1939.

Hofmann, Rudolf, et al. *German Attacks Against Permanent and Reinforced Field Type Fortifications in World War II*. Germany: Historical Division, Headquarters U.S. Army Europe, undated.

Grosses Orienterungsheft Frankreich: Ausgabe 1935/1936. Berlin: Oberkommando des Heeres, August 1, 1936.

Grosses Orienterungsheft Frankreich: Ausgabe 1935/1937. Berlin: Oberkommando des Heeres, August 1, 1937.

Lageberichte West vom 10. Mai bis 30. Juni 1940. Berlin: Oberkommando des Heeres, 1940.

Peyton, B.R., Colonel. "Organization, Defense and Attack on Fortified Zones such as the Siegfried and Maginot Lines." (Translation of a German magazine article of February 1941). Germany: Military Attache Report, March 31, 1941.

JOURNALS, MAGAZINES AND NEWSPAPERS

Adam, George. "Bristling Parapet of Peace." *Century* (April 1930): 264-270.

Balace, Francis. "Description détaillée des forts de la Meuse en 1914." *Liège: 1000 ans de fortifications militaires* (December 16, 1980 to January 16, 1981): 75-105.

Baldwin, Hanson. "Tank Traps Brace French Fort Line." *New York Times* (April 4, 1937): 9.

Callender, Harold. "The Bristling Line that Divides Europe." *New York Times Magazine* (November 5, 1933): 4-5.

"Daladier Promises France Will Guard Austria's Liberty." *New York Times* (August 28, 1933): 1.

"Five Held by France in German Spy Plot." *New York Times* (April 23, 1931): 13.

"France: Fortification System Insures They Shall Not Pass." *Newsweek* (September 9, 1933): 10-11.

"France Held Able to Enforce Edict." *New York Times* (March 13, 1936): 12

"France Holds Engineer Found with Forts Plans." *New York Times* (August 29, 1933): 1.

"France Plans Floods as Bar to Invaders." *New York Times* (February 18, 1930): 4.

"France's Mighty Wall Against Germany." *Literary Digest* (September 7, 1935): 13.

"France's Roman Wall on Land and Sea." *Literary Digest* (June 20, 1931): 13-14.

"French Fortifications." *New Outlook* (October 1931): 329-330.

"French Troops Try to Flee." *New York Times* (June 25, 1940): 2.

"French War Minister Views Border Forts." *New York Times* (October 7, 1930): 4.

Gaier, C. "Considérations pratiques sur l'attaque et la défense des anciennes places-fortes." *Liège: 1000 ans de fortifications militaires* (December 16, 1980 to January 16, 1981): 25-57.

"German Criticizes France's Defenses." *New York Times* (March 29, 1936): 28.

Gwyn, Major General Charles. "French Forts Held Peace Safeguard." *New York Times* (April 19, 1936): 35.

Heathcote, Dudley. "Painlevé's New Scheme of Defence." *Contemporary Review* (February 1929): 153-160.

Johnson, Thomas M. "Underground Fortresses Guard France from Invasion." *Popular Science Monthly* (October 1936): 14-15, 118-119.

Leurquin, Robert. "Crust of Gunpower Guards France." *New York Times* (September 4, 1938): IV-3.

McKenzie, V. "Underground Forts." *Literary Digest* (January 29, 1938): 17-18.

Phillip, P.J. "France Optimistic on Arms Position." *New York Times* (October 13, 1933): 4.

———"Bethlen in Berlin Upsets the French." *New York Times* (November 24, 1930): 2.

———"France Locks Door by Sending Men to Forts." *New York Times* (April 7, 1935): IV, 3.

Sauerwein, Jules. "Main Entrances Blocked, Side Doors Worry France." *New York Times* (December 10, 1933): IV-12.

"Swiss and Belgians Increase Defenses." *New York Times* (October 12, 1933): 1.

Thompson, Dorothy. "The Maginot Line: A Fort in Action." *Current History* (June 1940): 51-52.

Williams, Wythe. "The Great Chinese Wall of France." *Saturday Evening Post* (October 10, 1931): 18-19, 138-142.

WAR COMMUNIQUES

Translated and printed daily in the *New York Times*.

INTERVIEWS AND CORRESPONDENCE

Bernard, M. Interview at Zeitzerholz June 1979.

Dropsy, Georges. Interview at Fermont 1979.

Heymès, Raoul. Interview at Hackenberg June 1979 and correspondence 1979-1982

Maistret, Georges. Interview 1979 at Fermont and correspondence 1979-1984.

Mary, Y.V. Interview in Belgium June 1980 and correspondence 1979-1981.

Paquin, André. Interview at Fermont June 1978.

Truttmann, LTC Philippe. Correspondence, February 4, August 8, and November 1, 1982, and interview at his home in 1988.

Viennot, Colonel B. Correspondence March 5, 1981.

Wahl, Jean Bernard. Interview at Schoenenbourg June 1982.

INDEX

About the Authors

J. E. KAUFMANN is an Adjunct Faculty member at Palo Alto Junior College and a public high school social studies teacher.

H. W. KAUFMANN is Lecturer in Foreign Languages at the University of Texas at San Antonio.

ISBN 0-275-95719-5

HARDCOVER BAR CODE